MOTHER, I HAVE SOMETHING TO TELL YOU

Mother, I Have Something to Tell You

by Jo Brans

RESEARCH BY

Margaret Taylor Smith

DOUBLEDAY & COMPANY, INC.
GARDEN CITY, NEW YORK   1987

Grateful acknowledgement is made for permission to quote copyrighted material, as follows:

From *The Nature of the Child,* by Jerome Kagan. Copyright © 1984 by Basic Books, Inc., Publishers. Reprinted by permission of the publisher.

From *Prisoners of Childhood:* The Drama of the Gifted Child and the Search for the True Self, by Alice Miller. Copyright © 1981 by Basic Books, Inc., Publishers. Reprinted by permission of the publisher.

Library of Congress Cataloging-in-Publication Data
Brans, Jo.
   Mother, I have something to tell you.
   1. Mothers—United States—Psychology.   2. Mother
and child—United States.   3. Separation (Psychology)
4. Identity (Psychology)—United States.   I. Smith,
Margaret T.   II. Title.
HQ759.B755   1987   306.8′743   86-9028
ISBN 0-385-23132-6

To my mother and father,
Sammie Harlan Reid and Winton Samuel Reid,
who taught me to be a daughter

And to my children,
Erin Porterfield and Winton Porterfield,
who taught me to be a mother
J.B.

To my husband, Sid,

and our children,

Sarah Smith Hofheinz,
Sidney William Smith, III,
Susan Smith Whiting,
Amy Smith O'Connor
M.T.S.

Acknowledgments

A work of this kind necessarily comes to fruition only with the generous encouragement and aid of many people. First and most important, we want to recognize the brave women who dared to share their most personal stories with the hope of helping others, and whose experiences as mothers provide the substance of this book. To them, our unending thanks and admiration.

The Merrill-Palmer Institute of Wayne State University, where the research half of our team worked as Research Associate, became an academic base for the project. From the beginning, the study received the support of such respected members of the academic community as Rheta DeVries, Greer Fox, and Doug Powell. Anne Colby was instrumental in the inclusion of the data in the archives of The Henry A. Murray Research Center at Radcliffe College. Thanks too for the help of research assistant Pat Johnson and transcribers Eleanor Baldtuck, Barbara DiMaria, and Jean Palugi.

Molly Friedrich of The Aaron M. Priest Literary Agency gave new definition to the role of agent by bringing the writer and researcher together, a connection without which these pages would not exist. Fortunate in an agent, we were doubly so in editors; the enthusiasm with which Kate Medina bought the book was continued in Sally Arteseros, whose tact and editorial good sense saw it through to publication and beyond.

Tim Allis, who gave us our title, is one of the numerous friends and family members who listened, questioned, encouraged, suggested, read, criticized, believed, and otherwise cheered us on with their moral and financial support for the five years of this project. You know who you are: Thank you.

J.B.
M.T.S.

Contents

PART II SECOND SELF

STAGE FIVE Autonomy

STAGE SIX Connection

Preface
Second Birth, Second Self

We are mothers who speak to you here. We know that birth is violent, that blood must flow and flesh tear and hard bones bend to bring new life into the world. Upon our bodies is engraved the pain of Medea's cry, "I would rather stand three times in the front of battle than bear one child."

A new mother quickly forgets her pain in the pleasures of her child. She has not learned, as we have, that every child is born twice, the birth of the body and the birth of the self.

For some mothers, the second birth is easy. The grown child leaves its mother's house, but takes with it family customs and values, the intangible traditions behind the tangible gifts of Grandmother's silver, Aunt Dasha's tablecloth, or the bread tray Mama Harlan made biscuits in. These traditions span the generations, continue the family.

For us, the mothers in this book, the second birth was hard. The first birth did violence to our bodies. This second birth did violence to our expectations, to our hopes, to our dreams, to the inherited ideals we treasured. We have mourned for the child who didn't die as well as for the child who did.

But we do not own our children. We only live beside them. The time comes for all mothers when the self of the child will not be denied. We have learned to let go, to love without grasping, and once again to give our children's lives to them.

Setting them free, we free ourselves. We look past motherhood in the rhythm of our lives to the adventures that await. A mother too has a second birth, a second self.

Through the experiences recorded here, we have discovered the great truth of independence: that beyond the narrow confines of family tradition spreads a spacious realm of sympathetic selves, a world to move into. So we tell you our stories.

MOTHER, I HAVE SOMETHING TO TELL YOU

Introduction
The Secret Spell of Existence

Mothering is addictive. In ancient Rome, an *addictio* was a person who was "given over" to another, a slave. In modern America, women have all too often been encouraged to give themselves over to their children and to an ideal of motherhood. In a way hardly imaginable to those who aren't parents, to be good mothers they structure their lives to satisfy the emotional and physical needs of their children.

To be home with the children, women will give up a job they love. To provide for the children, they will take a job they hate. Mothers will hold a marriage together, change neighborhoods, choose their houses, their cars, their social circles, and their religions with the children in mind. From an excess of maternal love, they may lose their own identities in their children. Willing slaves, they put the children first.

Mothers may even come to forget that the child is distinct from the mother, and measure their successes by their children—their ability to learn, their readiness to make friends, their achievements. If a mother gives herself over to her child, the child becomes an extension of the mother. That's the catch.

And a very large catch it is. Consciously or unconsciously, when a mother devotes herself entirely to her child's well-being at the expense of her own, she anticipates a return. She has done her best for him, and in her heart of hearts she may expect him to make her happy by being the child she wants.

Suppose he doesn't? Suppose instead that an adored son or daughter makes a decision or enters a way of life that to a mother is distasteful, shocking, or horrifying? How does a woman who has made her family the center of her life cope with the disappointment and suffering that she feels?

In 1982, Margaret Smith, herself a mother, set out to answer that question through a series of interviews with American mothers. A trained sociologist who had chosen marriage and motherhood instead of a career, Margaret was motivated by past experiences with her own four children, all by then grown. She developed an irresistible compulsion to know how other traditional mothers, mothers like herself, coped with the "unexpected," "untraditional," and often "unacceptable" behavior of their children.

Each mother defined the terms independently in accordance with her own experience and standards, and the intentional ambiguity of a word like "unacceptable" allowed for a wide range of behavior in the children. However, Margaret deliberately chose to interview highly traditional mothers whose children were pioneers or victims of the sweeping social changes beginning in the 1960s. She wanted to focus on women who saw their children as having gone too far, not on mothers simply disgruntled with normal youthful rebellion. She believed that mothers whose lives had undergone a radical disjunction with the lives of their children had something to tell *all* mothers. And, as it turns out, she was right.

Over the next two years Margaret interviewed women who were generally like herself—wives of business and professional men, members of churches and clubs, community volunteers, and above all devoted full-time mothers, two of adopted children. Except for two who are Jewish and one who describes herself as an agnostic, they are Catholic or Protestant. All of them are white. Some say they are liberals, but in fact their liberalism is mostly theoretical or intellectual. F. Scott Fitzgerald's definition of a generation—a reaction against the past which occurs about three times a century—would group these women together. Though they ranged in age at the time of the interviews from forty-four to seventy, they shared essentially the same preconceptions and attitudes. They had married for life, had taken care of their homes and families, and had been unwilling or unable to have outside careers.

These mothers had tried to give their children the best of the world as they knew it: a traditional upbringing in loving but disciplined homes, with rules, curfews, chores, and manners. For the most part the women respected their own parents and the family heritage, and fully expected their children to do the same, to continue into succeeding generations the useful, industrious, circumspect life of upper-middle-class America.

To their dismay, they discovered that they had given birth instead to the rebels, the "freaks," and the flower children of the sixties and seventies. Not all of their children flouted the ways of their parents, of course, but many did. These children, characterized by woman after woman as "the cream of the crop," bright, affectionate, engaged with life, embarked as they grew up on conduct so aberrant in the eyes of their mothers that it went beyond the bounds of predictable teenage rebellion and demanded special attention.

The children came out of the closet as gays and lesbians. They formed rock groups, lived in communes, avoided the draft. They experimented with LSD and mescaline, smoked marijuana, became addicted to heroin and alcohol, and went to jail for dealing cocaine, as well as for armed robbery, theft, assault, and kidnapping. They "lived together," married across racial and religious lines, had sex-change operations, became unwed mothers or had abortions, joined the Moonies. Some succumbed to illnesses such as anorexia and bulimia, manic-depression and schizophrenia. Some overdosed with drugs and died. Others killed themselves. Eventually less than half of them had achieved enough equilibrium in their lives to be characterized by their mothers in the interviews as reasonably happy, productive, and independent. The rest had not.

The stories the mothers told Margaret were of exemplary American families, the families of *Life with Father* and *Leave It to Beaver,* beset by all the social traumas of the last quarter of a century. Here were parents, mothers in particular, who had to answer for their children's lives in the eyes of the community they lived in.

For it was the mothers, not the fathers, who felt they were blamed and who, at least initially, blamed themselves. The times they are a-changin', Bob Dylan sang. As more and more middle-class fathers involve themselves in the daily care and guidance of their children, both parents may feel they are equally responsible for a child's deviations from social expectations. But the women Margaret interviewed, who had come of age in the late forties and fifties, had been given nearly complete control of the home by busy husbands intent on careers. The husbands could judge themselves by business achievements, financial gains, promotions. For their wives, the children were *the* career, the only way they had by which to measure success in the world. As one mother told Margaret, "In the era we were raised in, the best thing you could do was to be a good mother. That was probably our primary goal. You get married, you have children, and your successes are told by the way your children turn out."

Alison Lurie puts the case well in her 1974 novel, *The War Between the Tates*. Erica Tate, whose children Muffy and Jeffo are going from bad to worse, reflects on the "separate spheres" of her husband Brian and herself:

> The worst part of it all is that the children are her fault. All the authorities and writers say so. In their innocent past Erica and Brian had blamed their own shortcomings on their parents while retaining credit for their own achievements. They had passed judgment on the character of acquaintances whose young children were not as nice as Muffy and Jeffo—but everyone did that. To have had disagreeable parents excused one's faults; to have disagreeable children underlined them. The parents might not look especially guilty; they might seem outwardly to be intelligent, kind and charming people—but inside were Mr. and Mrs. Hyde.
>
> It was agreed everywhere, also, that Mrs. Hyde was the worse; or at least the more responsible. A father might possibly avoid blame for the awfulness of his children—a mother never. After all, they were in her "area of operations," to use Brian's term. . . . He might advise Erica on important policy decisions, but ordinarily he would not question her management of the home, nor would she ever try to intervene in his professional life. If he lost his job . . . , it was his fault. If the children became uncontrollable, it was hers.

What happens to such women when the expectation of "my son, the doctor" becomes the reality of "my son, the drug pusher" or "my daughter, the Moonie"? A tragedy, or so it would seem; certainly, great pain. One moment all bright promise, the next broken bodies and ruined minds, with Mother left to pick up the pieces.

What happened instead is amazing. Many of these mothers Margaret Smith talked with rewrote the script. In their lengthy interviews with Margaret, these mothers revealed something that psychologists and journalists haven't taken sufficient note of and that in fact runs counter to the idealized view of mother martyrs prevalent in the popular imagination. Under crisis these mothers changed and grew. Faced with a child's maverick behavior, they moved through certain recognizable stages in the process of coping. Through this process, they learned, often for the first time, to separate their egos from the behavior of their children. They discovered that they could maintain the important bonds of affection and concern while relinquishing the shackles of unreasonable responsibility. Eventually, whenever possible, they turned their children's lives over to them.

In practical terms, this abnegation of excessive guilt and responsibility meant that the mothers came to accept for their children, although not for themselves, such formerly "unacceptable" behavior as homosexuality, biracial marriage, and membership in cults. For an addicted or alcoholic child, it meant that the mother did what she could to help the child while realizing that the addiction was the *child's* problem, not the mother's. Confronting even the irreversible tragedies of mental breakdown and suicide, the mothers managed to scrap a destructive load of guilt and to salvage good memories. In this process, they granted their children a second birth. They dignified the essential freedom and individuality of each child. And they set themselves free as well.

We live in an age of experts. Psychologists and psychotherapists, clothed in the authority of modern science, offer every parent who can read or turn a television knob a plethora of theories on child-rearing, on coping with crisis, and on personal fulfillment. But the experts rarely agree. As any parent turning to them for help with a troublesome child knows, every theory has its counter-theory.

Mothers are stronger and smarter than they think they are. Unlike the experts, basically the mothers whose stories are told here did agree. They learned something about child-rearing, coping, and personal growth the hard way, and they thought that what they had learned was worth knowing. In fact, many of these very reticent women were willing to be interviewed for just that reason: to pass on to other mothers the wisdom that came through their suffering.

Few of these women knew each other or had talked together. They varied considerably in personality and interests. They had sometimes vastly different ideas as to what constitutes acceptable or unacceptable behavior from a child. The fates of their children too differed. Some children came triumphantly through the crucible of social change; others emerged badly maimed; still others died at a tragically early age.

Nevertheless, as the women talked to Margaret about the experiences through which they had passed, a pattern revealed itself in interview after interview. In spite of differences in individual women, six stages emerged as basic in the process of coping with a child's untraditional behavior:

1. SHOCK. This stage is marked, for various mothers, by unrealistic expectations, denial, confusion, and anger with the child and at the unknown "cause" of his behavior. The mother feels an overwhelming sense of responsibility and guilt.

2. ATTENTION. The mother sees the real child who exists under the ideal child she had created in her mind. She tries to understand the child's true nature and then to interpret it to others, particularly to the father. Mothers at this stage often find they have unexpected skill in observing, listening, and communicating.

3. ACTION. Turning from feelings to action, the mother looks for help for herself in understanding and coping, for her child, and for the other members of the family. She consults doctors, ministers, teachers, support groups, friends, and parents in similar situations.

4. DETACHMENT. Having gone as far as she can in understanding her child and helping him to find resources for his own development, the mother recognizes the limits of her responsibility for her child. She and the father reach an agreement or a compromise on the

child's treatment. Lovingly but firmly she frees her child
from her expectations of him, and, whenever possible,
turns his life over to him.

5. AUTONOMY. Now the mother turns back to the only
life for which she is completely responsible—her own.
She evaluates it in the light of what she has learned, and
shapes it to accommodate her growth. She accepts full
responsibility for herself and to herself. This stage is
characterized by movement in new directions—new interests, a stronger role in marriage, possibilities for the
rest of her life.

6. CONNECTION. Bonds of love and concern connect
mother and child. Their relationship takes its place in
the network of independent selves to which the mother
belongs. Her child will always be part of her life, but
never all of it.

Some of the mothers interviewed could discern these stages, but
most couldn't. The pattern of the process gradually became clearly
visible, however, to the objective viewer. One younger mother,
horribly embroiled in the shock of having a delinquent and drug-
addicted son, cried through most of an interview. "Ever since he was
little," she sobbed, "he has commanded the situation in our home."
She was desperate to turn the tide. "But I'm not going to allow him
to grow up to be bad!" In these emotional sentences she suggests
the first three stages of coping: She's in shock, hence the tears. She's
paying attention with her analysis of the situation. She's resolved to
take action, though she doesn't yet know what action is needed.

The crucial step of detachment was hard for many mothers, who
found it difficult to give the burden of responsibility for a child's life
to the child himself. On the other hand, those mothers enjoying the
pleasures of the later stages of autonomy and mature connection
often actually had to be prompted for details of the earlier, trau-
matic periods. They had forgotten how bad things used to be. Time,
as many of them said, does indeed heal.

Nor was their progress through the stages regular or uniform.
Variations were created by the nature of the child's behavior and by
the mother's personality. Some women took immediate action,

while others spent a lot of time simply paying attention and deciding what action was required. Those mothers who had gained a sense of the process they were passing through tended to be stronger and more resourceful than others. They were comforted by the knowledge of their progress. Being able to recognize the steps in the process, they agreed, could help other women in similar situations.

Asking their friends for help, sharing their stories, these mothers came to believe that their experiences have universal application. Some of today's struggling parents may, like the children here, have themselves broken with tradition. Now, as they face similar problems with their own children, they can see those earlier events from the point of view of their mothers. Though this book focuses on the mothers of those growing up in the sixties and seventies, generational conflicts are a constant in American life, even in the more conservative eighties. Parents always have to cope with their young.

Every mother must discover at length what Nathaniel Hawthorne called "the secret spell of existence." An object lesson for mothers exists in that most mysterious and beautiful of American novels, *The Scarlet Letter*, and in the story of Hester Prynne, the guiltiest, most burdened mother of all, and her changing relationship with her daughter Pearl.

Because no one knows who Pearl's father is, in the eyes of Puritan Boston Pearl is entirely her mother's responsibility. At first, Hester too regards Pearl only as an extension of herself, the embodiment of the depths of her own nature. Looking into her child's eyes, "as mothers are fond of doing," she expects to see "her own miniature portrait."

Then Pearl's unpredictable antics shock Hester into awareness that she and her daughter are separate. "Child," she cries, "what art thou?"

"O, I am your little Pearl!" the child answers. "But, while she said it," Hawthorne adds, "Pearl laughed and began to dance up and down, with the humorsome gesticulation of a little imp, whose next freak might be to fly up the chimney."

"Art thou my child, in very truth?" Hester asks dubiously, wondering if Pearl is somehow "acquainted with the secret spell of her existence, and might not now reveal herself."

Hester has dropped the unthinking assumption that she and her child are one. She goes on to ask Pearl the questions that almost all women at some point in their lives as mothers want to ask their children: "Tell me, then, what thou art, and who sent thee hither?" Thus a mother begins the process of independence that allows her to see her child and herself as free and equal beings.

At the end of *The Scarlet Letter,* Hester and Pearl have arrived at a rapport that human mothers and children might well envy and try to emulate. Independent but connected, an "object of love and interest" to each other, each has taken up the secret spell of existence that legislates her life.

Hester is fictional. The women in the following pages are real. Though their names and some of the details of their lives have been changed to protect their privacy, they are neither imaginary nor composite characters. The stories that they tell really happened. The eloquent, humorous, angry words are their words. The pain which they express is the pain they suffered. The wisdom too, the wisdom that came through that pain, is theirs.

The crises in these families shed light on contemporary American attitudes toward the relations between children and parents and the functions of the community, the school, and the church. These stories also bring to life the most fundamental and universal issues of parenthood—responsibility and separation, care and communication, personal growth and connection. These issues have often been explored abstractly by sophisticated academic developmentalists. The words of these mothers give the issues life.

"Nothing is rarer," Simone de Beauvoir wrote in *The Second Sex* in 1949, "than the mother who sincerely respects the human person in her child, who recognizes his liberty even in failure." *The human person in her child.* De Beauvoir might have added the human person in herself as well: a mother cannot truly respect the person her child is or recognize his liberty unless she truly respects the separate person she is and recognizes her own liberty.

No mother, however devoted, can remain forever a vessel for her child, protecting him from the vagaries of fortune and from the consequences of his actions. Nor is a child a creature subject to his mother's total control. His mother influences him, but so do his father, his teachers, his friends. Everything that he meets in the world becomes a part of him, but he belongs to himself. The second birth acknowledges the child's ownership, "even in failure," of his own life.

Where does her child's second birth leave a mother? It gives her a second self, wiser than the first. No longer taking refuge in full-time responsibility for her children, she signs a new lease on her own life. She can, indeed must, seek fulfillment and happiness beyond motherhood, must set out to create a fate for herself. Once again, she is free to discover, as an independent human person, the secret spell of her existence.

PART I

SECOND BIRTH

Stage One

SHOCK

Facing unrealistic expectations, denial, confusion, anger, guilt, and an overwhelming sense of responsibility

1

The Double Cross

For twenty years or more the whole country was in shock, parents disappointed, children disillusioned. Their children double-crossed them, the mothers in this book claimed. The double cross comes in the gap between what they expected from their children and what they got—the gulf between dreams and reality.

The disappointment, the sense of being double-crossed, still exists below the healthy accommodation these mothers have made to their children's lives. How strong the disappointment is varies. For some women, it's deep enough to make them wish they had not had children. Asked what she would do differently if she had the chance to raise her children again, Bonnie Scott, mother of three, says that she would be the mother of one:

> I'd probably raise them the same way, but knowing what I do now—well, I've often told them, "You kids, you know, didn't ask to be born but if you had I'd have said no." I probably would stop with one.

Nor is Bonnie an unnatural mother. In 1976 Ann Landers posed the same question to her readers: "If you had it all to do over again, would you have children?" She reported the results of the survey in the June issue of *Good Housekeeping* that year: seven thousand of the ten thousand who responded, some 70 percent, answered "No!" in thunder. Many of these parents complained bitterly that their children had ruined their marriages and their lives.

How do parents feel that their children have double-crossed or cheated them? What have they expected from their children and what have they gotten?

Bonnie puts it this way:

> I loved raising them. I had them under my thumb then.
> When they were little, I was Mama and I loved it when they
> were home on vacation in the summer. I was the main man
> in their life, not their teacher or whoever. . . . I really
> liked being Mama.
>
> But when they got older they started rebelling—the kind
> that you raise to be independent and think for themselves
> and then they double-crossed me and went ahead and did
> it.

To amplify what she's saying a bit, here's the way the complaint of mother after mother in this study runs. Within the privacy of the middle-class nuclear-family home, the mother has taught her child certain basic liberal American values: The future is of your own making. You can be whatever you want. All of us are innately of equal worth. Racial and social discrimination is wrong. Money and position are less important than personal happiness and personal honesty. Discerning right and wrong is an individual matter. Let your conscience be your guide; your own heart will tell you what to do.

The mother means what she says. She is not insincere. But she assumes her child will also comprehend what she probably doesn't say, perhaps doesn't think she has to say: that such values are, in her mind, to be interpreted within certain implicit social norms, as, in fact, she has interpreted them in her own behavior.

Suppose her child takes literally what she meant to be taken theoretically. Racial discrimination is wrong? The child marries a black. Personal honesty matters? The child comes out of the closet. Let your conscience be your guide? The child drinks what he pleases, smokes dope, shoots up if he likes; his conscience says it's perfectly okay.

The mother feels double-crossed, when in fact she may have been obeyed all too well. One mother after another said, in effect, "I told

my child to think independently and to do what was right, but I
didn't mean to do *that.*" And she will almost certainly feel aggrieved
when the consequences of the child's actions deprive her of satisfactions she would normally expect to have as a mother.

Dorothy Wheeler, whose son Ned is a homosexual, says, "When
the first shock is over, you begin to feel cheated." She goes on to
explain:

> You don't feel cheated at first. You're thinking of the vic-
> tim's happiness. That strikes you first—"my poor child."
> And then it comes around to "poor me." When your
> dream is broken, shattered. And you expected that he
> would have a family.

Although "he has accepted it better than I thought he would," she
says, deep down her husband shares this sense of deprivation.

> Although he can hide his feelings very well, he would have
> preferred our son to have been straight, so that he would
> have grandchildren from our son. He had great dreams for
> our son. I certainly know how he feels. He knows he's got a
> great kid there. He just wishes he had gone another direc-
> tion.

What these mothers didn't count on was the ideological atmosphere of the times during which their children came of age, the
apocalyptic sixties and the swinging seventies. Events of these two
decades created an atmosphere that encouraged young people to
act out beliefs that they might otherwise have held quietly and
privately. The shock that one mother experiences when her child
behaves untraditionally was magnified millions of times, to affect
nearly all of America.

From the point of view of traditional middle-class parents, the
influence of the period created an indecorum, even a kind of crazi-
ness, in the young. Philip Slater, whose book *The Pursuit of Loneliness*
tries to explain the indecorous young to their parents and vice versa,
says that a principal difference in the two generations lay in the
older's adherence to social form and the younger's disregard for it.
These parents, products of the postwar forties or of the Silent
Generation of the Eisenhower years, didn't want to make scenes.
But their young, in order to display positions on social issues, did

make scenes. Coming out of the closet, putting on saffron robes,
taking a black bride home to Mother, or, as Slater says, referring to
the public protests of the sixties:

> Sitting-in at a segregated restaurant, occupying a campus
> building, lying down in front of vehicles, pouring blood in
> office files—all depended heavily on a willingness to make
> a scene and not be intimidated by a social milieu.

This willingness to put himself into the spotlight is, in fact, exactly
what Dorothy has found most difficult to contend with in Ned's
homosexuality. Twenty-four-year-old Ned informed his parents
that he was a homosexual the night before the large local newspaper
carried a profile of him, complete with his picture, announcing the
fact to the world at large.

Dorothy has mixed feelings. She had encouraged honesty and
self-knowledge in their home, but she didn't expect Ned to carry
those virtues to such lengths. On the one hand, Dorothy admires
Ned's openness. "He is more honest than anyone else I have ever
met. He always had to announce everything. He's a great talker."
On the other hand, she would feel more comfortable about his
sexual preferences if he didn't publicize them quite so much.

The Graduate, a youth cult film of the sixties, dramatizes this conflict between generations. The members of the older generation in
the film are seen by the younger as disenchanted with their lives.
They compensate by throwing themselves into unworthy business
enterprises, by quietly drinking too much, or by conducting discreet
and meaningless affairs of the kind the bride's mother, the Mrs.
Robinson of Simon and Garfunkel fame, has had with the young
protagonist, Benjamin. They don't make scenes.

For Benjamin it's another matter. In the climactic sequence at the
end of the film, as Philip Slater points out, Dustin Hoffman as
Benjamin breaks up a white, formal church wedding, surely the apex
of upper-middle-class form. In a direct challenge to the social attitudes and values which are responsible for the wedding, Benjamin
smashes into the church from the choir loft and grabs the bride. Her
long white veil flies out behind her as the two elope on, of all things,
a city bus.

Benjamin's action symbolized for the youth of America their own
relationship to establishment society. To take Slater one step fur-

ther, the key scene shows a deliberate imposition of the democratic on the upper-crust (All people are equal), a disregard for the accouterments of money and position (The qualities that matter are personal honesty and happiness), and a reliance on individual notions of right and wrong (Let your conscience be your guide). And in movie theaters across the country, young people cheered and stamped their feet encouragingly.

Alongside Benjamin and the symbolic destruction of a marriage, we might place Lois Wagner, a mother who came to support a marriage she had at first been "devastated" by. The feeling of being double-crossed and the dread of scene-making are both evident in her comments. "The guidelines [we gave our children] were, you know, be a good person, don't ever hurt anyone, do as well as you are able to do," Lois says. But when her son John took a black bride, her reaction was anger:

> I was angry. Why was I angry? Because he was doing something I didn't think he ought to do. Not that he shouldn't have, but I thought he shouldn't have. I think really the crux of a great deal of this is . . . not so much that the child does something wrong but that the child did something to put me in a position where I would have to face other people with a problem that I would rather not face. And I really do feel it's a very selfish, me-oriented kind of thing, because if I were only thinking of my child's happiness, I would have said, "Darling, I am delighted that you're married to someone that you love and who loves you," wouldn't I? But I didn't. I said, "How could you do this!" So I was thinking of me.

Lois was forced to see herself in a new light because of John's action. She saw the gap between the way she, as a mother, had told John to behave and the way she had actually expected him to act. She doesn't like herself for the unwitting hypocrisy, but she understands it:

> It's very easy to be liberal in your ideas when it's somebody else, very easy. And my husband always said, after this happened, "How could this not have happened?" because in our house we always said, "You accept people for what

they are as people, you do not accept them because of their
race, or their religion, or their origins, or any other reason,
but what they are as people." So he said, "If our son
decided that this was the person that he wanted to live with,
how can we say he shouldn't, because that is what we told
him all of his life."

Just the same, Lois "was devastated, absolutely devastated." Her
comments reveal the importance she has given social convention,
having "to face other people," in her thinking. They also show her
to have identified herself so completely with her son that his unconventional behavior became the cause of her social embarrassment.
She "cried and ranted and raved;" she says. "What has he done to
us, to me, how am I going to look in my community?"

Finally Lois got her priorities straight. "I decided, I cannot lose
my child, so I will have to accept [his choice]." She and her husband
Harold agreed that "our child's wife was going to be included in
everything that we did, just as he was."

All this drama occurred before she met her new daughter-in-law,
Anna, whom she found to be "charming, bright, and beautiful."
Shortly afterward this mother showed her support for John and
Anna with a statement as symbolic in its way as Benjamin's crash
through the choir loft. She and her husband gave a dinner party for
all their friends, and invited the young couple.

Lois is perfectly aware of the symbolic overtones of the gesture.
"She is our child now and there was no question that anybody would
think differently. I think that's the key to other people's acceptance."

It is almost impossible to understand the sense of being double-
crossed and cheated that these mothers feel without examining
briefly the differences in the generation that put on the wedding in
The Graduate and the generation that broke it up. What we see when
we look more closely at these parents and children is nothing less
than a conflict of cultures.

Most of the mothers in this study were central figures in a new
kind of family, the nuclear, suburban, middle-class family which
emerged in the aftermath of World War II. "Nuclear" is an apt word
to refer to this new image of the family, which was distinguished first
by its insularity. The family was reduced to its nucleus—father,

mother, and children—by the move to the suburbs. It had left behind, on farms, in small towns and familiar city neighborhoods, the extended family of an earlier America.

For these mothers, such insularity meant, to a very real degree, that they were on their own raising their children. Some nuclear families, like Dorothy's, maintained close connections with outlying relatives. Often, however, these new families lacked the level of supervision, the ready-made babysitters, the constant stream of advice and support and practical help, taken for granted by earlier families, when three generations, numerous cousins, aunts, and uncles, not to mention a slew of nosy or helpful neighbors, lived in close proximity.

The mother and father in the nuclear family of the late forties and fifties didn't set out intentionally to break with their families or with past modes of life. Like most venturesome Americans, they were simply pragmatic and mobile. They moved to take advantage of opportunities—jobs for the men in the cities, fresh air and space for the children in the nearby suburbs. Nevertheless, the dramatic exodus to the suburbs at the end of World War II and the creation of entire communities of similar nuclear-family groups delivered an atomic blast to traditional American life.

Bonnie Scott describes the traditional, protective small-town world in which she grew up. "I was brought up in a real little bitty town of twelve hundred. Our kids were brought up in a suburban town of thirty-five thousand. Everybody really knew me in that small town. When I was just a kid and was starting to smoke, you wouldn't dare to do it out anywhere where any of your mother's friends would see, because they'd be sure to call her up and tell her. . . . It was everybody's business to tell your mother when you were doing something wrong too. Everybody was sort of another mother."

Mothers didn't often have that kind of helpful and benign spy service available to them in the nuclear-family environment. "If just one person," Rosemary Dixon says, looking back on the years preceding her daughter Polly's horrifying suicide at the age of twenty-six, "if, say, the mother of Polly's best friend had come to me and said, 'Look, we are worried about her.' But no one ever did. . . . You go home at night and close your doors, and you and your family are a unit, and what is your business is your business, and nobody else's business."

In contrast to the earlier tradition-directed children in small towns and rural communities for whom "everybody was sort of another mother" or the "inner-directed" children whose inherited family values were the source of final authority for behavior, the situation of suburban families created what David Riesman termed "other-directed" children. These children, Riesman wrote in *The Lonely Crowd*, one of the most popular books of the fifties, were "cosmopolitan." Responding to signals from a wide circle of influences, they sought direction from "others" rather than from tradition or family. In particular the children sought to emulate each other, to accept the standards and mores set by their contemporaries. Their parents, themselves conforming to what Riesman calls "the larger signals of the group," tried to protect their children by moving to "nice" neighborhoods with "good" schools, attempting to keep them away from "bad" influences. Then they hoped for the best.

And the level of this hopefulness, the optimism of the mothers in this study, was high. "The irony is," Rosemary says with a sigh and a little laugh, "that I was so determined that I would have a healthy family." For, in addition to its insularity, the suburban nuclear family possessed another distinguishing feature: confidence in its own perfectibility.

Mothers, on whom the burden of perfection largely rested, could create within the bastions of the suburban home a small, private Eden. Here, perfect freedom of expression—no "repressed conflicts" for this Freud-wise generation!—could join perfect love in an enlightened and harmonious whole. Never was a generation of mothers more ambitious to succeed at motherhood.

Betty Friedan, in her book *The Feminine Mystique*, published in 1963, gives the term "nuclear family" another connotation in the reason she suggests for this renewed commitment to home and family: the feeling of powerlessness generated by America's use of the atomic bomb at the end of World War II. The predictable baby boom that resulted when the war was over and the men came back was followed, surprisingly, by an even greater baby boom in the fifties. As Friedan explains this phenomenon, in the presence of the Bomb Americans turned away from the outward, uncontrollable arena of social and political involvement, and turned toward the inward, presumably more controllable arena of family life.

The American spirit fell into a strange sleep; men as well as women, scared liberals, disillusioned radicals, conservatives bewildered and frustrated by change—the whole nation stopped growing up. All of us went back into the warm brightness of home, the way it was.

The husbands of the mothers in this book, the upper-middle-class men of the Silent Generation, concentrated their energies obsessively on professional success, on making money and raising the material standard of living for their families. The mothers took on, single-handedly, the task of raising the children in an atmosphere of "togetherness," one of the catchwords of the times. Every child mattered; respect for the individual went hand in glove with mutual and shared concern for all members of the family.

In spite of the fact that many of these women were as well-educated as their husbands, except for the business entertaining that came with success, the people of this class completely separated business and home life. Like a warrior, the typical husband in this study went to battle every morning; he was away in the city from nine to five, or, more truthfully, from seven to seven. His day was long and arduous, with a commute on each end. The ideal for the women, when the children were small, was to have them fed, bathed, and garbed for bed so that Daddy could see them at their sweetest for an hour before bedtime.

Women's magazines of the fifties advised women to pretty themselves as well as the children before their men came home, with a bath, fresh, feminine clothes ("It doesn't matter what you have on, so long as it's not what you were wearing when he left!"), and scent behind the ears. Most of these young mothers tried to comply. They wanted perfect marriages, perfect homes, and, of course, perfect children.

As the children grew older, many men began to make frequent business trips in their ascent to upper-middle-class success. As an extreme case, Rosemary's husband was "in a job that kept him in different parts of the world and away from home for months at a time." She was of necessity left to handle their five children alone.

Dorothy's husband traveled too. She wonders now if her husband's frequent absences had anything to do with Ned's homosexuality.

I felt that he was away from home too much when our son
was little and I would say that's when it first started. Traveling and being away, and I was responsible for the five alone
except for gala weekends and outings for them—fishing
and trips to the coast and things like that. But I felt I was
responsible full-time.

The home world, miles and miles of peaceful landscape, was inhab-
ited almost entirely by women and children. Mother, a remarkably
resourceful and energetic woman, held the whole edifice together.

What was this woman, the mother of our book, like? She was first
of all a mother, in spades. The birth rate rose in the United States
after World War II to reach its postwar height in 1960, and then to
decline—there were about three births in 1960 for every two in
1981. (Meanwhile, from 1950 on, the number of births was falling in
France, Norway, Sweden, the U.S.S.R., India, Japan, and other advanced nations.) Girls in the United States married young, half of
them before they were twenty, and had babies young.

Slightly older, educated women had increasingly large families,
especially if they were Catholic. Half of the mothers in this book had
four or more children. Both Rosemary Dixon and Dorothy Wheeler
had five; one mother has six; another, seven; still another has, including three stepchildren, a grand total of nine.

Mothers responsible for families the size of these could hardly be
expected to work outside the home unless family needs made it
absolutely necessary. Nor had most of them seriously considered
lifetime careers as a possibility for their lives. They would work for a
year or two before they married or until the children came, they
assumed, and that would pretty much be that. Even higher education of the time assumed that women would forfeit careers in order
to marry and raise their children. As enlightened a liberal thinker as
Adlai Stevenson conformed to the prevailing doctrine of feminine
domesticity. In the commencement address at Smith College in
1959, he advised this female intellectual *crème de la crème* that Smith
graduates could best exercise political power through their influence as wives and mothers. In a variant of the old "The hand that
rocks the cradle is the hand that rules the world," Stevenson suggested:

This assignment for you, as wives and mothers, you can do in the living room with a baby in your lap or in the kitchen with a can opener in your hand. If you're clever, maybe you can even practice your saving arts on that unsuspecting man while he's watching television. I think there is much you can do about our crisis in the humble role of housewife. I could wish you no better vocation than that. [Quoted in Friedan.]

Elizabeth Janeway, in her book *Cross Sections,* describes the dilemma of well-educated women of the fifties:

"What am I doing here?" graduates of the Seven Sisters were asking themselves as they sorted the laundry. . . . Perhaps even more often the question was "What was I doing there—listening to lectures on Seventeenth-Century French Poetry, Organic Chemistry, and Money and Banking—when I was fated by the Destiny of Anatomy to end up here?" For the decade of the fifties was not one in which the graduates of even the most prestigious women's colleges easily contemplated a change in their fate, their status or their occupation. Married they must aspire to be; housewives they must expect to become.

Was a college education for women a complete waste of time, then? No, because *the home,* in its movement toward perfection, would benefit from the cultivated artistic, intellectual, and moral qualities of educated mothers. Some of the women here, like Ann Rourke, a mother of seven with a degree from Vassar, regretted that they hadn't had courses designed for future parents, instead of or in addition to their liberal arts courses. "I would have trusted myself a lot more," Ann says, "and it was really lack of confidence in myself, you know, thinking that there was really some big mystery [to being a mother] that I didn't understand."

In lieu of such courses, many women turned to that wonderfully comforting guru for parents in the fifties and sixties, Dr. Benjamin Spock. Originally published in 1945 and sold for twenty-five cents a copy, Spock's *Baby and Child Care* has now sold well over thirty million copies. It was nothing for the college-educated mother of a large family in the fifties to go through several copies, wearing threadbare particularly useful passages on everything from infant colic to toilet training to discipline.

Spock was comforting to the novice mother from the first sentence, "You know more than you think you do," because he told her to trust her own judgment and instincts. After all, she was a mother, and mothers instinctively know best! All she had to do was *be there*. She could relax about toilet training, she could feed her child when it was hungry, she would know what to do in crises.

A symbol of reassurance for mothers and permissiveness for children, Spock nevertheless set forth a philosophy that reinforced the dominant view at the time of the mother's role in child-rearing: her full-time presence was indispensable. Why? Because of the malleability of the child. A mother could virtually create her child in the image she envisioned; therefore nothing less than total dedication was acceptable. If she tried hard enough, she could make a perfect child.

As Philip Slater puts it:

> From the very beginning Spock's books have encouraged Pygmalionesque fantasies in mothers—stressing the complexity and importance of the task of creating a person out of an infant. His good sense, tolerance, humanity, and uncanny ability to anticipate the anxieties that everyday child-rearing experiences arouse in young mothers seduce them into accepting the challenge. Deep in their hearts most middle-class, Spock-taught mothers believe that if they did their job well enough, all their children would be creative, intelligent, kind, generous, happy, brave, spontaneous, and good—each, of course, in his or her own special way.

In their efforts to create perfect children, these idealistic, energetic, educated, earnest women set out to create perfect homes. They succeeded perhaps too well, so well that their children often were devastated when they discovered the unpleasant realities of the world outside the home—the poverty, the violence, the racism, the hypocrisy and shoddiness of much of America. Mother never told them it would be like this. Often Mother, isolated in her pleasant home, didn't know. And neither Mother nor American society generally was ready for the violent break with tradition generated by the inconsistency between the ordered, insular home and the chaotic world outside.

WHAT THE CHILDREN WANTED

If the mothers felt double-crossed, more than likely many of their children did too. In response, as these children grew up and discovered what the world outside the home was like, they invented a counterculture. As their mothers had tried to create perfect homes, they tried to create a perfect society, a world of their own making.

Steven Tipton in *Getting Saved from the Sixties* places the responsibility for the rise of the counterculture with its alternative religious movements squarely on the ethos of the middle-class family of the period. The amount of leisure time in the middle-class home and the separation of the home from business and economic self-interest made it, as Tipton writes, "a refuge of intimacy and tenderness, love and duty." Within the home there was time to express feelings, to enjoy pleasures, to get to know oneself, and to have what the sixties dubbed "meaningful relationships" with others. Sincerity, openness, trust, mutual respect, and love were valued rather than the authority and obedience of an earlier time.

A young person coming from such a home was often ill prepared to encounter the vagaries of society. He was apt to become disillusioned both with society and with his parents, according to Tipton:

> Many of the upper-middle-class sixties youth whose families and educations most developed this new ethos rebelled not so much against their parents' values as against the larger society's failure to enact these values in its public policy or bureaucratic structure. They charged their parents with hypocrisy for failing to enact the values they espoused *in the home* once they went outside of it.

"I don't think our daughter rebelled against us so much," says Bonnie of the civil rights activism of her daughter Sheila that led to Sheila's biracial marriage, "as she was really rebelling at society . . . and jumping on the bandwagon for the black people."

"Never trust anyone over thirty," youth of the time cautioned each other, believing that older people and American society generally had sold out. But, as Aristotle noted centuries ago, the young are often disenchanted with their elders and vice versa. What made the youth revolution of the sixties different? First of all, the vast number of young people who were involved. Because of the baby boom after World War II, half of America was under twenty-five. As they turned eighteen, they left home and family for the by then common American experience of college. Away from home, they joined forces to become, as Morris Dickstein puts it in *Gates of Eden*, "an amorphous mass spread out across thousands of colleges and communes, in the country and the city, whose culture enshrined music and films and drugs more than books."

Parents, seeing their children turn radical in college, were often inclined to blame the reading and teaching in the college classroom. Not so, says Dickstein:

> It's safe to say that few kids became radicals, hippies, or freaks in the sixties from reading *Eros and Civilization* or *Growing Up Absurd*. . . . [T]he tremors of the sixties, which shook institutions in so many remote corners of society, were generated from society's own deep core, from all those problems neglected in the fifties that could no longer be wished away.

Ironically, the financial success of their parents gave them what the generations before them had certainly never had in such numbers: the leisure in the college community, the detachment from the work world, to look at the country they lived in and to see more or less objectively the national problems they began to address.

Lois remembers how John, now a successful lawyer, was in college:

> Until he decided to go to law school and to become part of the establishment, we didn't know which way he would go. He was very angry. He was angry at the whole world. Because he felt here was a world that should be a good world, and he's still growing up, and he still has a whole life to lead, and what's going to happen to this world. And the outward signs were a beard and long hair. . . . It was an

intellectual rebellion. . . . "We're in a rotten world and it's not of our doing and what are we going to do about it?" What they did about it was scream and holler and no matter what we said—oh, we always had great discussions in our house—we were always 100 percent wrong. . . . "Mother, you don't understand what's going on. You're naive. You've been very protected all of your life."

Aside from the tremendous power in numbers the youth had, the sexual permissiveness and proliferation of drugs of the period made this youth revolution socially more significant than those of the past. Every generation thinks it invented sex, and this one was no different. What gave these kids a sexual freedom unknown in the past and allowed them to change the sexual mores of the country perhaps permanently was, of course, the pill.

How was a mother from the buttoned-down fifties supposed to deal with a child's, particularly a daughter's, promiscuous sexuality? Members of the generation of the forties and fifties were not necessarily celibate, but they tended to be faithful. The constant possibility of pregnancy made fidelity to a single partner essential, at least for women; hence the double standard. Now the pill allowed women too the privilege of sex with as many partners as they liked. This practical license caused a fundamental rethinking of the whole subject of sex. Everything was up for grabs, even *The Scarlet Letter:* a scholarly journal of the seventies ran an article entitled "Hester Prynne and the Pill." Forget sin, forget guilt. Here at last was sex without consequences, sex without the responsibility of children.

The change in sexual mores had sweeping and unpredictable effects on the lives on these young people. Agnes Price, for example, firmly believes her daughter Phoebe became anorexic when Phoebe's standards about chastity, learned at home, came into conflict with social permissiveness toward sex. As Agnes explains the situation:

> She was a very round and firm and fully packed young lady, and the boys loved her, and she always had high moral principles. She would go out with some boy, and she'd come in and say, "Wow! I can't go out with him again. I can't handle it." And so I think [the anorexia] was one way to avoid it. She was sick and tired of beating off the boys.

When she got thin and anorexic, all of a sudden . . . the
periods stopped, the boobs deteriorated, the whole thing.
She did not have to fight off the boys.

Drugs were an unfamiliar and terrifying aspect of the youth movement for most parents. "Dope was never anything I'd even heard of.
I mean, I knew nothing about dope, and I don't think my husband
knew anything about dope," says Margot Morrison, whose son Paul
died of an overdose at nineteen. Jazz musicians might smoke "reef-
ers" or use cocaine or heroin, but ordinary people in the years
before the sixties knew nothing about drugs.

Then here were the young of the sixties touting exotic or previously unheard-of substances—marijuana, heroin, cocaine, LSD,
mescaline, hashish, Methedrine, amyl nitrite. They spoke of these
substances as consciousness-raising devices, tools of mind expan-
sion which would allow perfect rapport between people, a sense of
oneness with the universe, and even a mystical experience with God.

What was a parent to say? Ruthanne Mowbray's daughter Beth,
the youngest of four children, began experimenting with drugs in
high school. "I did find occasion to talk to her about the dangers of
drugs," Ruthanne says, "and she defended them."

Beth, a top student, stayed straight enough to graduate from high
school with excellent grades. She went away to college in the fall of
1969. Soon she was in trouble. Ruthanne says, "She told us later she
had some very bad trips with LSD." After several suicide attempts,
once slashing her own throat, once drinking gasoline, Beth had a
complete breakdown. She is still mentally incapacitated and will
probably always be dependent on her parents.

Ruthanne doesn't believe the drugs are entirely responsible.
Bright, smart, outgoing, Beth, her mother says, "had a borderline
personality. She was a fairly sensitive child. . . . She was aware of
everything, asked questions about why are we here, and about God,
a little more introspective . . . than her brothers and sisters."

But in such a vulnerable person, the use of drugs precipitated a
crisis, her mother thinks, that might have otherwise been averted.
Hallucinations and other experiences that could perhaps have been
resisted by another kind of person had an unfortunate and overwhelming effect on Beth. "I think if she had not had those bad trips,
she would be all right today. A borderline personality, who with a

very normal life might not have been mentally ill. At any rate, today, ten years later, she is a mentally ill girl."

It was not only parents who could often see difficulties in the supposedly mind-liberating drugs. In his wonderful parody of sixties language and behavior, *Snow White*, published in 1967, Donald Barthelme reveals the nonsense in the chemical path to enlightenment through the experience of Edward, one of the seven:

> Edward was blowing his mind, under the boardwalk. "Well my mind is blown now. Nine mantras and three bottles of insect repellent under the boardwalk. I shall certainly be sick tomorrow. But it is worth it to have a blown mind. . . . Those cream Corfam shoes clumping overhead. I understand them now, for the first time . . . their sacredness. Their centrality. They are the center of everything, those shoes. They are it. I know that, now. Too bad it is not worth knowing."

But for many of the young, drugs were an aphrodisiac, a tranquilizer, a study aid, and a tool of philosophy. Dropping acid together was a religious ritual, in which two or more people could move through the same spiritual experiences simultaneously. Drugs were believed to open what Aldous Huxley called "the doors of perception," and their effect on the counterculture was immeasurable.

What was the counterculture like? Because of the pill, the generation of the sixties was perhaps the first generation ever that didn't have to devote its youthful creativity to raising kids, and it gave its primary attention to making the world better. Tipton describes the basic tenets of this alternative to establishment society proposed by the young in the lives they led.

Its conception of reality began with the individual, "a personality that experiences, knows, and simply *is,*" or, as the catchphrase of the time had it, "the way to do is to be." For these individuals, the goodness of an action was measured by the level of satisfaction it yielded, so that "If it feels good, do it" was regarded as a generally reliable guide to behavior. When Mick Jagger sang, "I Can't Get No Satisfaction," he was uttering a spiritual plaint.

Consistency was not viewed as a positive quality. Spontaneity and self-expression were valued: "Let it all hang out." Different behavior was appropriate for different situations—"Go with the flow"—

and for different people—"Different strokes for different folks."
Instead of setting up moral absolutes for life, one should pay attention to what was happening from moment to moment and do what
felt most fitting in response.

Feelings were all-important, the key to the truths held by the
universe and the natural world of which man was a part. The hippies
took the position of Rousseau, that man in the state of nature is
good. Consequently, to be "in touch with your feelings" and then to
do what was spontaneous, honest, and natural would be to do what
was right.

Wholeness mattered, as in "the whole earth" (which could be
catalogued) and "the whole person" rather than a collection of
social "roles."

The counterculture then set itself against what it saw in America:
technological sophistication achieved at the expense of the fragmentation of human life and the alienation of human beings. It
valued intuition and feeling, personal experience, tolerance, and
acceptance of others.

There was nothing particularly alarming or even particularly new
in these ideas stripped of their cultural decor. Nevertheless, the
ideas and the behavior that accompanied them caused one of the
most serious schisms ever experienced in American life. The schism
was made more serious because neither parents nor "the experts"
could, at the time, make sense out of what was going on with the
young. A chasm divided young and old, long-haired and short-
haired, bearded and clean-shaven, students and administration,
youthful behavior and the law, and, with the advent of the Vietnam
War, doves and hawks. Parents were separated from the hearts and
minds of their children. How could a mother respond properly to
what she couldn't comprehend?

Rebecca Winslow, an admittedly stern mother who once scolded a
girlfriend of her daughter Kris for wearing curlers to the family
dinner table, says that Kris found something with her "group," a
vaguely religious cult, that she never got at home. "The group," a
whole colony of people who have followed each other over the years
to various small towns along the eastern seaboard, has for all practical purposes become Kris's family. They live near each other,
though not always together, share each other's money, conduct

various artistic and business enterprises together, tend each other's children.

From a mother's point of view, too, group membership has advantages.

> Once a New York *Times* reporter came [to visit the community] and questioned our daughter. She said that she didn't need drugs, because she got high on the experience [of the group]. So she found, I guess, what she was looking for, but I never quite discovered what it was.

Nevertheless, Rebecca regards the strength of Kris's attachment to the group as a rejection of her family, and has lived with confusion and jealousy about this ongoing part of her daughter's life.

> I suppose I was jealous to a certain extent. I think probably all parents are. They question why their children need this. I asked my daughter why she had to be there. What had been missing in our home life that she felt she had to have this? Was this going to be her family from now on?

Kris has tactfully refrained from answering, but Rebecca knows the answer. "Our daughter's loyalties were always to the group before her family," she says sadly.

Kris's silence is typical. A difficulty in closing the schism between these generations has lain in the distrust of language or the inadequacy with it exhibited by the young. They frequently felt that it was impossible to communicate in language the insights they gained. The journalist Joan Didion, in "Slouching Towards Bethlehem," describes an acid trip she witnessed in Haight-Ashbury in 1967:

> At three-thirty that afternoon Max, Tom, and Sharon placed tabs under their tongues and sat down together in the living room to wait for the flash. Barbara stayed in the bedroom, smoking hash. During the next four hours a window banged once in Barbara's room, and about five-thirty some children had a fight on the street. A curtain billowed in the afternoon wind. A cat scratched a beagle in Sharon's lap. Except for the sitar music on the stereo there was no other sound or movement until seven-thirty, when Max said "Wow."

Inarticulation became the mode. Initiates, the reasoning went, understood without words, and all the words in the language could not pass the experience along to the uninitiated.

This distrust of language was compounded in the dispute between the factions in America over the Vietnam War, the major catalyst of the conflicts of the sixties. Whatever one thinks about America's role in Vietnam, no one seriously disputes the fact that a whole vocabulary of deception (and self-deception) arose in the political and military operation of the war. War was never officially declared, so people were dying in what was described as "a police action" or "a conflict," implemented through powers given to the President in a tame-sounding congressional "resolution." Soldiers went to Asia "to win the hearts and minds of the people." We were "advisers" to the South Vietnamese, and the "Vietnamization" that began in 1970 ostensibly meant that they would do the fighting rather than American troops. "Rooting out the infrastructure" meant killing not only Vietnamese soldiers carrying weapons but also their civilian relatives or suspected sympathizers. The "pacification program" referred to the same practice. The cozy "carpet bombing" meant a bombing pattern designed not to destroy recognizable military targets but to wipe out all life on every square inch of an area. Such euphemisms deepened the young's suspicion of language itself and of the people who used it so glibly, and widened the gulf between the establishment and the counterculture.

Many parents agreed with their children on this issue. Upper-middle-class parents, even those from hawkish backgrounds that might previously have used the military life to straighten out an errant child, regarded the prospect of sending a son to Vietnam as unthinkable. When Paul Morrison and his father got into a pitched battle over Paul's drugs, Paul had to go out on his own, the second-worst thing he could have done, according to his mother, Margot. The worst would have been to go to Vietnam. Margot says:

> The horrible part was the period he lived in. Had he lived twenty years earlier, there would have been problems, but I don't think it would have led to his death [of a drug overdose at nineteen]. I remember my father always saying [when a crisis arose], "Well, probably the best thing in the world would be to have him join the Army. That's what I

did, and it made a man out of me." Well, unfortunately, this
was the Vietnam War.

Bonnie Scott believes that her middle child and only son, Fred,
was completely and permanently derailed by Vietnam, even though
he didn't go himself. Fred, who graduated from high school in 1969,
"had a cousin that he was very close to that was killed over there six
weeks after he arrived. We went to his funeral in a military cemetery,
with all the white crosses. And Fred was very impressionable; he's a
sort of artistic child. And he hated Nixon, and he got into the drug
bit, and lived in a commune right after high school. He just made a
mess of his life."

Although his parents supported the war, Fred registered as a
conscientious objector. "We had a World War II mentality," Bonnie
says. "We just didn't realize what kind of war that was. But Fred
started working on a deferment before he was eighteen, got all the
information and got the letters written, whatever he had to do, and
he did all this without our help. I think now he was a lot smarter than
we were." But Fred has never recovered from his disillusionment
with American society and perhaps with his parents as well.

The sixties and seventies were the best of times, the worst of
times. And when the scenes of these turbulent decades had played
themselves out, some of America's children were victims and others
were pioneers. Many of the mothers whose stories are told in this
book consider their children victims. Victims of their own natures.
Victims of a misplaced idealism. Victims of their innocence, of their
capacity to feel, even of lessons of achievement and dedication and
fairness learned in the family which somehow let them down in life.

A disinterested observer will not always agree. Some of these
children—proud, courageous, and independent—who are regarded
as victims by their mothers, can clearly be seen as pioneers of freer
and better ways of living. But mothers are bound by rules of the
heart which may prevent clear vision.

Oddly enough, it is often as difficult for the mother of a pioneer to
cope with her child's behavior as for the mother of a victim. Pioneer
or victim, the untraditional child causes his mother to move from
the initial shock to attention, action, and detachment, until finally
she reaches the plateau of autonomy and mature connection with
her child. Like all mothers, along the way each mother ponders the

causes of her child's behavior and her own responsibility. Each regrets the child's decisions. Each dreams of a more perfect future for her once perfect child.

We can distinguish between victims and pioneers by the level of responsibility in their behavior. The victims challenged tradition with behavior that was irresponsible to themselves and their own talents and to their families. Rosemary's daughter Polly knew that suicide was irresponsible. When a close friend of hers committed suicide, Rosemary says she burst out, "How could she have done that? I could never hurt my family that way." But she did. Suicide, dope addiction, alcoholism, membership in a cult, anything which limits growth, destroys the power to choose, and denies human love —clearly these are irresponsible paths. The pioneers, on the other hand, challenged tradition responsibly, in ways which made them larger, stronger, more loving.

As the mothers speak to us in the coming pages, it is our turn to ponder, to regret, and to dream. What mystery of human personality turned some children into pioneers and others of similar backgrounds and equal talents into victims? What remorseless fate turned the struggles of some mothers into triumphs and those of others into tragedies? Surely the suffering of these women gives them the right to ask: What made the difference?

But no resonant, ringing "Why?" will call forth a cosmic answer. We can speculate, but we can never know for sure.

2

Rosemary for Remembrance

Shock is an almost inevitable part of life for mothers. When the phone rings at two in the morning, most mothers sit up instantly, awake and full of dread: Johnny? Susan? Where are they and what has happened to them? We ready ourselves for disaster. But no mother can ever really be ready for some of the shocks that children deliver.

Item: Two days after her fiftieth birthday, Myra de Shazo flew to Florida from her home in Pennsylvania to begin decorating a condominium she and her husband had bought as a retirement home. Two days later, her husband surprised her by deciding to join her. "He called and said, 'I'm coming in.' I was thrilled!

"But the first thing he told me was that Ben had been arrested. And I said, 'Oh, dear, what for?' And he said, 'Selling cocaine.'" Bail for Ben was set at $85,000, and he subsequently served eighteen months in a federal prison.

Item: One cold Friday night in November of 1976, Kate Barnes, who was suffering from a mild case of the sniffles, had a warm bath and crawled into bed with a book. Everyone else in her family, her husband Nicholas and their three children, had gone to the high school football game. The police called. Debby, the eighth-grader, had been found in some woods behind the school, barely able to give her name. "She had drunk a tremendous amount of vodka and beer in about an hour and a half," Kate says.

Nick and Kate sped to the hospital, where all night long Debby's stomach was pumped. About four o'clock in the morning, the doctor stepped out and told Kate he thought Debby would live.

Item: That lazy Sunday afternoon Margaret and Van Bentley were catching the last of the Masters on the big television set in their family room. The door opened, and Nan, a college sophomore, came in from the garage. "She had her new gray suit on, and I said, 'Hi, honey! Gee, you look so great!'

"She walked over and turned the TV off, which was most unusual, because she was such a nice kid, just so thoughtful and just a joy. . . . Then we became aware that there was somebody behind her, this girl. And Nan turned around to us, I'll never forget it, and she just looked at us and said, 'This is Tricia. We are lovers. She loves me and I love her, and I want you to let her live with us.' "

Item: Margot and Paul Morrison were taking their family to Mexico for a long weekend. They were especially pleased because Paul Jr., who'd been having some problems and was under the care of a doctor, had agreed to come along and to bring his girlfriend, Sandy. On Friday night before they were to leave on Saturday, Sandy called Paul to say good-night and to find out what time they'd leave the next morning.

She missed him by about fifteen minutes. In that fifteen minutes Paul bought and injected the drug overdose that killed him.

However aware a mother might be of her child's difficulties, as three of the four mothers here were, events like these are an overwhelming blow. Shock is always there, but the level of shock varies. The greater the gap between what a parent has learned to expect from a child and what the child actually does, the greater the shock. When parents expect only good things from a child, experiences like these can devastate. In time, a mother may recover from such a shock, but she will never forget it.

Rosemary and Robert Dixon had learned to expect nothing but the best from their daughter Polly. "Outsiders always considered Polly the perfect child," Rosemary says, an opinion in which she and Robert concurred. And the Dixon family standards for perfection are high. Five members of Rosemary's immediate family have graduated from Columbia University: Robert and two sons, Bob Jr. and

Philip, from Columbia, she and her only daughter, Polly, from its affiliate, Barnard.

The Columbia connection is significant. Other facts about the Dixon family can be altered to preserve their anonymity. We can change their name, can settle them in Utah or California or Texas instead of their native Connecticut. We can find employment for Robert in marketing or space technology or education instead of television, and we can assert, truthfully enough, that Rosemary's two youngest sons have chosen other schools. But the salient fact remains that Columbia University has been a constant presence in the life of the Dixons for nearly four decades.

What does this mean? It means first of all that the family belongs to an intellectual aristocracy, an elite based not on money or family but on educational achievement. To have one or two Columbia grads in two generations confers status on a family. To have five indicates a remarkable climate of intellectual energy and a genuine intellectual tradition in the family.

Second, obviously it means that Columbia played a role, probably a vital role, in shaping the character of such a family. If a university is more than the sum of its buildings, as schools like Columbia rightly insist they are, then Columbia has a tacit but real responsibility for the quality of life of its graduates. And Columbia has had every right to be satisfied with the successful, progressive, responsible Dixon family.

Rosemary Dixon, Barnard 1947, is a strikingly elegant woman, dressed the late-April morning of the interview in a smart navy linen suit, with pearls at the neck of her white silk blouse. Her dark hair, lightly streaked with gray, is pulled back sleekly into a bun at the nape of her neck, a severe style which suits her pale madonna face. Her face, in repose, is sad, her manner reserved and controlled. Most of the time during the conversation she speaks tentatively, almost as if working out a difficult academic exercise. But when she talks about Polly's early life she smiles lingeringly at the memories of her "perfect child."

Rosemary was proud of Polly. If Columbia created standards for the Dixons, Polly, the oldest of Rosemary and Bob's five, went above and beyond any standards set. Polly was a winner. From childhood on, Polly was totally serious about her activities. "I don't think you can realize," her mother says, "what a strong force she was in our household, even at six or seven.

"Whatever she'd do, she'd do with such thoroughness. She decided she wanted to be a coin collector at one point, so she had more and better coins than anyone else—they were all over the place. And another time, she started studying wildflowers. Before long she knew more wildflowers than anyone else. We could mention any little thing, and she would just take it and go!"

Aside from their pride in Polly's accomplishments, the Dixons enjoyed Polly. Her four younger brothers looked up to her and emulated her, and her parents delighted in her. "This was a joyous child to have at home," Rosemary says, "humorous and close, a child who needed to stay close." Polly wasn't the least bit stiff or stodgy. "She was funny, really funny," Rosemary remembers, "such a klutz. Everyone enjoyed her klutziness, and she did too. She tripped and spilled—you could just follow her trail around the house."

Rosemary chuckles at a recollection. "I remember when she was a teenager, her coming downstairs in her Frye boots with the big heels, tripping down the steps, and dropping a cup of coffee. And everyone hears the crash all over, and this scream, 'Oh, shit!' " For a moment it seems as if pretty, klutzy Polly is in the room.

Academically Polly was brilliant, at the top of her class every year. Her parents had enrolled her from the first grade on in a small, private girls' preparatory school, where she was with the same friends, children from backgrounds like her own, through high school. At first a little inclined toward shyness, as Polly grew up she began to make "lots of friends, close, caring friends."

Rosemary's pleasure in Polly was intensified by Polly's competitive spirit in the swimming pool. Rosemary herself had been a diver in college, and she loved seeing Polly follow in her laps. By the time Polly was in junior high school, she had become a nationally ranked junior competition swimmer. Her parents, especially Robert, encouraged her, but were never really "pushy," Rosemary claims.

> How do you develop a superchild? You start off with [lessons from the neighborhood teacher] in something in which other people in the family have an interest. And then the teacher sees that this child can go a little more, and

recommends a better teacher. You end up driving miles to get to the teacher, and the teacher sets up a routine, and the child thrives on it, loves it, becomes compulsively addicted to it, whatever you want to say.

Rosemary didn't realize at first how passionately devoted to her swimming Polly was. When Polly was twelve, Rosemary made what she now considers a "destructive" demand of her athlete daughter.

It had to do with a social situation at our summer cottage. It's a very small, tight community, a club arrangement of houses, so that good manners are just essential. People wanted her to participate in an intra-club swimming and diving competition, and she didn't want to do it.

I said, "You *have* to do it in this situation. They are expecting you to." So she did it, but she behaved in a sullen way, and made it obvious that she didn't want to be there.

As most mothers would, Rosemary admonished Polly for her bad attitude. "I said, 'You really shouldn't have behaved like that.' " A mild enough chastisement, but then Polly had rarely received criticism. Later Rosemary was to reproach herself for putting social expectations above her daughter's feelings.

Rosemary had little else to reproach herself with. She was a conscientious, loving mother, and she never let the high level of her participation in community affairs interfere with her top priority, the welfare of her children. A highly intelligent woman, she deliberated over the way she treated the five of them. Because Robert's business trips often made her the only parent in charge for weeks at a time, she felt she had to be especially scrupulous.

She thought long and hard, for example, about her brother who had killed himself during the trauma of World War II and the effect that such a family story might have on children. Early in Polly's life, Rosemary wondered what to say about the shadowy figure in the family album. She and Bob talked it over and decided not to let their children know their uncle was a suicide. "I had read that suicide becomes an attractive, romantic image, when people dwell on it," Rosemary says, reflectively smoothing the skirt of her suit. She was confident that she could escape the past and create her greatest desire, "a healthy family."

Healthy, brilliant, happy Polly went off to Barnard, her mother's school, in 1968. Rosemary still remembers vividly the day Polly and her parents arrived at the campus. "It was a wildness, things were crazy. We had this pretty, clean girl, with nice-looking clothes, and we dropped her at this prestigious university. These filthy people were sitting along a dusty, dirty corridor. Here we were, parents coming in with a new girl, and not one of these dirty-haired, unattractive people even looked up with any interest."

As that first semester wore on, Rosemary became concerned about her daughter. Polly made constant phone calls home. "At that time, buildings were being burned, campus presidents' offices stormed by students. She would be just unbelieving of things going on in the dormitory—actual orgies, she said. Where there's a bathroom at the end of the hall, and boys and girls are in there taking showers together and flailing things around and screaming and having a regular orgy—and she's down the hall listening in!"

Rosemary's fastidiousness verifies her own description of herself as an overly protective mother, but any mother would be dismayed at other experiences that Polly had that fall at Barnard. She was grabbed off the street and dragged into an alley by an "Indian" who tried to rape her. She escaped by kneeing him and running. Her room was broken into. She was getting into a car with a bag of groceries, when a black boy came up, knocked her to the ground, and grabbed her wallet. Groceries went everywhere. "It was just a wild, horrible environment," Rosemary says.

Finally the crisis came. "She called home one night and said, 'I'm afraid. I went to the top of this tower and got to thinking, what if I were to jump? I was afraid I might jump.' "

For the first time Rosemary realized that Polly's problems were internal as well as external. She and Bob took action quickly. They made an appointment for Polly in another city with a nationally respected psychiatrist specializing in adolescent problems. After he had talked to Polly, he told her parents, "She has to be hospitalized immediately. This girl has never developed an ego." His diagnosis was that Polly's whole personality structure would have to be broken down and rebuilt.

Rosemary was shocked—and skeptical. She wondered how a child could be that defective without the parents knowing it. She recoiled too at the doctor himself, "the most physically and socially unattractive man. Our stomachs turned at the sight of him." Nevertheless, she and Robert put Polly into the hospital on a voluntary commitment, which meant that she could be released on her own request. In two weeks Polly was out, "having convinced everybody that she could handle life on the outside again." She came home to Greenwich for the rest of the school year.

That year Bob was working away from home, but Rosemary stayed behind with the children. Once she was back in Greenwich, Polly seemed to be doing fine. Twice a week she drove in to see a psychiatrist in New York, with whom she developed a wonderful intellectual friendship, though, Rosemary says, in retrospect, it "did her no good" psychologically at all. The following fall, with everyone's encouragement, Polly went back to Barnard. This time, in spite of the continuing campus unrest, there were no hysterical phone calls or desperate letters home. Polly was apparently okay. Better than okay: for the next four years she succeeded brilliantly in her studies.

Rosemary quit worrying. She knew that during her college years and afterward Polly saw three or four different psychiatrists. As Rosemary explains it, she would see one for a while, then move on to another in order not to "do whatever the doctors told her to." But her mother wasn't terribly concerned. She wasn't sure what sort of useful advice Polly could have gotten anyway from a doctor like the first psychiatrist they'd taken her to. Polly was so intelligent, so successful, so much in command of her life, that Rosemary believed her daughter knew what was best. "I had such respect for this person that if she had told me she was seeing a psychiatrist in Johannesburg, South Africa, I would not question her." She trusted Polly to work it out.

After her graduation, Phi Beta Kappa and *summa cum laude*, from Barnard, Polly landed, one after the other, a series of positions which were highly prestigious for a young woman. An extremely talented commercial artist, she went from one excellent post to another. She never stayed in one place long enough to reap all the benefits, but every move was a move up.

Her family didn't view the job-jumping critically. It was natural for a girl of Polly's talents to escalate quickly in her profession, they thought. "None of us looked upon it as a failure, never. But the length of stay got shorter and shorter."

And the pattern was always the same, Rosemary says, until the last job of her life as art director of a national publication. "In her final job, which she worried about getting, which she got, which she didn't want to take once she had it, she worked about eight or ten weeks, and then drove off and committed suicide." In 1975, three years after sweeping the field for honors at her college graduation, Polly checked into a motel alone and took a fatal overdose of sleeping pills.

"It was an unbelievable shock," Rosemary says, sitting up taller in her chair and crossing her slender legs nervously. As soon as she could really take in the fact that her perfect child was dead by her own hand, she went into agonies of speculation about the cause. Why, why, why?

She thought immediately of the years of protective silence she and Bob had carefully maintained about her brother's suicide. In spite of it, here was Polly, with all her solid achievements and all her bright promise, dead at twenty-six. Could there be a genetic factor at work? "It would be really easy to rationalize that it has something to do with depression in the genes."

Recent scientific experimentation lends credibility to this idea. For Rosemary, however, it was too easy, and Rosemary has never taken the easy way out. That answer didn't satisfy her.

She was also inclined to blame what she considered the baleful influence of the sixties. Polly's first breakdown had come when she was faced with the chaotic Columbia atmosphere of her first semester away from home. Might not the period itself have driven a bright, sensitive girl over the edge?

Rosemary still believes there's something to this theory. To make the case, she recounts what happened to the ten or so girls who were at the top of Polly's graduating class in her exclusive prep school. One was killed by a hitchhiker she and her boyfriend picked up as they drove through Colorado. One died of a drug overdose. Another had a drug-related mental breakdown and continues to be unstable. Two of them are lesbians. Polly is a suicide.

The two girls in the top of the class who seem to have done best for themselves are, to her chagrin, the daughters of the families Rosemary describes as "materialistic," interested only in living in the right neighborhood and belonging to the right club. "The two daughters of those two families have been conservative, followed traditional patterns of behavior, caused no problems, and are now married to 'the right kind of men,' and have never done one thing to my knowledge that their parents wouldn't have wanted them to do."

So Rosemary's soul-searching inevitably led her to blame herself. How, in spite of all her efforts as a mother, had she failed her daughter? Had she, echoing the period, been too liberal with Polly?

Rosemary both does and does not consider herself liberal. Socially she is an activist, giving much of her time to worthy volunteer causes. "I think you would consider me a liberal in my views on politics, sociology, and social and human behavior."

But she insisted on old-fashioned good behavior from her children. "When it comes down to the family, I'm not a liberal. I believe in good manners, I believe that everyone has to have limits when they live with other people."

Perhaps, then, she had not been liberal enough? After Polly's suicide, Bob looked for clues to the reason in the diary that she had left. He discovered that for years suicide had been on Polly's mind. At the age of twelve, she had written a full description of the time that Rosemary had forced her to swim in the club competition and then had scolded her afterward for her bad attitude. This passage contained the first mention of suicide in the little book.

Surely that was an unrealistic response to a mother's simply saying, "Oh, come on, be part of the group." But Rosemary still blames herself bitterly for this lapse, as she considers it, on her part. "What I realize now," Rosemary says, "is that when someone is as serious and dedicated to what they are doing as she was, they can't fool around. I obviously didn't understand the depths of her belief."

Most of all Rosemary regrets that she did not take the advice of the psychiatrist who told them, on the occasion of her first breakdown, that Polly "had no ego" and needed serious and extended help. She berates herself for her failure to pay attention, for her willingness to look at Polly's successes and to gloss over the reality of Polly's inadequacies and fears. But Polly was amazingly successful, so successful that she persuaded those who could have given her help that she didn't need it. She deceived her doctors and she deceived her mother.

If she had it all to do over, Rosemary insists, she would commit Polly to the hospital and to the treatment of that first psychiatrist, socially and personally repulsive as she found him to be. Polly was only nineteen at the time. An involuntary commitment, which would have been easily possible, might have saved her life. But her admiration for her child was so great that Rosemary even trusted Polly to continue treatment for mental instability on her own.

Bob believes, however, that treatment might have been futile. He thinks that Polly could never have accepted a traditional pattern for her life, according to Rosemary. "Any life she ever led he feels would have been very eccentric. She was really torn—between a conservative upbringing and a wild culture around her, and societal pressures to be a wife and mother and societal pressures saying, 'A Phi Beta Kappa from this institution. You're not a wife and mother. You have to go out and beat down the world!'

"And I know she felt right in between all this. She always had very interesting men, very interested in her too. She'd say, 'I should just forget all of this and get married.' "

The journalist Vivian Gornick, in an essay written in 1973, "Why Radcliffe Women Are Afraid of Success," explored the ways in which the kind of atmosphere which Polly had just left contributed to those tensions for women graduates. Pointing out that remarkably few of these "brightest, most talented, most serious young women in the country" went on to responsible jobs after graduation, Gornick attributes this failure to certain revered features of Harvard life, particularly the house system, from which women by virtue of their sex were excluded. In the residential houses provided for Harvard men, students and professors had meals together and enjoyed an easy camaraderie, a casual daily contact that opened doors for enterprising students. Gornick quotes Carol Kay, Radcliffe class of 1967:

> "Yes, we shared classes [with Harvard men], but the institution always gave out the signals, and those signals said, 'You don't belong. You're not really a part of things.' Because we lived in dorms, we never ate lunch with the men and the faculty. As a result, you didn't make those contacts, those easy friendships, that led to being able to work with your favorite professor. When you graduated, your department was behind you as it was behind the men. But it didn't look forward to placing you. You hadn't made the friendships that counted.

"The doors were never closed, but you never felt free to walk through them. The feeling I was left with after four years here was, 'We train leaders, and women aren't leaders.' "

As her thesis in the essay, Gornick cites the work of the sociologist Matina Horner, who became president of Radcliffe in 1973. As Horner put it to Gornick a year earlier, the women she studied were "anxiety-ridden over the prospect of success. They were not simply eager to fail and have done with it; they seemed to be in a state of anxious conflict over what would happen if they succeeded. It was almost as though this conflict was inhibiting their capacity for achievement."

Barnard and Radcliffe were not alone among prestigious schools in unwittingly permitting defeatism in female students. The women in the first Horner study were at the University of Michigan. The writer Nora Ephron, who graduated from Wellesley College in the class of 1962, points an angry finger at the "feminine" behavior encouraged there:

> I am still amazed at the amount of Christian charity that school stuck us all with. . . . How marvelous it would have been to go to a women's college that encouraged impoliteness, that rewarded aggression, that encouraged argument. Women by the time they are eighteen are so damaged, so beaten down, so tyrannized out of behaving in all the wonderful outspoken ways unfortunately characterized as masculine; a college committed to them has to take on the burden of repair . . . to force young women to define themselves before they abdicate the task and become defined by their husbands. *What do you think? What is your opinion?* No one ever asked. We all graduated from Wellesley able to describe everything we studied—Baroque painting, Hindemith, Jacksonian democracy, Yeats —yet we were never asked what we thought of any of it. *Do you like it? Do you think it is good? Do you know that even if it is good you do not have to like it?*

Certainly factors other than her Barnard education, factors Polly brought to Barnard with her, contributed to Polly's tragic death.

Rosemary knows that the emphasis on achievement in the family
may have been detrimental (though we must not ignore the fact that
in this family the parents too were educated at Columbia). She
describes an experience with Polly's younger brother, who

> seemed early to be just a golden child, the kind of child that
> the gardener would come up to me on the lawn and say,
> "That boy's going to be president someday." And he went
> through a period of overt rebellion. And he tells me that
> one of the most destructive things that I could do, and have
> done, is to make him think he is so good, when I have said,
> "Well, you can do *anything*." That is threatening to him,
> because he feels that he cannot measure up to my expecta-
> tions of him.

Pondering this mother's brave, honest words, we can speculate that
Polly may have tried too hard to please her parents and others, at
the expense of herself. Ego depends on acceptance of the entire self,
of the unpleasant parts of one's life and personality as well as the
pleasant. Did she feel that exhibiting her anxiety, fear, despair, she
was something less than perfect Polly? In any event, when she faced
those feelings, death must have seemed the only solution.

Yet how clearly difficult for Polly also was the social milieu of the
sixties, the factor in a young adult's life which psychologists often
regard as definitive for behavior. After the suicide Rosemary
learned that, although Polly had only twice in fourteen years mentioned suicide to her parents, with her friends at college she had
talked about it.

"A brilliant young man came and stayed with us after her death,"
Rosemary says, "and he said, 'Oh, yeah, we talked about suicide a
lot.' And we said, 'Where on earth would she ever have gotten this
idea? To do this?' And he said, 'Well, of course, this is what we all
talked about. That's life.' "

Her family knew nothing about all this. After Polly made what
Rosemary believed to be a full recovery from the 1968 breakdown,
Rosemary quit worrying about her. Polly's relationship with her
parents was remarkably intimate and apparently open. She called
her mother almost daily, up until the day she died, from wherever
she happened to be working.

Maybe too much dependence, Rosemary thinks now, but at the

time, like so much else that Rosemary now broods over, it seemed natural. "She did that. She was on the phone all the time talking to people. And you know that the day she died, we know people she called *after* she had been to the drugstore to get the sleeping pills she took."

With so many factors at work, too many to fix blame anywhere, Rosemary recognizes now that all her intellectualizing will not allow her to comprehend Polly's death. "I have studied and analyzed, studied and analyzed. . . . I still don't understand what happened."

But she believes a significant part of the motivation lay in Polly's own personality, in Polly's ongoing insistence that nothing in her life was ever good enough.

> If you were to talk to the mother of her best friend in high school, that mother would tell you there had been a lot of stress between me and my daughter. There hadn't been! If you talked to me, you would think that there was a lot of disappointment in the friendship between the two girls. But the girl wouldn't think there were problems in the friendship.
>
> In other words, nothing was ever right. Any work that she did wasn't up to her standards. Any award that she achieved meant nothing. . . . It's like getting excited to go to a party and then not having a good time. She looked forward to things, and then didn't enjoy them when they came.

Talk, talk, lots of talk. Intelligence and articulate communication are high priorities in the Dixon household. Rosemary, intelligent and articulate as she is in the interview, worries because she doesn't talk as well as her husband. "Sometimes I think the children question the level of their mother's input, but they don't have any doubts about his intellect. He communicates very well." Her eyes darken and she closes them as if in pain. "I think we intellectualize a little bit too much," she says wistfully.

ROSEMARY'S ROAD TO RECOVERY

For a long time after the first shock of the tragic and untimely death
of her brilliant daughter, Rosemary could do nothing but intellectualize. Ordinarily, a mother begins the process of recovery from a
great shock given to her by a child by forgetting herself in trying to
understand and help her child. Rosemary was frustrated in her own
recovery because Polly was gone. By the time Rosemary realized her
daughter needed help, Polly was beyond the reach of any help her
mother could give her.

Since the temporary breakdown six years earlier, Rosemary had
not really worried about Polly. She respected Polly. She had idealized Polly, had believed that Polly could handle anything. Now, too
late, she began to pay attention to the darker side of Polly's personality. Confronted by the irrevocable fact of Polly's death, Rosemary
began to think about signs and symptoms that had not seemed
crucial before but gained in significance because of their now clear
importance to Polly. With Polly's successes put into perspective by
the overwhelming fact of her suicide, she saw Polly as she was.

Polly's achievements had become a trap for her, Rosemary realized, because they were never enough. With all of Polly's intellectual
brilliance, Polly was frightened, confused, unsure of herself. To get
out of situations which threatened the façade of success behind
which she hid her fears, she "programmed herself for failure,"
Rosemary says. "She would work at a job until she didn't want to
anymore, and then would program herself so that she could get out
of it. Something would 'come up.' " Easier to change jobs—or doctors—than to admit the possibility of weakness.

Rosemary now had the understanding that she needed to help her
daughter, if Polly had been alive. But Polly was dead. If we have
seemed to dwell on the causes of Polly's death, it's because Rosemary did. The stage of attention, the endless "studying and analyz-
ing" that Rosemary spoke of earlier, could not give way for this
unhappy woman to action, the next necessary stage in a mother's
healthy progress from shock to independence. What action could
Rosemary take for the best interests of Polly, who was no longer
around to benefit? Because she could not go on to take action to

help Polly, Rosemary's psyche was doomed to wander for a time in a state of shocked attention.

The effects of Polly's death on other members of the family were devastating also, especially on the Columbia-educated brothers. The "golden child," a brother just younger than Polly, was graduated from Columbia after going through four years of college stoned, according to Rosemary. Bright as he was, he finished, Rosemary says, "merely *cum laude*. . . . Something like eighty percent of the student body graduated *cum laude* then." Eventually he went into the import business, and became very successful. On a trip to Rome, he met an Italian girl whom he subsequently married. He has become, his mother says, "a part of her big, warm, loving family, a family where they hug and kiss. He likes it, and it's good for him."

The second son was still in Columbia at the time of the interview. "He is in an environment where her name is known and is often reminded of her successes and is under tremendous pressures to work, yet he often doesn't work—and I think maybe sees a terrible loss in the work that she did. 'Why bother to study twenty hours a day and read every book in the library if you are going to kill yourself in the end?' That's what he says."

Polly's father, Bob, threw himself into his demanding work and the travels that went with it. Rosemary didn't mind his going. She wanted to be alone to face her grief, and still thinks that the enforced separation may have been a blessing to the marriage. "Maybe by being alone I was better off. . . . There wasn't any opportunity for stress between us because we weren't together, and each one had the chance to try to heal in his or her own way."

As for Rosemary, she retreated into herself. In fact, she describes her greatest source of strength initially as "aloneness," and says that she was "sort of like a little animal going off into the woods to get better." Typically, she did a great deal of reading, "really studying to see what I had missed, reading case studies of the kind of behavior accepted as being normal but eccentric." Although she lost a lot of weight, she didn't otherwise suffer physically.

But she suffered emotionally, and was especially sensitive to the comments, no matter how well intentioned, of other people.

> It was really difficult for me to go into a group of people, because I didn't want someone to come up to me or say

anything. I really had horns out all around me [with one hand she describes an arc in the air in front of her face] to keep people away. . . . I wanted people to leave my private problems to me. . . . Their tentative kinds of approaches really turned me off.

Friends helped most when they communicated support "without talking about my problems." Although Rosemary believes that "sympathetic support from friends bolsters the human spirit," she emphatically did not want to talk Polly over with anyone outside the family.

I don't understand it, and I certainly know that if I don't, no one else around me does either. And I'm not interested in gossip, and it's too late now to do anything about it. The only thing I can do is try to be more supportive for the rest of the family. That's all I can do now.

This self-imposed silence extended to the clergy. She would not have dreamed of confiding in a minister, though in "a very minor way" her Lutheran faith helped her—"at least I'm a part of something."

Unable to take positive action to help Polly, she turned her considerable energy back to the service of her Greenwich community. As her husband had thrown himself into his work, Rosemary threw herself into her usual volunteer activities, carrying out the responsibilities that preceded Polly's death. Eventually she was spending a good half of every week in doing useful, unpaid work for others. This work brings her into contact with other people, but allows her to retain the privacy that is so much a part of her attitude toward life.

Not so typically, she began selling real estate. During the library hours she spent reading case histories that would help her understand Polly, she also "started reading every word of the *National Real Estate Investor, Realtor News,* and *The U.S. Real Estate Letter* and getting really interested in the market. I decided to see if I could make some money."

Why such an interest for a woman who earlier spoke with disdain of materialism as an index of success? "I threw myself into something that was totally mine, something I wanted to do for myself, and spent a lot of time doing it. I got interested and involved, and it totally took my mind off other things. I thought, Well, it's time to do something for *me.* "

With her community service and her rabid interest in real estate, Rosemary gained control of her own life and reached a new level of autonomy. She has never consciously abandoned the questions she asked about the meaning of Polly's suicide, but as time passes she has found herself putting them aside. Certain incidents still trigger memories and bring up the inevitable rehashing. But more and more she is able to detach herself from the unhappy, guilty thoughts, and remember Polly as the brilliant, lovable klutz they all adored. She longs for a time when her whole family, together, will be able to look back at Polly's life "with happy memories and be able to talk about it all."

> I wrote this in a letter to a friend whose husband commit-
> ted suicide, and I believe it too. I said, "Someday your
> family will be sitting around the dinner table, and your
> children will feel free to say, 'Remember when Dad did
> this? Remember?' And you'll talk freely and openly about
> it." We are not quite there—in our house.

Such a scene represents in Rosemary's mind a genuine detachment, a final relinquishing of excessive responsibility for Polly's death.

It also represents a need in herself that she does not often ac-knowledge, perhaps cannot "safely" acknowledge—the need for openness. Rosemary finds it hard to receive comfort and help from others, even from her husband and certainly from friends. She also finds it difficult to give help. She is pleased to report that she recently issued some warnings, based on her own experience, re-garding a troubled child. "In the past few weeks a young man has been exhibiting very, very destructive behavior, self-destructive be-havior, and I've spoken to a couple of people about it. 'Do some-thing before it's too late!' " But, interestingly, she did not go di-rectly to the boy's parents; instead she spoke to a psychiatrist friend, who is also a friend of theirs.

She is almost wistful, however, in her desire to help others. "I know of a family where there's a child exhibiting very, very destruc-tive behavior. I've said to Bob, 'Do you think I should say some-thing?' And he said, 'No, you shouldn't. They'd just resent it, and you probably won't be able to help.' And I don't like to interfere.

But I do feel, though maybe I feel it now, maybe I wouldn't have felt
it then . . . that I wish someone had interfered with me." She
pauses a moment and sighs deeply, then she says softly, "And I just
may do it."

As a parent, Rosemary has learned some lessons from the experience of Polly's death. She thinks she inclines toward being overly
involved in her children's decisions. Laughing, she says, "Knowing
me, I will always be trying to encourage them to do anything for
which I feel they are qualified." But she thinks that Polly's dissatisfaction with herself might be linked to her mother's high expectations, so Rosemary is more careful now with her boys.

> I always thought you should encourage children, build
> them up and not tear them down, but now I have to watch
> myself, don't I? When my son says something like, "Oh,
> this is really hard, I don't think I can do it," I cannot leap in
> and say, "Oh, yes, you can, you know you can." It appears
> that that is destructive.

She acknowledges the importance of not playing God, of knowing
when to step back and turn a child's life over to the child. "People
are people," she says, "and you're not going to change them." She
applies this healthy acceptance to her family: "Everyone in the family should be able to say it, and I would hope"—she laughs ruefully,
thinking of her own nature as a mother—"that I would be able to let
them say it. 'I am what I am. Take me as I am.' "

The interview is over, and Rosemary looks tired. Almost certainly
this is the first time she has talked openly and at length to anyone
outside her family about Polly's death. In the long conversation she
has recapitulated all the stages of the process of independence
through which she has been moving for the last six years—the shock
of the completely unexpected suicide, the long months of attention
which could not be translated into action, the detachment with
which she is coming to view those things about Polly's life which
cannot be changed.

She has shown evidence of increased autonomy by taking up an
interest in real estate "for myself" and by recognizing the limits of
her responsibility for all of her children. Describing the difficulties
that her reticent, intellectual, striving, loner's nature makes for her
as a member of the human family, she has expressed a wistful desire

that she will someday be able to give and receive help. Thus she looks forward to new kinds of connection with the world that grows at once bigger and more inviting with intimacy.

What about her connection with Polly? One can ask what hopes a mother may have for a living child; one cannot ask the same question of a mother whose child is dead. Surprisingly, Rosemary brings the question up herself, in the "casual" way with which we often raise our deepest concerns.

As she slips into her spring coat, she mentions D. M. Thomas's novel *The White Hotel,* which she has just read. Life is horrifying, she says. Look at Anna, the heroine, and "the life that that woman works through, the struggle for an existence, a life, and bang!"—she snaps her fingers—"it's over!"

Maybe not, the interviewer suggests gently. "I saw her as a very noble woman who could not have been noble had she not gone through this struggle. Her life was a victory. It was not a defeat."

Rosemary brightens. Then she mentions the meeting of Anna and her mother in Paradise at the end of the novel. Tears come to her eyes. "I did think, wouldn't that be nice to happen to me. To get there, and there she is, waiting for me."

3

Fathers—Part of the Solution or Part of the Problem?

In all of the families in this book, the mother believed she noticed the child's untraditional behavior first, often long before anyone else. It would seem strange if she did not. After all, the children were considered primarily her responsibility. For years she spent her days paying attention to their habits. Naturally she soon became aware of any deviation from the norm.

Just as naturally, faced with behavior she had trouble understanding and accepting, the mother turned first to her husband for help. She hoped he could bring a more objective mind to the situation, perhaps make some suggestions based on his wider experience of the world. At the very least, she expected him to be interested and sympathetic, sympathetic to her, sympathetic to the child.

But the response of the fathers in these families varied considerably. In some cases, a mother found that her husband was not only ready and willing to help but in certain ways more able than she herself. In others, the wife found the father seemingly indifferent, slow to take alarm, or ineffectual. In a few cases, she found him actually detrimental to the child's welfare, a hindrance to her own efforts to cope, part of the problem rather than part of the solution. These women whose husbands were part of the problem undertook to deal not only with the shock of a child's unexpected behavior but also with the shock of the abandonment or betrayal of a husband.

Before turning our attention to this second kind of shock, let us take a look at several able fathers, fathers like Kenneth Brooks, for example. When young Tom Brooks came to trial for assault and theft, it was Kenneth, rather than Tom's mother Jean, who went to court every day, listened to the witnesses, conferred with Tom's lawyer, gave constant encouragement and support to Tom. "I just could not do that," Jean says, "but Kenneth managed to handle it beautifully. He's unflappable." But the trial took its toll, even on such "a remarkable man." "He would come home so drained," Jean remembers, "that he didn't even want to talk."

Nor was Kenneth Brooks the only exceptionally resourceful father. During their daughter Debby's problems with drugs and alcohol, Kate Barnes learned to appreciate that, in their family, "Nick really is the strong one." Kate realized, especially after the family went into group therapy, that she had been far too protective of Debby, running interference unnecessarily between the girl and her father.

"I had to learn to back off and allow him to come forward," Kate acknowledges. In group therapy, the Barnes family was advised to let Nicholas take the lead for a while in dealing with Debby. "We were together in this," Kate says, "and we discovered that we function better as a couple than most people. We're fortunate—we were strengthened by that."

No father could have been more giving than Nick Barnes, but then not all fathers would have had the funds to be as generous as Nick, who is an investment lawyer. Debby's therapy for the first two years of treatment cost the family over sixty thousand dollars. She is still in therapy, and the expense is still terrible.

Debby herself feels guilty about this inordinate drain on the family finances, but Nick discourages guilt with his matter-of-fact affection. When Debby brings the subject up, her father, Kate reports, "always says that it is his privilege to provide for her."

Strong fathers take the lead in ways other than signing checks. Lois Wagner says that it was her husband Harold who moved her toward acceptance of their son's biracial marriage. Harold, deter-

mined that John's marriage to a black woman should not be allowed
to split the family, cut through Lois's tears and what she calls her
ranting and raving. "I fell apart. I cried, I hollered, I screamed. . . .
I pushed John aside. I wanted nothing to do with him. He was in our
house when he told us, and he tried to comfort me, and I said, 'Don't
you dare! Just leave. Go!' "

Very rapidly Lois changed her attitude, largely through Harold's
ministrations. John had been born when Harold was forty, and he
was "terribly important to my husband," Lois says. "And John was
his only son, another Wagner to carry on the family name." Harold
insisted immediately that they accept John's bride as they accepted
John himself, with nothing held back. His strength kept the unity in
the family.

Lois attributes that insistence on family unity in part to their
Jewish heritage. "For so many thousands of years, the Jewish people
were ostracized. They lived in small, self-contained communities,
ghettos. Their children were their entire lives. . . . They had a
terrible past, their present was dreadful, and they could only look
toward the future. For all of us, our children are our future." Harold's quick acceptance of a black daughter-in-law looked toward the
future of the family.

Still another father, William Baron, helped his wife conquer the
crippling emotions to which she fell prey because of her child's
untraditional behavior. Joy Baron was overcome with shame when
her youngest child, fourteen-year-old Toni, became pregnant.
When Toni decided to have the baby and to give it up for adoption,
there was no question but that the family would support her
throughout her entire pregnancy. But Joy's feelings almost got the
best of her.

"Oh, the shame!" she remembers. "Perhaps my biggest fault is
that I—I rely too much on appearances . . . and you don't hide
pregnancy. It is so apparent. . . . The shame and humiliation, that
was the worst."

Then her husband William stepped in. "My husband saved me,"
Joy says. "This is the man who took his nine-months-pregnant
daughter to a restaurant for lunch on the day that the baby was born.
[Toni] was physically a very young-looking person. She has the
freckles, the blond, curly, baby hair that always makes people look

young. At the time she delivered the baby, she looked like she was about twelve.

"We walked into the restaurant that day. There were a lot of people. The headwaiter was going to give us a bad time, because at that point we didn't look like the kind of people who ate there. But Bill said, as soon as we walked in, 'We would like a table for three, please. And my daughter is not feeling well today. We would like a very comfortable table and very nice service today, because it's an important day to us.'

"And we walked through the crowd with our daughter big as a barrel. I couldn't have done it alone. He is the one who carried me through. And he is the one who gave me the passage from Isaiah that saved me."

To illustrate the significance of "the passage from Isaiah," she describes another incident. Early in Toni's pregnancy, Joy and Bill had to pay a requisite annual visit to Joy's parents in California. They had decided not to tell Joy's parents about their problem because "if I'm conscious of appearances, my mama is even more so," Joy says. "They matter to her."

On Sunday morning Joy, Bill, and Joy's parents went to church together. The small church was very crowded, and Joy sat alone a couple of rows ahead of the others. During the service, to her horror, she found herself in the tears which engulfed her constantly during those troubled times. "My biggest problem was always in church. I'm half dissolved all during the whole service and I'm having a very bad time." She wondered how she would ever compose herself sufficiently to face her parents when the service was over.

As they moved to the communion reading which concludes a Catholic service, Joy was startled to see an open missal appear at her hand. "Bill reached through the people with his book—it's just the way he is—and handed me the book. He was pointing to the passage: 'Look up to the Lord and smile and you will never be ashamed.' And that literally carried me through the next two years, whenever things would be very, very bad."

"If I hadn't had him, I couldn't have made it," Patricia Wentworth says of her husband Murray, in a touching testimonial to the power of a husband's love and to the importance of a strong father in a family. Patricia is recalling the years after their son Joe's suicide.

"There isn't a doubt in my mind about that." Murray, she believes, "thinks much more of me than I think of myself. If I hadn't had his support and his love, I could never have made it."

Patricia's heartfelt claim is probably not true, although Patricia doesn't know that. Women can manage without their husbands' support, whether they know it or not. For some women, the shock of their children's problems is compounded by the shock of discovering that their husbands are selfish, insensitive, or inadequate to the burdens of parenthood. But these women do not buckle. With commendable fortitude, they take up the slack, to meet alone, as well as they can, the challenges their children present.

Some of them become understandably angry or disgusted at the additional burden created by such a husband, though very few feel as strongly about it as Margot Morrison. Margot's son Paul got into drugs in the early sixties, when few parents understood addiction and the drug culture. Like most other families at the time, the Morrisons were ill equipped to handle Paul's problem. Nevertheless, Margot is still angry with her husband for Paul's death at nineteen:

> I do know one thing I could have done, and it would have saved his life. I probably should have done it, but I didn't have it in me to do it.
>
> I can remember my father saying to me at one time that his Aunt Somebody-or-other had three baby boys, and that she left her husband to raise the boys. Then after she'd raised the boys she went back to her husband. I think that was the closest he ever came to suggesting that I might try to go it alone, you know, raising my kids. . . .
>
> But by the time Paul was in his teens it was too late.

Paul didn't lack men in his life, she says, but "he lacked men who cared about his well-being." She believes that both she and the men in Paul's life let him down.

> I feel that I lacked strength, and that the men in his life were selfish. He had two grandfathers and a father . . . and a mother. I think I was not strong enough. I was not definite enough. I was not realistic enough.
>
> And his two grandfathers and his father were selfish in

their handling of him. I think they used him, rather than helping him. That's really my belief.

Clearly enough, when a father refuses to be part of the solution, he becomes part of the problem. The kind of shock that a mother undergoes when she realizes that her husband is part of the problem is illustrated by the experiences of Lucy Carpenter. In a Freudian web that has taken this slight blond mother years to untangle, Frank Carpenter, a high school teacher in Orlando, Florida, and his son David, the youngest of the three Carpenter boys, actually competed for Lucy's attention in a struggle to the death.

"David had almost no relationship with his father," Lucy says. "Frank had problems from the beginning." Even as a baby, David, accident-prone and asthmatic, needed more of his mother's attention than the other boys had. "I felt there might have been jealousy," Lucy says, "that he required so much attention that my husband really resented it."

As David grew into an older child, things didn't improve. Frank thought that Lucy pampered David, who was extremely attached to his mother. Lucy, on the other hand, regretted the distance that developed between the boy and his father. "There was nothing that they could do together, that they got along doing for very much time. . . . There was just constant friction between the two of them."

When David, at the age of fourteen, was picked up by the police for burglarizing houses with some of his friends, Frank was instructed by the court to go to a group meeting for counseling with other parents. "It was something my husband could not deal with," Lucy says. "He went once, and then he didn't follow through."

This important failure in responsibility on Frank's part presaged a complete split between father and son. Lucy believes that the breaking and entering itself may have been David's suit for attention from his father. "Maybe he wanted to see how much attention his father would be willing to give him."

Very little, as it turned out. When Frank refused to go for counseling after the first session, the boy felt rejected. He didn't talk to his father about it, but he talked to his mother. "He didn't understand why not. He felt that . . . you should just follow through with something like that, but my husband just didn't seem to be able to face that. . . . He said he didn't have the time to go, which was not true. It was obvious he didn't *want* to go."

David became increasingly depressed and antisocial after this episode. A year later, David, a bright boy and a good student, failed chemistry. It was a failure guaranteed to get the attention of his father, the chairman of the high school chemistry department. Frank was disgusted with his son. It confirmed his expectations of David. "Frank just always felt," Lucy explains, "that if something was going to go wrong, David would be instigating the whole thing. And David didn't disappoint him."

Faced with this fiasco, David grew more depressed. Not only had all of his friends taken the final chemistry test and passed, but his father was a chemistry *teacher*. Humiliated and realizing how further alienated from him Frank would be, David made two clumsy suicide attempts. First he swallowed a bottle of aspirin. This just upset his stomach. Lucy thought he had flu, and discovered only afterward what he'd done.

When the aspirin overdose failed to get attention, David took more drastic measures. Lucy describes what happened when he came home from school that day.

> I went upstairs, and he was in the doorway of the bathroom. He turned to me, and he showed me his wrist, and there was a deep gash, very deep, almost like a big hole. And I said, "What happened!"
>
> "Well, I was in a fight at school."
>
> I said, "I can't imagine a wound like that. How is that possible?" I said, "Well, it's wide enough to go to emergency."
>
> My husband had just come in from school himself, and I thought, well, he would go with me. He didn't.

At the hospital Lucy learned that David's wound was self-inflicted.

> I got very, very upset, and I tried to talk to David. I said, "What's the problem? I can't really understand—why did you do this?" And he really had no answer. He was in quite a bit of pain, and so they had to call in a surgeon. . . . It was a very delicate operation, and he could have lost the use of his hand because he almost hit the main artery. . . .

What was significant was that I called home to tell my husband and he didn't come to the hospital. I took David at three-thirty. The surgeon got there about nine o'clock that night and performed the operation. When my husband arrived it was around eleven o'clock, after David was out of surgery. . . .

When we walked into the room after he'd been taken back, he told his father he didn't want to see him, he didn't want him there, he didn't want to have anything to do with him.

David relented and did see his father during the two weeks he spent in the hospital for observation. On one occasion, a hospital psychiatrist told Frank Carpenter, in Lucy's presence, "You had better get involved with your son, or he very well could kill himself."

His arm healed, David returned home. The next Saturday, David made an overture to his father. As Lucy tells it:

He said, "Let's go bowling, Dad," and Frank said, "No, we're playing backgammon." And I was very upset. I was angry. I said, "How much importance does a backgammon game have when your son asks you to do something?"

And then afterwards I asked Frank, "Why did you refuse?" And he said, "I think he's manipulating me. I think he's using this illness as a pretense to have me do something. He knows I always play backgammon on Saturday afternoon. Why couldn't we go later in the day?" Because, you see, David wanted to go right then, and he couldn't see why his father wouldn't drop everything and do that for him. And so later wasn't good enough.

By this time two psychiatrists had seen David. Whether or not the Carpenters played tournament backgammon together on Saturday afternoon became an issue. One psychiatrist, Lucy says,

told me to stop playing and to stay home with my son. He needed my attention, but not my husband. Because, you see, my husband kept right on playing, going to tournaments, going out of town. But I stopped for over six months.

Enter the second psychiatrist. This doctor agreed with Frank's manipulation theory. He speculated that the sixteen-year-old boy wanted to separate his parents, and told Lucy brutally, "You must get him out of your bed."

He advised her to start going again to backgammon tournaments with her husband. "The conflict was terrible," Lucy says.

> Who are you to believe? An absolute difference of opinion between two professionals. I got quite confused after that. I didn't know—I thought, "I'd just better do what my instinct tells me." But then I felt [the second doctor] could possibly be right. I needed to spend more time with my husband, because the anger and resentment was quite great, and this could not help the whole situation at home, there was no question about it.

David was subsequently hospitalized for his psychiatric problems. Lucy got involved with a parents' group that met every Thursday night at the hospital. In the three months that his son was in the hospital, Frank Carpenter attended the parents' group meeting only twice.

> He said he didn't want to talk in front of a lot of people. He didn't want to talk about this child. He didn't feel it was necessary, he didn't feel it would help, and therefore he wasn't going to go.
> But I did go, because I felt, "Well, maybe I will gain some insight." Because there were parents of two other children who were depressives and [potential] suicides, and I felt maybe we could help one another.

For Lucy, the shock of David's behavior was magnified a thousand times by the shock of her husband's childish resentment of his son and his unwillingness to help. She felt caught in an impossible cross fire between father and son, without the help that any mother might legitimately and fairly expect from the father of her child.

SHARON ALL ALONE

As unhelpful under crisis as such fathers are, only one of the mothers represented in this book gave up on her marriage entirely. Sharon, born a child with "too much love," learned as a woman to live—and to cope—alone.

At first Sharon Marsh really had no choice. Donald Marsh, her husband of twenty years, abandoned her and their four children. "God didn't mean me to have all these children," Donald, an independent oil producer in Phoenix, told Sharon. "Just because people are family doesn't mean that you have to love them. All I want to do is get rid of you."

When Donald moved out in 1970, Russell, the second of the Marshes' four children, had just started taking drugs. Russell was twelve years old. Sharon received two nearly simultaneous body blows. As she dealt with the shock and pain of her husband's betrayal, she faced, alone, the shock and pain of Russell's gradually increasing waywardness.

Yet that horrendous watershed year and the difficult decade that followed have given Sharon formidable strength and assurance today. After the times she has come through, she says she knows that "I can do anything. If you asked me to go be president of IBM, I wouldn't hesitate. I'd say, 'Sure, I'll give it a shot and do the best that I can.' "

As she laughs and pretends to roll up the sleeves of her beige blazer in order to take on IBM, Sharon radiates casual self-confidence. She is a big woman, almost six feet tall, with an ample and voluptuous body. Her wide mouth laughs easily, her gestures are expansive, and even her voice booms in a way unexpected in a woman. Pushing her brown hair back, she crosses her long legs carelessly, and studies the toes of her brown pumps as she describes the girl she was and the woman she has come to be.

Sharon Marsh was born Sharon Trachtenberg in 1936, the only child of a sixteen-year-old girl and a father whom her mother divorced before she was born. After her birth, her mother brought the baby home to Sharon's grandparents. The first twelve years of Sharon's life, in a very small town in rural Tennessee, were idyllic:

My grandparents did nothing but think of their family.
Everything was done for me, with me. I learned about the
woods and squirrels and trees and all the beautiful things
in life. . . . I grew up with too much love. I mean, every
pencil mark, everything I did was wonderful, beautiful. I
was the most beautiful, wonderful child in the world.

When Sharon's mother went away to college and left Sharon with
her grandparents, Sharon did not suffer. Her mother called, wrote,
visited constantly. "We adored each other, I think because she was
so young. We had a wonderful relationship."

During World War II, Sharon's mother married again. Sharon's
stepfather was in the diplomatic service. Sharon was six and just
starting school. Her new father—"as far as I'm concerned, he is my
father"—"was being transferred every three months, just hopping
around, and . . . they felt it wouldn't be good for me to be pulled
out of one school after another." So Sharon continued to live in
Tennessee with her doting grandparents. She spent summers in
Washington with her parents, and had the best of both worlds. And
she formed a firm idea of what family life should be.

I thought of raising my family, making Halloween or
Christmas decorations for the windows, doing fun and loving things with my family. . . . Being raised in a small
southern town, the thing to do is grow up, get married, and
have a family, and that's all I ever wanted.

When Sharon was twelve, her life changed, but her ideas about
life didn't. She joined her parents, who traveled where her stepfather's career led them.

We traveled all over the world. I lived in Europe; I lived in
Japan; at the age of twelve I was learning to defend myself
because of the Communist riots in Europe. During the
Berlin airlift, I lived in a dormitory in my school in Ger-
many, and we learned how to handle guns.

Nevertheless, she remained the girl from a small town in Tennessee.

I was one of the few kids in that school who didn't sneak
out. My roommate and I had a room with a little window
that you could climb out of, and all the other students used

our room to get out and go to the *Gasthaus* and have their
little mugs of beer. I never did things like that. My grandparents never drank and smoked. I never had a desire to.

After four years of private school, Sharon went to college in
Arizona at seventeen. Two years later she was married, at a very
unripe nineteen, to Donald Marsh, older, worldly, handsome, popular with debutantes in Phoenix, his hometown, to which the young
couple moved. It was a marriage of opposites, the man-about-town
to the beloved baby. Sharon says, "I couldn't even write a check
when I got married. I didn't know how to drive a car. I would say I
was probably behind myself in many things."

To make matters more difficult, she soon realized that, after a
childhood of love and praise, she had gone into a marriage of chill
and blame.

The contrast was unbelievable. I went from people who
thought I was wonderful to a person who thought I was
terrible, couldn't do anything right, didn't know how to do
this or that. If I learned to play a piece on the piano, it was
the wrong kind of music, or I played it too loud. . . . I felt
like a little nail. I had been a very tall nail when I got
married, but . . . I was pounded into the ground. Nothing I did was right.

Soon she was pregnant. With the birth of Kathy, her only daughter, and Russell, a little over a year later, Sharon began to see that
Donald's coldness extended to the children also. Once when Kathy
was eighteen months old, she reached up to the stove and pulled a
pot of boiling water down over herself. Sick with dread, Sharon
began to pull off the little pajamas:

My reaction was: Get her to the doctor immediately—because all of her skin came off with her pajamas. Donald's
reaction was: Put her to bed, punish her, she did something
wrong. He was taking her to bed. I said, "My God! The
child is hurt! She has to go to the hospital."

So I grabbed her out of his arms. I picked up Russ—he
was maybe three months old—at the same time, and ran
downstairs, and threw him in the arms of our landlady.

Then I ran next door, and a neighbor took me to the
hospital. Kathy had very severe burns all over her legs.
    It's like Donald's mind closes. . . . He wants everything
to be on an even keel, no ups or downs. He made a comment to me once that I never forgot. He said, "Sharon, I
envy you your highs and your lows." He obviously never
experienced feelings, emotions.

A third child was born. Sharon had the family she had always
wanted. "I took pride in my little family," she says. "I was a very
young mother, with a lot of little babies, but I was a loving, caring
mother." She cooked, took good care of her children, made clothes
for herself and Kathy.

As the children got a bit older, Sharon became involved in community activities, helping at the school and working in Junior
League. She also took craft classes of various kinds, baked special
things to take to school for the children, studied jazz, took a course
or two. "You name it. I did it."

But, as she tells the story, Donald wasn't satisfied with her. "You
just can't stick to anything, can you?" he said.

"What do you mean, can't stick?" she told him. "I'm having a
wonderful time. . . . I'm touching a little bit of everything in life."

"But I think he saw me as a person who did nothing. He told me,
'I want a woman who does something.' "

So Sharon, ever the obliging wife, decided to do something. "I
thought for months and months. What is needed? What am I good
at? What can I do? I came up with this idea and approached a friend.
We started a business, a sewing shop. We sold fabrics, and we taught
sewing and needlework, we arranged quiltings, we patented two or
three basic patterns with embroidery and appliqué designs. And the
department stores sent us customers. It was just terrific."

Three months after they started the business, Donald came to
Sharon and said, "You've worked long enough now."

"I looked at him, and I said, 'I don't think you understand. I've
invested every penny my grandfather left me. This is not a volunteer
project. I'm in business with another person. I've invested my sav-
ings and she has invested hers.'

"But he said it was time for me to quit. He wanted me back home.
He saw that I was doing something, and I was doing it too good."

Sharon didn't quit. More and more she saw that Donald's constant dissatisfaction with her was nothing she could remedy.

When the two had been married a little over ten years, the bottom began to fall out. First came a series of deaths. Her whole family, which had given Sharon so much love and support all her life, was decimated within the space of a year, and Sharon was left with only her children and Donald. Sharon's adored and adoring grandfather had already died. Now her mother, to whom she was devoted, died very suddenly at the age of forty-seven. Her stepfather died the following year, and shortly afterward her grandmother, her "second mother."

Throughout Sharon's mourning, Donald was less than supportive. "I came home from my mother's funeral in Washington. Donald was getting ready to fly out on a business trip. I said, 'Please just come and sit with me for a few minutes.' He said, 'If you think I'm going to sit there and be morbid with you, you're crazy,' and walked out."

In the middle of this emotional chaos, Sharon became pregnant with Roger, her youngest child, who was born in 1968. "Donald did not talk to me for nine months. He had told me if I ever got pregnant again he would divorce me, as if I did it to myself. And he did not acknowledge that Roger existed for his first two years of life."

When Roger was a little over a year old, Sharon discovered that Donald was having an affair. She had believed that, whatever his personality problems were, he loved her as much as he could love anyone, and so she had made allowances for his bad treatment of her. Then there was her dream of family stability. More than anything she wanted to hold her family together.

But she was recovering from a miscarriage and the emergency surgery that followed it. Physically debilitated, exhausted from the trauma of the last two years, Sharon took the knowledge that her husband was involved with another woman hard.

> I'd wake up in the morning like I'd had a terrible nightmare, and I couldn't get it out of my mind. . . . I would go to the grocery store and just sit in my car in the parking lot. I could not make myself go into the store.

At the same time she also realized that her oldest son, Russell, at the age of twelve was experimenting heavily with drugs.

He had been one of the most perfect, well-behaved little boys you could imagine, always wanting to please, and saying, "Mom, I'll do anything you want me to." Extremely handsome, above average; a sweet, loving, sensitive child. . . .

Then he began coming home very tired and sleepy from school, and I would say, "Oh, my poor child, he's really working too hard," which showed my naiveté. . . . He was into the first step of drug abuse, marijuana.

Russell's drug use quickly accelerated. "Our life turned into a nightmare," Sharon says.

The door would open and we'd stand there waiting for Russell to walk in, not knowing what state he was going to be in. Usually it was a very stoned state, just—you know— slurring of words, not being able to move, weaving back and forth, abusive verbally, and of course all the other children watching. It was just devastating.

"Russell is not the kind of son I want," Donald told Sharon. Shortly afterward, he told Russell himself, "told him to his face that he didn't love him." Then Donald left his family. Sharon, strained to the limit, spent three months in the hospital with a complete nervous breakdown.

"When I came out," she says, "I looked in my mirror and I didn't like what I saw. I was a vegetable. I'd lost a considerable amount of weight. I had always been a really happy person, and now I was just shot. I looked at myself, and I said, 'Lady, either you're going to swim or you're going to sink.' "

She swam. She had to. Four children, the youngest only two, depended on her. But it was upstream all the way. First she decided to get a divorce and move ahead. She missed Donald less than she had expected to. "Once he moved out, nothing changed—nothing except stress and worrying about how he felt about me and was I pleasing him and all that. Suddenly I didn't have to worry about those things."

But she hoped that Donald would keep a relationship of some kind with the children, particularly with Russell, who seemed to need him most. "The fact that his dad didn't like him was just like a

big dagger sticking in the pit of his stomach all the time," according
to Sharon. Years later, after therapy, Russ told his mother, "I don't
know if I hated my dad so much or loved him so much. I just wanted
him to accept me. I kept wondering: What do I have to do to prove
myself to Dad?"

Some fathers who leave are more responsible to their children
away from the trauma of a bad marriage. Not Donald. "I'd have
them all set and dressed, waiting for him to pick them up, and he'd
call and say he couldn't. . . . They always did have great love for
him. It isn't there anymore."

When Donald did come by for an occasional visit, as usual he
wanted the surface of life to be smooth. He was certainly not eager
to help with family problems, and by now Russell was a problem, a
serious problem. As he moved into high school, his condition wors-
ened. He was heavily into drugs, and became cross-addicted to pills
and alcohol, "a mixture of everything."

Sharon was desperate for help.

> I started making phone calls, and I came up against brick
> walls constantly. Nobody knew where to go for help at that
> time [in the early seventies]. I'd go to doctors. I called the
> church. I'd call hospitals. They couldn't advise me where
> to go or what to do, and it was the most frustrating situa-
> tion I've ever been in. And it was just getting progressively
> worse.

Sharon asked Donald for help. "He would be there, and I would
say, 'Please help me.' I'd say, 'He's sick. He's totally sick.' " Russell,
a strapping six-footer by this time, was a great deal for a woman
alone to handle. The occasion arose when Donald could see for
himself that Sharon needed help with their son.

> It was the first time Russell was in any way abusive physi-
> cally. Donald was there, and Russell pinned me to the
> door. Donald just walked right out and got in his car,
> leaving me pinned to the door.
> And at that moment I knew that we would never get help
> from him.

All alone, Sharon set out to do something for her son. Unlike
Rosemary Dixon, who discovered the seriousness of her daughter's

problems only with Polly's suicide, Sharon had found out what was
going on with Russell in time to avert total catastrophe, or so she
hoped. Rosemary, frustrated of action, endlessly asked why. For
Sharon:

> It wasn't just asking why, why, why, why. It was trying to
> handle the situation and just going from each day to the
> next day and the next day. I don't know that I ever sat down
> and said, "Why did this happen?" It was just "Let's get this
> taken care of. Let's get him some help."

Help was not easy to find. Sharon went to physicians, but in the
early seventies doctors knew very little about drugs, nor were there
resources through churches and social agencies of the kind available
to parents today.

> There was no place to go. What do you do with a child
> who's about to kill himself or is threatening suicide, trying
> to jump off buildings, and you find out later his friends
> have held him back because he's hallucinating? . . . I
> can't tell you how many times I was called to hospitals
> because of overdoses, and standing there, and the nurses
> and doctors would say, "Please stay with him to make sure
> that he doesn't stop breathing, and if he does, call us."

On at least one occasion Sharon saved Russell's life.

> One of the worst situations that we experienced was one
> time he was home and in a very bad state. For some reason
> his father was there and they got into an argument. It
> became physical, the first time they ever had any physical
> encounter.
> I guess it was too much for Russell, for whatever he was
> on at the time. He literally expired right on the floor. I
> screamed and called the emergency corps. Then I went
> over and I said, "I'll be damned if I'll let you die now." And
> I jumped on him and started pushing the air in. And Don-
> ald just sat there, rubbing Russell's arm gently, saying,
> "Oh, it'll be all right. He'll be all right."

As Russell sank deeply into a state in which drugs ran his life, in
which he could not distinguish between hallucination and reality,

his whole personality changed. He became more and more violent. Sharon, who loved creating holidays for her children, regretted the spoiled family festivities. "So many of our Thanksgivings and Christmases were marred by him walking in totally out of his mind."

He destroyed family antiques, "shattered beautiful Kaiser chairs and Queen Anne plant stands. I walked in once to what looked like a bombed-out area, where he had gone berserk."

Another time Sharon came home to something even worse. The other children were away, and Sharon hoped that with Russell and her alone, he would be calmer. She went to the grocery to buy the fixings for his favorite Mexican food. When she returned and pulled the car into the driveway, she saw a small mound of something white lying at the garage entrance.

> It was pure white, and I said, "My goodness, what's that bag of flour doing out there?" Then I saw about a nine-inch dagger covered with blood and blood all over, and I didn't know what— It was the cat. He'd stabbed the cat to death.

Afraid for her life, Sharon took the knife and retreated to a motel for the night. The next morning she went home very early. Just as she walked in the door, the phone rang. The police had Russell.

> They said they found him on the corner, just hallucinating, and he had a three-inch slash on his face. . . . They had him in jail. I went there and talked to him. And he said, "I had to kill the cat because it was full of germs."

The stress for his mother was dreadful. "Your whole body is just tense, so tense that it's rigid. You don't even realize how tight you are until you get into bed and you can't unwind. Your body—it feels like a branch on a tree, it's so tight and hard," she remembers. "I was angry at Russ. I would try to talk to him, you know, but I just truly didn't have a grasp of the situation. I just didn't—I just didn't know."

What she "didn't know," she says, was what addiction really means. "You can only help yourself so much with this drug abuse. You can't just say, 'I'm stopping,' and with alcohol, too. It's a disease. I know that now."

Now Sharon attributes Russell's addictions to his physiology.

When he started experimenting in the sixties and seventies like so many kids, he was unfortunate, because his body chemistry is different. . . . My daughter experimented. She told me. She said, "Mom, I experimented like everybody else in those days, but only once or twice, and that was it."

But with Russ, whatever his body chemistry is, he became hooked. It was an addiction that he just couldn't let go of.

And, you know, I think of my friends who smoke and they can't give up their cigarettes, or how hard it is for me to lose ten pounds. What in the heck is he going through, trying to give up alcohol and drugs? . . .

I have to *understand*. It isn't like a kid who just does something defiantly. Russ has a disease.

But ten years ago, Sharon didn't understand all this. Since the sixties, Americans have grown steadily more sophisticated about addiction. At the onset of Russell's problem, Sharon didn't have the benefit of such readily available information and support. She understood only how badly she and her son needed help. When she didn't get help from doctors and ministers, Sharon "approached a couple of friends." There too she struck out. "I didn't tell them all the circumstances, but just enough, and . . . I never talked to them again about it. It was like they didn't want to hear it. It was so foreign and frightening . . . so I didn't share it with anyone. I think that was a mistake, although I got through it."

Feeling she could not help Russell unless she got some help herself, Sharon started to attend Al-Anon meetings. For the first time help presented itself, not only for the suffering mother but also for her child. She learned about a place where addicts could go to dry out, and made arrangements for Russell's placement.

It's a working farm . . . for about twenty-six individuals— they call them residents. They have to work, milk the cows, bring in the eggs, do all the things that people do on a farm. . . . Russell stayed there eight months and made terrific progress, and came out.

But the unfortunate part was that I expected too much. I thought, "He's cured. Our troubles are over." It was the first time since all the problems started that I could breathe easily, live in peace, and not worry about him on the streets.

When Russell left the farm, he "had a slip," as Sharon says. He went back to his old habits, and they were worse than ever. He had a head-on collision in his car, which ruptured his liver and nearly severed both his leg and his tongue. He was in such bad shape that they couldn't take him directly to the hospital. The medics worked over him for an hour on the road, an hour during which Sharon, waking from a restless sleep, heard nonexistent sirens.

> My second son came in around one . . . and I started to say to him, "Did you hear those sirens?" but I knew that there really weren't any sirens. . . . Three hours later we received a phone call from the hospital, and Russ had his accident about the time that I thought I heard those sirens.

This time, when he came out of the hospital, Sharon sent Russell to a facility for alcoholics and cross-addicts. He was there for a long time, and came out stronger than ever. Again, his mother expected too much. Again, she was wrong.

Her dreams were destroyed when Russell was arrested for trying to break into a gas station. "He never got in . . . he was so loaded and stoned and out of his mind at the time, but we still had to go to court."

There was a trial by jury. Russell had gone into another hospital with a drug-abuse center, and he was released from the hospital to stand trial. Sharon knew Russell's feelings better by this time, and her own feelings were deeply engaged with her son. She had witnessed his sufferings from the knowledge of his addiction.

> He has cried many nights over the fact that he can't give it up—you know, just can't give it up. . . . And he says, "Mom, I'm going to go through life saddled with this. . . . You don't know what it's like." And he's cried, he's cried. He said the struggle—and I know that he's thought of suicide, I mean, just as an easy way out, because he said, "You don't know the feelings inside, how it feels."

Unlike Jean Brooks, whose husband Kenneth was on hand every minute of his son Tom's trial, Sharon had no husband to be there with Russell. Russell had no stalwart pillar of a father to offer constant support and counsel. Sharon alone stood by her son, hard as it was for her.

> You want to scream and yell and go up there and tell that judge that he doesn't understand, and knock that prosecuting attorney across the— I mean, I'm not a violent person, but if I ever wanted to hit anyone, it was that prosecuting attorney, because . . . here's your child struggling to live, and [the prosecutor] is trying to say all these things and twist them around and confuse what's been said. I—I felt violence within me. Maybe it was the mother instinct, but I wanted to go up there and protect my child.

At the end of the trial, when Russell was declared guilty and the police officers came forward to take him away to jail, Sharon actually did find herself obstructing the arm of the law.

> It's strange what mothers will do. I found myself standing in front of Russell between two state police officers and saying, "You're not taking him. He's sick, and he has to go back to the hospital." And I must say how sweet and understanding they were.

She got her way. The judge decreed that Russell should serve his term in the drug-abuse center at the hospital. Months later he left the hospital on probation.

Once again he turned to drugs. By this time his habit had become expensive, and he had no money. Sharon's losses were material as well as emotional now. He cleaned out the house, stealing ten thousand dollars' worth of heirloom silver, jewelry, and a watch that had belonged to her mother. Sharon located some of the items at a pawnshop, but to protect her son she didn't report them stolen. Instead she tried to buy them.

Sharon had paid the high cost of Russ's hospital stays. If there is no Kenneth Brooks in her family to attend his son's trial, neither is there a Nicholas Barnes, a father who feels "privileged" to pay for his child's treatments. But, though Sharon pays for Russell's treatment, her profits from the sewing shop, which supported the family after Donald's departure, don't allow for the purchase of valuable silver and jewelry, even her own.

But her mother's watch was a different matter. That, for sentimental reasons, she felt she must have. Even in 1982, she was still trying to get it out of hock. "I'm paying a little bit each month to get it back, but it's been almost two years now." Her laugh is bitter as she explains it has been two years that she's tried to scrape up six hundred dollars, "believe it or not."

Pressed for funds, Russell got in over his head with a gang of dope dealers. When he owed them money, they put out a contract on his life. As Sharon recalls the horror of that time, the phone would ring and a voice would say, "This is Russell's murderer. Your son is dead. This is it." She was afraid not only for Russell but for the lives of her other children as well. Everything began to run together for her:

> The first couple of incidents you remember clearly, but after that, one police station after another, waking my boys up in the middle of the night, going to a police station to get him out, the accidents. . . . It's been an earth-shattering experience, horrifying times, totally horrifying.
>
> When I hear a siren, I tense up and I wonder if it's Russ. If the phone rings after eleven o'clock at night, I can't tell you how my adrenaline shoots. . . .
>
> I guess my greatest fear was always that he was dead. . . . The fear was—death was pending, it was just around the corner and everyone knew it.

When the dope peddlers put out the contract for Russell, Sharon knew he would be dead in days. He was living away from home, Sharon didn't know where, but he called her every day to check in so she wouldn't worry.

> When he called, I could hardly stand it. He was on something terrible, really terrible. He couldn't speak, slurring words, falling asleep right on the—you know, I just wanted to reach out and bring him home. . . .

One Friday the call didn't come until five in the morning. It wasn't from Russell but from a downtown hospital. He had been found unconscious in the street.

> They wouldn't tell me on the phone if he was alive or if he
> was dead or what was wrong. I got the boys up . . . , we
> went down there, and . . . they said he had pneumonia,
> but . . . whatever drugs he took had paralyzed his lungs.

Sharon stood by him again in the trial for violating probation which
awaited him when he came out of the hospital. But the ordeal of the
trial, with its numberless anxieties, delays, and postponements, took
something out of her.

Russell refused further treatment, and, as by now he was well over
twenty-one, Sharon could not legally commit him. Without protest
she saw him led away and placed in a work-release program in a
minimum-security prison.

At the time of the interview Russell was still in prison and his
mother was not at all sure of the future for him. "I don't have any
answers. He's twenty-four now and still in trouble, a recovering
alcoholic, an addict, fighting for his survival. . . . I don't know
where it's going to lead." In the stage of detachment in the ongoing
process of coping with her son's behavior that Sharon has reached,
having him safely ensconced, even in jail, helps her peace of mind.

For mothers, there's some peace in knowing rather than wondering. "You know the night Abby died, when the police called me and
told me?" says Selena, the mother of another troubled child in
Grace Paley's short story "Friends." "That was my first night's sleep
in two years. I *knew* where she was." And Sharon has more comfort
than Selena, who has definitely lost her child. As Sharon says:

> I know he is where he should be. . . . I know that he can't
> harm himself, that he is not going to be in trouble, and it's
> a great relief for me. . . . The relief is unbelievable. I can
> go to sleep at night and know that he is in a controlled
> situation, and I don't have to worry.

This lesson of detachment has been hard for Sharon. For years
the Al-Anon group, which had been virtually her only support during all of her struggles with Russ, had urged Sharon to "detach."
"But I didn't understand," she says.

> It took me a long time to know what they were saying. They
> kept telling me, "Detach. Detach. You must detach yourself
> from Russell."

I thought they meant detach myself, walk away from him completely . . . and I argued. I would sit at those meetings and argue with that. I said, "Do you mean to say that if I was on a beach and saw someone on a bridge about to jump, that I wouldn't get out of my comfortable beach chair, and go over and try to help them? I couldn't do that."

But what they meant was, "Don't detach yourself from *Russ,* but from *his problem.*" And I have done that. I have finally been able to do that for the first time in my life. It's just happened in the last few months, not even a full year. But I've reached a point where I know, intellectually, emotionally, whatever, I know that I have done as much for Russ as I can do. I can do no more. There is nothing more that I can do, financially, physically, mentally.

I can continue to love him, which I will do; support him; be by his side at all times. But he must assume the responsibility for his actions now and know that if he takes a drink or pill, *he* is going to pay the consequences.

I hurt for him. I just cry, and I'd die for him. I can do no more for him.

For Sharon, the shock of her son's behavior was made infinitely harder to bear because of her extreme isolation. The grandparents and parents who had made her early life so joyous all died at the time she needed them most. Her husband, who by all rights should have helped, was part of the problem rather than part of the solution. Alone she paid attention to the child and recognized the illness that caused his behavior.

Sharon was resourceful and strong in action, in handling the various crises of Russell's illness while he, as a minor, was to some degree under her control. She saw to it he got the best help she could provide at every step of the way.

Once, dramatically, Sharon threw herself between her son and the law, and pleaded to the court for greater understanding of his problems. But now that Russell has reached an age at which Sharon herself can no longer put him into a hospital or drug program, she has wisely recognized the limits of her responsibility for him. She has detached herself, not from him, but from his problems. Now he must commit himself to get help. He is responsible for himself.

And Sharon is tired. "I'm truly tired. I'm tired of problems." She realizes she had lost something of herself in the ongoing battle for Russell's life. "One day on the tennis court I was up at the net, and I realized that I was a woman on stilts. I wasn't Sharon standing at that net. I was like a big lemon with two sticks for legs, and my heart was not singing. From childhood, I always had this thing about my heart singing, you know, when I felt happiness within. And that was not there. That was gone."

She is ready to pay attention to herself. "There has to be a time for Sharon, and the time has come. Twelve years is a long time."

Recently she tried to describe her new feeling of independence to her children. She told them, "There's a difference between needing and wanting. I don't need my house, my car, my job. I don't need a lot of things. I may want them to make my life more pleasurable, but I don't need them.

"And I don't need you children. I don't need you in my life to live."

She had to explain, particularly to Russ. "It was during one of his clear moments, and he thought I meant I didn't love him." She goes on:

> But I said, "Wait a minute. Listen to what I'm saying. I don't need you in my life to live, but I want you in my life. Because I love you."

The conclusion to Russell's story is open. He must write it himself. But whatever happens to her son, Sharon, if need be Sharon all alone, will survive.

Stage Two

ATTENTION

Seeing the real child under the ideal, and interpreting the child's true nature and needs to others

4

"Is It My Fault?"
What the Experts Say

Listen. Look. Learn. As the first shock of a child's unexpected behavior eases, a mother begins to pay attention. She does what the mother of a newborn does—she experiences her child from a different point of view.

After giving birth, a mother must reconcile the child in the womb with the child in her arms. The child's contours and movements she now sees objectively rather than feels as parts of her own body. She can listen to his cries. She can look at him and trace family likenesses in the lineaments of his face. She can learn to understand his habits and his nature.

Like a new mother, the mother of an untraditional child must listen, look, and learn. She spends as much time as she can simply paying attention to her child, letting him talk, not judging but listening. What is it like, she asks herself, taxing her empathic imagination, to be this person, her child? And she tries to see her child, not as she wants him to be, not as she has assumed him to be, but as he really is.

As attentively as she listens to what he tells her, she also looks for clues as to what he's not saying. To learn all she can about him and his puzzling or shocking behavior, she may turn to experts. She will perhaps visit doctors, lawyers, teachers, or, less frequently, minis-

ters and priests. Almost certainly she will read. As Jean Brooks said,
"I pulled on what I had all my life—reading."

Karen Matthews, for example, learned her daughter Elisa was a
manic-depressive. After a horrible experience during which Elisa
had to be straitjacketed and hospitalized, mother and daughter
embarked on a reading program. As Karen tells it:

> During her periods of depression . . . Elisa would go to
> the library and bring stacks of books home, all about
> manic-depressives, because she wanted to learn as much
> about it as she possibly could, and of course I would read
> them too. It . . . really helped a lot about understanding
> what—what it's all about.
>
> And she said, "Oh, Mom, I'm in good company. Abra-
> ham Lincoln was one, Churchill was one." And she named
> the list of all the well-known people through history that
> were manic-depressives. Many, I'm sure, were, but were
> never diagnosed as such. It was good to be able to read it.

Such reading will help mother and child place the child's difficulties
in perspective. As perspective is apt to be the first thing to go under
trauma, its restoration is a necessary part of coming to determine
what action the family must subsequently take.

Before a mother can give her full attention to the child himself,
however, she must reckon with her own guilt. To what extent is she
responsible for the behavior and perhaps the unhappiness of this
stranger, her child?

MOTHERS "ON THE HOOK"

Feeling guilty came naturally to the mothers in this study. "I asked
myself a million questions," Lois Wagner said. "You know, you go
back to the year one and say, 'What did I do?' Guilt feelings! . . . I
guess Jewish mothers are always guilty." Nor is this feeling of overwhelming responsibility and guilt confined to Jewish mothers. "I
always blame myself," Bonnie Scott, a Presbyterian, says. "I always
think it's my fault. I did something or I didn't do something."

The mother's dilemma in a nugget: "I did something or I didn't do something." What mother can ever be sure that what she is doing —or not doing—with her child is right, unmistakably, irrefutably *right,* at any given moment?

This guilt has been unfairly augmented by so-called experts. Dr. Paula Caplan and Dr. Ian Hall-McCorquodale, of the Ontario Institute for Studies in Education, recently reviewed one hundred and twenty-five articles in journals of clinical psychology from 1970, 1976, and 1982. They found "mother-blaming" rampant, regardless of the sex of the author, the type of journal, and the year of publication. Seventy-two kinds of disorders were directly attributed to mothers. Mothers were related to a child's problems five times as often as fathers.

The time has come to take mothers off the hook. Successful mothering depends on a mysterious amalgam of personality and circumstance. What works with one child will not work with his sister. In the families described here, children who are now happy, independent, and productive grew up with brothers or sisters whose lives seem to their mothers to be, to use a word that keeps recurring in these interviews, "wasted." And, as different as the children have turned out, the mother is not aware of having treated them in the least differently when they were growing up.

In fact, the child who comes to grieve the mother most may have been, like Polly Dixon, the one who showed the most promise. If a manic-depressive is, as Elisa and Karen discovered, in good company, so are children with other forms of aberrant behavior. Because they are curious and courageous, the most promising children often behave the least traditionally. They have everything going for them—intelligence, talent, concern for others, an appetite for life. They are accustomed to success. Small wonder that these young people are so often the ones who find defying tradition easy and tempting.

When they succeed, their mother does not take the credit. When they fail, should she take the blame? Whatever other questions a mother may ask the experts as she begins to pay attention to her child as he really is, the one great spoken or unspoken question for every mother is, "Is it my fault?"

The answer she gets depends on which expert she asks. Just as Lucy Carpenter found the psychologists sharply divided as to whether she should play Saturday-afternoon backgammon with her husband after her son David's first suicide attempts, experts differ greatly on the question of a mother's responsibility for her adult child's behavior and success in life. Let us look at relevant theories recently expressed by three developmental psychologists.

Exploring the basic issues of responsibility and separation, Dr. Alice Miller, a respected German practitioner of the Freudian school, says it *is* the mother's fault. Miller defines the plight of the sensitive, alert child whose very early and consistent adaptation to his parents' emotional needs causes him in adulthood to lack the ability to experience immediate, authentic feelings of his own. She holds psychically weak parents, especially mothers, responsible, and by implication argues for stronger, more independent parenthood.

Dr. Jerome Kagan, a professor at Harvard, takes exactly the opposite tack. He argues that the human capacity for change, for personal growth, rules out the inexorability of early childhood experience. Nothing can be called a mother's fault with any certainty, Kagan insists. The influence of the family on the child's development, he explains, has never been satisfactorily measured at all. A child's *interpretation* of family influence matters rather than the influence itself, which is anyway far more "subtle and complex" than is recognized in the Freudian camp and elsewhere.

Concerned primarily with the issues of care and communication, Dr. Carol Gilligan, also a professor at Harvard, argues that women should be given credit for forging and maintaining the connections between people. Gilligan sees women as primarily devoted to human relations rather than to abstract "male" justice. A concerned woman can reconcile conflicting points of view, and thus can hold a family together. For Gilligan, women demonstrate their greatest strength in their ability and desire to care for others.

The three writers differ so markedly in approach and theory that one can hardly conclude any is "right" to the entire exclusion of the others. They all represent tendencies already existent in popular thinking and in the minds of the women in this study.

MILLER: EXPRESSING THE "TRUE SELF"

The least palatable of the three for any mother is Alice Miller. Miller, whose book *The Drama of the Gifted Child* was translated from the German and published in English first in 1981 as *Prisoners of Childhood*, adheres staunchly to the Freudian doctrine of the overwhelming importance of the experiences of childhood. Her thesis is that the "gifted," that is, the most empathic and sensitive, child loses touch as he matures with his instinctual "true self" because of the necessity he feels for conforming to his mother's unconscious plans for him. Acting out of needs which remain unsatisfied from their own deprived childhoods, parents, especially mothers, unintentionally and unconsciously manipulate their children so that the most alert children will try, also unconsciously, to satisfy the repressed, narcissistic needs of the parent.

Rather than accepting the expression of all aspects of the child's personality, a typically imperfect mother can accept only the behavior in the child that she finds rewarding, pleasant, and unthreatening to herself. She "loves" the child when he behaves well, and withholds love when he behaves badly. Because of his great dependence on his mother's love and approval, as the child grows he learns to repress whatever feelings or qualities he might have which will lead to her rejection of him, and to exhibit only the feelings or qualities she accepts. Gradually, by denying part of his nature, he becomes "narcissistically cathected" or divided. He takes on an entire "false self," with many of his true feelings so deeply submerged that he may have lost the ability even to feel them.

In this state, the adult child may be, indeed often is, successful in the world. Because his achievements provide his mother with great satisfaction, he early learns the habits of achievement. Emotionally, however, he remains a child, subject to the twin perils of "grandiosity" and "depression." Miller describes these extremes, of which there are many gradations:

> The person who is "grandiose" is admired everywhere and
> needs this admiration; indeed, he cannot live without it. He
> must excel brilliantly in everything he undertakes, which
> he surely is capable of doing (otherwise he just does not
> attempt it). He, too, admires himself—for his qualities: his

beauty, cleverness, talents—and for his success and
achievements. Woe betide if one of these fails him, for then
the catastrophe of a severe depression is imminent. . . .
One is free from depression when self-esteem is based on
the authenticity of one's own feelings and not on the possession of certain qualities. . . . Although the outward
picture of depression is quite the opposite of that of grandiosity and has a quality that expresses the tragedy of the
loss of self to a great extent, they have the same roots in the
narcissistic disturbance. Both are indications of an inner
prison, because the grandiose and the depressive individuals are compelled to fulfill the introjected mother's expectations: whereas the grandiose person is her successful
child, the depressive sees himself as a failure.

Grandiose and depressed persons have other points in common
in addition to those already mentioned: a fragility of self-esteem;
perfectionism; a great willingness to conform in order to secure
love; envy of the healthy; oversensitivity; a readiness to feel shame
and guilt; strong aggressive tendencies that are separate from the
visible "false self"; and restlessness. Most important, they also lack
"vitality: the freedom to experience spontaneous feelings."

It is part of the kaleidoscope of life that these feelings are
not only cheerful, "beautiful," and "good"; they also can
display the whole scale of human experience, including
envy, jealousy, rage, disgust, greed, despair, and mourning. But this freedom cannot be achieved if the childhood
roots are cut off.

To be healed, such persons must become children again. According to Miller, they can regain the "true self" and access to the full
gamut of human emotions only by reliving, in analysis, the unacceptable behavior of childhood and having it accepted by the analyst
in his or her role as surrogate parent. Intellectual understanding
alone will not suffice for this catharsis. The damage was done on the
level of the emotions, and healing must take place there as well. The
analyst, to whom Miller's book is largely addressed, must cultivate
in herself or himself the qualities of the ideal, accepting mother.

As Miller acknowledges, the ideal, accepting mother does not exist in nature and is only a creature of legend and dreams:

> A mother such as we once urgently needed—empathic and open, understanding and understandable, available and usable, transparent, clear, without unintelligible contradictions—such a mother was never ours, indeed she could not exist; for every mother carries with her a bit of her "unmastered past," which she unconsciously hands on to her child.

The analyst, approximating the ideal mother, tries to create the healthy situation for emotional growth that was lacking in the patient's childhood.

From a mother's point of view, there are serious difficulties with Miller's schema. The determinism always apparent in Freudian thinking here catches the mother in a real double bind. On the one hand, she has to accept nearly total responsibility for her adult child's traumas. He suffers because she, hamstrung by her own psychological inadequacies, failed to be the all-accepting mother "once urgently needed." Because of her failures, only thorough analysis can help him to health, just as only thorough analysis could have made her an ideal mother.

On the other hand, in spite of her guilt in the situation (and remember that nearly all mothers are guilty), her manipulations of her child were unconscious and unknowing. Given her own psychological state, she couldn't help what she did, and in fact may never realize that anything was amiss in her treatment of her child. On the contrary, because of the obvious successes of her child, she may very likely see herself as a good mother, conscientious in exacting from him the best use of his talents.

Her child too will cling to the myth of the good mother, resisting her domination only in unconscious ways. For example, Miller credits political action to an unconscious resistance to the tactics of domineering mothers.

> Political action can be fed by the unconscious anger of children who have been so misused, imprisoned, exploited, cramped, and drilled. This anger can be partially discharged in fighting our institutions, without having to

give up the idealization of one's own mother, as one knew her in one's childhood.

Thus it is possible to interpret the civil rights and anti-establishment movements of the sixties and seventies, which involved many of the children in this study, as motivated by unconscious anger against mothers.

These ideas, interesting as they are, make the striving, admittedly imperfect mother feel as if she is caught in iron cobwebs. Perhaps the best she can do, short of going into analysis (which may come too late anyway to help her children), is to work to create a good family situation. For Miller, the characteristics of that situation, in simple terms, are:

1. The parents are self-confident and independent enough not to be threatened by the aggressive impulses or strivings toward autonomy of the child.
2. The child does not have to be "special," so he can experience and exhibit ordinary impulses, such as jealousy, rage, or defiance, as they develop in each phase of his growth.
3. The child, separate from the narcissistic needs of his parents, learns to accept his parents and himself as "both good and bad," and to display ambivalent feelings.
4. Thus he can integrate all of his emotional needs and doesn't have to resort to repression or splitting, or to the good opinion of others, in order to esteem himself.

Any parent might benefit from keeping these principles in mind. A mother who neither counts too inordinately on her child's successes nor too greatly fears his failures liberates her child to find his own way, to be himself.

KAGAN: A COMPLEX OF INFLUENCES

Jerome Kagan in *The Nature of the Child* (1984) would agree with Miller that the child is often a target for misplaced parental hostility.

Kagan acknowledges that a punitive mother typically rationalizes to herself and to others that the child has violated a standard of some kind. She punishes him, putatively to serve his development, actually to vent her own anger and frustration.

Kagan's basic concerns lie elsewhere, however. As an epigraph to his book, he has affixed: "Every age has its myths and calls them higher truths." In the text he is intent on providing a critique of several myths or "idealistic assumptions" about the child and family which are currently held to be true.

American families (and Freudian psychologists) assume, for example, that a child's course is set for life in the first few years of his existence. Parents see physical affection and firmness as the vital ingredients. Give a small child visible love and strong guidance, the reasoning runs, and he will become a self-confident, disciplined adult. To Kagan such thinking is simplistic. He presents an alternative point of view.

Rather than accepting the premise that family influences single-handedly produce the child and that, as Wordsworth had it, "the child is father of the man," Kagan sees the individual human being as a complex brew of influences. He uses a metaphor from biology to make the point:

> The evolutionary tree may be a good metaphor for psychological development. Biologists do not explain the appearance of man by pointing to protozoa, even though in the remote past the existence of protozoa made humans a little more likely. Rather, scientists point to the entire evolutionary sequence. Similarly, one cannot explain a ten-year-old's phobia of horses or Proust's aestheticism by listing their respective experiences as infants. Each person can be understood only as a coherence of many, many past events.

To Kagan, American parents believe in a connection between early childhood and later development largely because they want to rather than for any scientific proof on the subject. He gives six reasons for the American predisposition to this belief. First, it makes the future knowable and secure. Training a small child well, to those who hold a belief in connectedness, Kagan analogizes, is rather like gathering wood for the winter.

Second, this belief simplifies the human being, makes him neatly mechanistic and predictable, operating on a strict cause-effect sequence. Third, the belief is egalitarian, because it implies that similar experiences, with similar results, can be arranged for all children. So the belief guarantees a democracy of childhood.

Fourth, the belief in the direct connection of childhood with adulthood is sustained by our language. English adjectives, descriptive words which give us our sense of ourselves linguistically, apply equally well to a person of any age. In English, for example, a baby, an adolescent, or an adult can all be described as "intelligent," as if the meaning of the word were not altered by growth. In Japanese and certain other languages, Kagan points out, *different* words are used to describe the quality of intelligence in children and in adults. Thus English implies a stability of character, as Japanese implies change.

Fifth, this belief satisfies a "book society," in which reasoning and written knowledge generate the sense that everything has a fixed, scientific explanation. Finally, our acceptance of the ranking of children in and out of school, with a concurrent emphasis on the *building* of skills, inclines us to accept a similar idea regarding the building of character.

Kagan argues for the importance of change or disconnectedness in human development. Once he has pointed out the ways in which Americans are conditioned to a satisfying belief in connectedness, he specifies four major conditions for change which are powerful influences at various periods of development in the individual.

1. The infant or small child is influenced by the genetically programmed changes in his central nervous system.

2. The normative regimens of society, such as going to school between five and six, learning to drive at fifteen or sixteen, and going to college at eighteen, lead to significant changes in the older child.

3. Historical events, such as economic depression, war, revolution, natural catastrophe, or inventions like television or the computer, most strongly affect older adolescents and young adults. For example, the demonstrations against the Vietnam War in the 1960s more seriously influenced Americans between the ages of fifteen and twenty-five—that is, the age of most of the young people in this study—than those who were older or younger.

4. After the age of thirty, the first three factors become less im-

portant, and unexpected or unpredictable events, such as a divorce, an illness, or an accident, become much more important in causing change.

QUALITIES OF THE AMERICAN FAMILY

Of particular relevance to the present study are Kagan's conclusions about the role of the family in his last chapter. He begins by asserting that little can be stated flat-footedly about the consequences of parental behavior, because "the effects of most experiences are not fixed but depend upon the child's interpretation. And the interpretation will vary with the child's cognitive maturity, expectations, beliefs, and momentary feeling state." Instead of attempting to measure the essentially immeasurable quantity of family influence, then, he goes on to explore the qualities of American family life.

He cites four qualities which distinguish American and other families of the modern Western world from the centuries of families that preceded them as well as from families in other parts of the world today. First and perhaps most important, he believes that the significance of the family in our society is slowly being superseded by the significance of the individual. The individual, not the family, has become the basic unit. In other societies, the conception of self depends on the status of the family. In America, more and more young people have begun to conclude that their future lives depend on their personal abilities and ambition. "This attitude may be historically unique," Kagan remarks. Although there are questions about the form of the earliest families,

> no anthropologist or historian has ever suggested that the majority of adults living in older societies believed that their survival, personal reputation, and material success did not depend primarily on their family of rearing. Thus, each American adult must acquire a special state of mind which most families, consciously or unconsciously, train for from the earliest months of life.

The second significant characteristic of American and contemporary Western society is the high position of women, and, with it, the importance given to maternal love. Dr. Kagan is particularly acerbic in describing the vaunted power of a mother's love. In our society, he says, this power has

> a parallel in the potency attributed in other societies at other times to spirits, loss of soul, sorcery, sin, gossip, God, and witchcraft. . . . A mother's love for the child is treated as a mysterious force which, if sprinkled plentifully over young children, guarantees salvation. But for the child who is not fortunate enough to have had a loving mother, the future is poisoned.

Clearly Kagan discredits this whole line of reasoning, which is part of the burden of undue responsibility from which the women of this study have had to free themselves.

Kagan describes how the totem of mother love came into being:

> It is natural to award sacred qualities to those who represent the ideals of the society. As European middle-class women began to assume primary responsibility for the child's character and to adopt the Enlightenment virtues of charity, kindness, humaneness, and unselfishness in the service of husband and children, they became candidates for sanctification. Men did the evil work of the world; women, by loving, did God's work.

But there may be a drastic difference, Kagan warns, in what the mother feels and what the child experiences. The most loving mother may be misinterpreted by her child. Then too the child and mother do not live in a vacuum. There are influences other than the mother's on the growing child. Thus this myth obviously imposes an unfair and impossible psychological burden on women. However loving a mother may be, she may fail in the child's "salvation."

The third unusual quality of American families is the degree to which they glorify the freedom and selfhood of children. All societies value children, some more than others, but in most societies the child is also taught to feel loyalty and obligation to parents. "The special ingredient in the American form of child-centeredness," Kagan claims, "is its one-sidedness."

Parents are supposed to sacrifice for their children, while
the children are expected to grow increasingly independent of their parents. For many middle-class families, the
child is a beautiful young bird to be cared for until it is
ready to fly free in the forest.

Finally, unlike the families of China and Japan, American families
value sincerity and honesty above social harmony. Children of the
Orient are taught to show respect for their elders and others in
authority, to suppress anger, and to avoid telling a painful truth:
these are the qualities of maturity. The West considers this behavior
obsequious and dishonest, and believes that venting one's feelings
is necessary to the emotional health and integrity of the individual.

If, as Kagan asserts, these four qualities exist in American families
generally, they exist more markedly in middle-class families. Because working-class parents value job security, they stress conformity and other qualities which they think will guarantee it. They are
more likely to believe in the adherence to outside authority rather
than internal control when the child faces temptation. Living closer
to economic stress, they are more apt to recognize the extent to
which destiny is shaped by outside forces.

But college-educated, middle-class, economically secure mothers
of the kind in this study communicate to their children a strong
belief in self: freedom of choice, intellectual independence, control
of one's own destiny. In a sense all these children were acting out
their mothers' instructions when they took their maverick paths. "I
told him to be independent, to think for himself, and to do what *he*
thought was right, no matter what other people might say," wailed
the mother whose adored only son had made, she thought, a disas-
trous mistake, "but I didn't mean *that!*"

GILLIGAN: THE LADDER AND THE WEB

A discerning reader of Kagan's book who was already familiar with
Carol Gilligan's *In a Different Voice* (1982) would be led to comment
that three of the four qualities of American families that Kagan
points to might be what Gilligan would term aspects of male moral-

ity. Gilligan prefaces her discussion by saying that the voices she designates "male" and "female" throughout coexist within each person, male *and* female. She is characterizing modes of thought rather than gender, she says. In all of us there are two voices, one advocating autonomy and separation from others, the other advocating concern and connection with others.

In American society, however, she argues, the voice advocating autonomy speaks more forcefully to men; the voice advocating connection speaks more persuasively to women. Thus, three of the four qualities Kagan describes—emphasis on the individual rather than the family, on the overweening freedom and selfhood of children, and on honesty and sincerity even when they are upsetting to social harmony—all belong on the male side of the ledger. If Kagan has characterized American society accurately, Gilligan would say Americans live in a milieu based on "male" values. Love alone, in Kagan's description especially the overblown, pseudo-mystical maternal love of popular mythology, belongs on the female side.

Gilligan is aware of this imbalance in American thinking and eager to see it corrected, to see men learn to value "female" qualities and women learn to cultivate "male" qualities in themselves. Her thesis is that the moral development of women has been misunderstood and found wanting for years because women have been measured against male standards of morality, which are essentially and drastically different from female standards.

She bases her conclusions on three psychological studies she has done: a college student study, of randomly selected college sophomores in a moral and political choice class; an abortion study, of women of diverse ages, backgrounds, and situations all considering abortion; and a rights and responsibilities study, of men and women matched for age, intelligence, education, occupation, and social class across the life cycle. Her conclusions help in comprehending the motives and actions of the women whose stories are told in this book.

Women, she concludes, believe relationships between people to be the highest good. They rely on an ethic of caring. Men want their rights. They rely on an ethic of justice, and define morality as an absolute standard of right and wrong. Women would try to change the rules to preserve a relationship. Men would accept the rules and count on replacing the relationship.

Gilligan uses two apt illustrations from the Old Testament. Through the patriarch Abraham, who was willing to sacrifice the life of his son Isaac to demonstrate the strength of his faith, the male voice speaks. The abstract concept of obedience to a "higher truth" takes precedence over a single child. The woman brought before Solomon whose child is being claimed by another woman cries out, "Give her the child, but spare him!" Thus the female voice speaks. Wise Solomon, pretending to be ready to sever the child to satisfy each, recognizes the mother, exactly because she is ready to relinquish both the truth and her rights as mother in order to save the child.

Two images taken from male and female fantasies help in understanding these divergent views of the world, according to Dr. Gilligan. Men, she says, see life as a ladder or a hierarchy. One advances from level to level, rung to rung, leaving behind whatever will impede the progress to the top. Women, however, see life as a web or a net, where all relationships are interconnected and safely caught. The images of the hierarchical ladder and the web, Gilligan says,

> convey different ways of structuring relationships and are associated with different views of morality and self. But these images create a problem in understanding because each distorts the other's representation. As the top of the hierarchy becomes the edge of the web and as the center of a network of connection becomes the middle of a hierarchical progression, each image marks as dangerous the place which the other defines as safe. Thus the images of hierarchy and web inform different modes of assertion and response: the wish to be alone at the top and the consequent fear that others will get too close; the wish to be at the center of connection and the consequent fear of being too far out on the edge. These disparate fears of being stranded and being caught give rise to different portrayals of achievement and affiliation, leading to different modes of action and different ways of assessing the consequences of choice.

Because women value relationship, they tend to deplore selfishness, which they view as its enemy. Many of the women in Gilligan's study mistakenly see themselves, all-loving and all-giving, as the "candidates for sanctification" that Kagan speaks of. But the best relationships exist only when one considers oneself as well as the other. In women unaware of this basic principle, "unselfishness" can take control altogether. A woman may entirely suspend her own needs, and become incapable of making a choice, any choice. A life lived only in response to others' needs yields no way of acting assertively that could not be construed as "selfish."

Such a woman, like Alison Murray in Margaret Drabble's *The Ice Age,* may be effectively frozen in what Drabble has referred to as "the ice age of inactivity." Alison is paralyzed by the competing demands of her two daughters, her lover, her work in the community, and her employment. "I can't split myself in two," she protests at length. But in fact, like many "unselfish" women, she has tried to do just that—to split herself in two, in three, in whatever portions of her time and energy it would take to go around, with very little of either for Alison herself. "Unselfish" to the bitter end, she's left bereft at the conclusion of the novel.

No one reading such fiction by women, or the painful and profound reflections of the women interviewed by Gilligan or of those in the present study, can believe for long that women exist at a lower level of moral development than men. What does become clear is the truth of Gilligan's thesis: women value relationships more than they value abstract and non-situational notions of right and wrong. Making the right choice for a woman means creating a delicate balance, continuing the human connections with the greatest good and the least hurt to everyone involved.

USING WHAT THE EXPERTS SAY

How can we bring the apparently discrepant insights of these three psychologists to bear on the experiences of the women in the present study? If we accept the fatalistic, even tragic, view of the mother-child relationship—that a mother will inevitably damage her child because of her own unconscious needs—that is expressed in Alice Miller's theories of mothering, we can only use the stories of the mothers here as cautionary tales and look to what they tell us not to do: How do the mothers here wrongly seek ego gratification from their children? How do the children covertly rebel against the insidious domination of their mothers? One has only to listen to mothers like Lucy or Sharon or others presented here to know the wrong-headedness of this kind of thinking.

Yet Miller is helpful to mothers in her implication that they should not set standards of "specialness" which children feel compelled to meet. Mothers should provide models of independence by being independent themselves, by serving their own ego needs, rather than expecting the child to serve them. The relationship between the mother and child then allows the child to be valued aside from his pleasing qualities and the mother to be respected aside from her needs.

Kagan acknowledges that only by behaving responsibly themselves can parents encourage responsibility in a child. By setting attainable goals in an environment where he can succeed, parents can allow a child to value himself. But Kagan counters Miller's fatalistic assertion that a mother inevitably shapes her child by citing two significant factors which Miller leaves out.

First, there are important influences on the child outside the family. The monumental influence on the children in this study, their mothers say, is the period in which they grew up. They claim that the zenith of individual freedom reached in the sixties and seventies, with the accompanying ideological and social changes, undeniably shaped their children.

Second, Kagan recognizes that the child always interprets his mother's treatment of him. He determines and defines his own character in the way he interprets the influences upon him. Whatever—good or bad, right or wrong—a mother does, the child must choose his response to her.

Gilligan asserts the special moral skills of women, skills shown in action in the mothers here. Women, she says, can see and comprehend all sides of a situation. They can respond intelligently and sensitively to a view of the world they don't share. And like the mother before Solomon, they value life itself more than they value an abstraction about life: "Give her the child, but let him live!"

Thus when a mother like Elizabeth Rowe begins to hear the first anguished murmurings of the real child under the ideal child that has existed in her mind, she listens. She pays attention.

5

Elizabeth Choosing Life

MOTHER IN THE MIDDLE

The year her daughter Judy turned thirteen, Elizabeth Rowe found herself in the middle, standing between her child and the world. This situation is not uncommon for women. Mother gets in the middle in family after family exactly because of the female abilities that Carol Gilligan describes in *In a Different Voice*. Mother has the ability to listen; the ability to talk about emotions with candor and without embarrassment; the ability to empathize with others' feelings; the ability to see both sides of an issue. Because of these heightened skills in communication, she may quickly find herself interpreting her child to her husband and to others.

Women understand that they have these skills, but they aren't sure what to think about them. Many women measure themselves against a stereotype that they assume, rightly or wrongly, to be the prevalent male opinion of women. Ignoring the clear evidence that it is largely their own articulate concern that keeps their family intact, they worry reductively that they "talk too much."

To assess such attitudes, to discover what the women in this study think about themselves, about others, and about reality, what they are concerned with, how they interact with others, and how they manage their impulses, the mothers interviewed here were given the Loevinger Sentence Completion Test. This test was developed over a decade of effort and experimentation by Dr. Jane Loevinger, a psychologist at Washington University. It determines with considerable validity and reliability the level of ego development that a person has reached.

Deceptively simple to take, the LSCT consists of thirty-six incomplete sentences that the test-taker is required to complete. Each sentence completion is then subjected to a complex scoring technique that, cumulatively, yields the person's ego stage. In this study, the results of each test were measured by an experienced scorer in The Henry A. Murray Research Center at Radcliffe College.

The scores of the women in this study "are all quite high," the scorer writes. Twenty-seven of the thirty-two showed a higher-than-average level of ego development, and none was below average. These are strong, confident women. But in the two completions on which there was greatest consensus, even these exceptional women described themselves negatively. Twenty-two of them saw female communication skills as a detriment rather than a benefit to life. An equal number asserted that men think women are inferior to men in some way.

First, the value of communication skills. A resounding two-thirds of these women didn't fully appreciate in themselves the skill in relationships that Gilligan regards as the greatest female asset. Instead, they saw their ability to talk well less as a source of help and comfort for others than as a handicap to an untroubled life. They completed the phrase "What gets me into trouble is . . ." with some variant of the communication of feelings: "perhaps being outspoken," "my tendency to speak too truthfully," "talking before I think," "talking too much," "wearing my heart on my sleeve," "speaking too freely," "my tongue," "my mouth." Somehow these women have learned to devalue candid, sensitive, and spontaneous response to others.

How they have learned this negative valuation, whether through personal experience or through social conditioning, isn't established by the test. It may be significant that an equal number of women believed that the skills of women are not appreciated or valued by men. Two-thirds of the women concluded the phrase "Most men think that women . . ." with some variant of the inadequacy of women in the world outside the home: "are less intelligent than men," "are to be at home," "are slightly inferior," "aren't capable of making major decisions," "belong in the home," "are inferior" (used, without any qualifications, by several), "are not as smart as they," "are second-class citizens," "are helpless," "should be submissive."

Only two of the women were able to believe that women's differences from men might be unequivocally positive in men's eyes. To "Most men think that women . . ." one added: "know more about raising children," another: "have different areas of expertise than men."

Only Joy Baron, who scored at the highest level of ego development in the group, voluntarily put these two factors together. Joy, though she needed her husband's help in dealing with her "shame" at her teenaged daughter's pregnancy, nevertheless suggests that a man might not have the last word on a woman's value. To "What gets me into trouble is . . ." Joy responded: "My father and my husband would answer my big mouth—but I think not."

"But I think not." Strong, independent Joy is saying that the men in her family don't know something she knows. With these four words, Joy intimates her agreement with Carol Gilligan—that the female ethic of caring for human relations, of listening, of talking, of paying attention to feelings, cannot be accurately assessed by male standards. The whole process of coping with the behavior of an untraditional child depends initially on someone's willingness to inhabit the middle ground between discordant elements. That someone is usually a mother.

PAYING ATTENTION TO A "SPECIAL CHILD"

Elizabeth Rowe is a majestic, matronly woman with the aquiline features and wiry black curls of an Old Testament warrior princess. And like some Old Testament heroine, Elizabeth received a vision as a child, a vision that the grown-up Elizabeth believes to this day was sent from God.

In a dreamlike state, half asleep, half awake, young Elizabeth remembers lying in her narrow young girl's bed. "There were all kinds of people around my bed. I couldn't understand what they were saying exactly, but there was a realization that I was going to have a special child."

Alarmed, Elizabeth herself behaved like the normal child she was. "I remember sitting up and pulling my knees up and I started calling for my mother."

But the boundaries between dream and reality dissolved. "And then I was [awake, and,] in fact, sitting up in bed calling for my mother—I was around thirteen at the time—[and asking], 'What kind of a special child? Who knows, really?' "

The "special child" was born some fifteen years later to Elizabeth and her husband, Victor Rowe. After a miscarriage early in the marriage, Elizabeth had difficulty conceiving again. When little Judy, a beautiful, lively, healthy daughter, made her appearance in the fifth year of their marriage, she was very welcome, and very special indeed to her young parents.

"We knew she was bright," Elizabeth recalls, "but we didn't know how bright [until] . . . she was about four years old. We were in a drugstore and she was looking at a dog toy and trying to figure out whether the label said 'dog chope' or 'dog chop.' Until then I didn't know she could read."

Very intelligent, very "inward," Judy went to sleep every night in a bed piled high with books. But she had problems in school. "Emotionally," her mother says, "she was at one level, mentally she was at another, and she was just bouncing back and forth." By now Elizabeth was also busy with a second child, James, three years younger than Judy. But she did what she could to help her daughter make her way with her schoolmates. She saw to it that Judy had counseling to help her overcome her shyness and alienation from the other children, and Elizabeth herself became a Girl Scout leader so that Judy would go into the Scouts happily.

Though the Rowes "encouraged socialization," Judy was "never a very social person" nor did she go along with the crowd in dress or behavior. Pretty and petite, with dark curls and big brown eyes, "she preferred to be dressed in jumpers or skirts with tights, at a time, in the sixties and early seventies, when all the girls went to school in jeans. . . . She dressed as a girl," Elizabeth remembers. "The only time she would wear slacks was on a gym day, and she hated gym, because she had to change."

But Judy didn't often complain, and she continued to be highly successful in her academic work. When she was going into the eighth grade, Elizabeth and Victor decided to take her out of public school. They enrolled their gifted child in an academically challenging private school. After being in the new school a week, Judy told her mother the new school "was the first place outside her home where she was treated like a human being. And that was really the first time," Elizabeth exclaims, "that we knew she had been dissatisfied!"

Imagine their surprise then when, as she became an adolescent, their quiet, disciplined daughter turned strangely intractable. The Rowes are Jews. They keep the Sabbath and set a kosher table. Approaching thirteen, the age at which Elizabeth herself had had her premonitions of "a special child," Judy decided she wanted a bat mitzvah. This religious ceremony, which was introduced into Jewish ritual life only as late as 1922, marks for Jewish girls from twelve to fourteen an entrance into religious adulthood. Girls who choose to undergo the ceremony—and not many do—symbolically become "daughters of commandment."

Not only did she want a bat mitzvah; shy Judy wanted the bat mitzvah to have the attributes of the bar mitzvah, its much more common and centuries-old counterpart for thirteen-year-old boys. Her bat mitzvah, she requested, should be held on Saturday morning, during the principal day of worship, in front of the whole congregation.

"Well, Judy was very proficient in Hebrew," her mother says. "She was just as qualified as any boy I know who had a service." Unfortunately, their synagogue in Philadelphia at that time would not permit a girl to have a bat mitzvah on Saturday morning. So the family arranged for a bat mitzvah in the small Pennsylvania town where Elizabeth's parents lived. In the synagogue there, girls were allowed to have the full service that boys have.

Plans for the service were going along fairly well, when Judy came to her mother with a change of plans. "I do not want to be called up as a *bat* mitzvah," she told Elizabeth. "*Bat* means daughter. I am not a girl. I am a boy in this body."

Shocked to the core of her being, Elizabeth learned for the first time just how special her "special child" really was. Judy wanted a *bar* mitzvah, making her a "son of commandment" rather than a "daughter of commandment." She insisted to everyone concerned that she was not female but male. The rabbi wanted nothing to do with such a thing, so the ceremony was called off.

At the same time, Judy announced that she would no longer respond to her female name, Judith. She wanted a male name, and had settled on Nathan, which was Victor's father's name. Elizabeth and Victor were completely flabbergasted. Without understanding in the slightest, they tried to respect their child's wishes, but "it was hard," Elizabeth remembers. "The 'she's' would come in, the 'Judy's' would come out. But we did start trying, you know, to use the word 'Nathan' or 'Nate.' He came under a lot of fire from a lot of people, but he stood his ground." By "he," she means Nate, formerly Judy.

Elizabeth tried to understand. She saw how much it mattered to Judy, white-lipped and tense in her determination to be "Nate" and to gain recognition as a male. Always reserved and controlled, Judy was suddenly passionate in her demands. "So," Elizabeth says, laughing, "after I picked myself up off the floor, we talked about it."

"We" means Elizabeth and Judy. In the first shock, Victor had acquiesced. Now, he "had a very hard time dealing with it," and refused to take Judy seriously. He thought that Judy was using the outrageous claim that she was male to get even with her parents for some imagined slight or to manipulate them to get something she wanted. Elizabeth found herself caught in the cross fire between her husband and her child. "It almost killed the marriage," Elizabeth says. Like many of the women in this study, she became a "mother in the middle."

From the beginning, Elizabeth listened to her child. She never believed that Nate, as she tried to call Judy, was fabricating. Perhaps she knew she had to pay attention to Nate because he needed her so much. He was terribly depressed. He told his mother he could not go on living as "Judy," that it put him in an absurd and hypocritical position.

"Mom," he pleaded with her, trying to make her understand, "what if you woke up one morning and you found that your body was that of a horse? And you were treated like a horse and you had to live like a horse.

"And suppose your mind told you, 'I am a human being. . . .' But you couldn't get anyone to understand what you were saying.

Because you looked like a horse, you had to *be* a horse." And he insisted again and again that he was not a girl, but a boy.

"But you never wanted to dress boyishly," Elizabeth responded, feeling slow and stupid. "You always insisted on dressing in a very feminine way. Why?"

Nate paused and looked at her for a moment, his brown eyes measuring her reaction. "I was trying to prove to myself I could *be* a girl. Well, I can't." The feeling, he told her, had been present as far back as he could remember. When people referred to him as a girl, he would want to argue, but he didn't know how to verbalize it.

At first Elizabeth was incredulous. Nate's feelings were obviously real, but maybe he was exaggerating them. She wondered if this was just a normal phase in her child's development. "I was a tomboy myself, and I can remember thinking, 'Gee, I'd much rather be a boy.' Was this what he was going through?

"And I knew at this point in his life that he didn't like his teacher. He didn't like the girls in his class—in fact, he couldn't stand them. I was thinking, 'Has he turned against being a female because he doesn't want to be like any of the females he knows?' "

But as the weeks went by she became convinced that Nate's strange story was true. There was something here beyond the normal. However the situation might appear to others, Nate truly felt he was a male trapped in a female body.

Incidents from the past came to her mind, with new and telling significance. There was the time when "Judy" was seven or eight years old that she said she'd rather be an animal than a person. "Can doctors put a tail on a human being?" she asked her mother. "They could put one on," Elizabeth told her, "but it wouldn't work like a tail." Amused, she told Victor what their highly imaginative child had come up with.

"She wasn't really asking about a tail," Elizabeth says. "That was the first time she actually expressed this. . . ."

At thirteen, however, Nate was less concerned about adding a tail (that is, a penis) than with getting rid of the breasts that, as "Judy," he was beginning to develop. With the onset of menstruation, Nate was growing desperate, and he turned to his mother for help.

"My feeling?" she recollects. "I was just torn up." Like most mothers, she felt that she must be responsible for her child's problems in some way, a feeling that added to her stress. "Everything just turns topsy-turvy. You wonder, 'What did I do wrong? Is it something I did?' My first question was, 'Was it the cortisone I was on when Nate was conceived?' "

But such abstract issues were soon lost in her horrified realization that her child's life was at stake. "My fear was, 'Is he going to kill himself?' He made threats, not necessarily [of] killing himself, but 'if doctors don't remove these breasts, I'll remove them myself.' And transsexuals have been known to mutilate themselves if they can't get help. My main object was just keeping him alive, and not letting him hurt himself.

"The mental stress—it's very hard to describe. It's—oh, it's hell."

Nor was her hell made easier to bear by sharing it with her husband. Victor Rowe is a scientist. As a geologist for a large oil company, he deals with facts every day: What is the composition of this soil? Does this location merit drilling? He had a lot of difficulty understanding and accepting his child's bizarre demands, and he thought Elizabeth was far too patient with "Judy."

At the same time, Elizabeth rapidly ran out of patience with Victor. "When you're sitting and talking to your thirteen-year-old about why he should go on and live, why he should not cut certain appendages off his body, why he should try to find answers: 'The answers are out there. Let's keep trying to find them. Let's find someone to help you.' And this is going on every night. Ten, eleven, twelve o'clock you're sitting there talking to this kid, and you're emotionally drained, completely drained.

"And you go in to go to bed, and you try to express this to your mate. And the answer is, 'If that's the decision the kid's made, that's her life. If she wants to mess it up, she's just going to have to kill herself, and don't feel bad about it. If we have sex, *you* will feel better and everything will be fine.'

"That was the answer. And you don't—you stop talking to him. You don't want to be near him. Period. [Somebody like that is] no help."

Elizabeth developed terrible migraine headaches and a chronically upset stomach. "Every system in me," she says, "went into knots," though when she was actually talking to Nate, a curious calm descended on her. Nevertheless, Nate himself was hard to handle. Sometimes he deliberately refused to understand what she said to him. "I'd say, 'Look, there are doctors out there who can deal with this. We may have to search, but we will find one.' And he'd answer, 'I want one NOW!' That type of thing made me angry."

She was particularly terrified to overhear Victor discussing the situation with his two sisters, Nate's aunts, who both hold advanced degrees in psychology. Elizabeth puts her head in her hands at the recollection. Even now, the memory overwhelms her. Their advice was, "Put the child in an institution, the sooner the better, and have her rehabilitated." Victor seemed to be acquiescent.

"I knew that wasn't the answer," Elizabeth says. "I mean, this was a functional human being."

In fact, Nate was more than merely "functional." In spite of the stress they were all under, he continued to be an exceptional student. His papers had always been good; now they were eloquent, especially on the subject of individual differences in people. An English composition concludes with a plea for the human transcendence of sexual differences:

> No matter how much society's definitions of masculinity and femininity change, any definition that attributes some qualities exclusively to males and others exclusively to females automatically limits the innate human potential to develop the full range of human traits and behaviors. Perhaps some day society will realize this. Then a man will be defined as a male human being and a woman as a female human being, and being human will be the most important thing to achieve, whether one is a man, a woman, or something else.

An amazing anticipation of Gilligan's ideas, written by an adolescent six years before her book was published!

"You don't institutionalize someone," Elizabeth says, "who is writing papers on being an individual and what it means to be an individual. You don't institutionalize people like this." Instead she set out to find the answers and the help that she kept assuring Nate existed.

"FROM WHENCE COMETH MY HELP?"

She tried to find books on the subject, but there weren't many. Unable to talk with her husband, she talked to others around her. Her gynecologist expressed concern and sympathy, but he was quick to say he didn't know anything about problems of this kind. Elizabeth turned next to her rabbi, a gentle, elderly man. He told her, "Don't worry. She'll outgrow it. A lot of girls go through this sort of thing, but time will take care of it."

By now Nate was discussing the various methods of suicide open to him. From the family doctor, Elizabeth got the name of a female psychiatrist who dealt in problems of adolescence. This expert's diagnosis was that "Judy" resented leaving the nest. Judy needed to be pushed out of the home. She would have a very difficult adolescence, but if the Rowes pushed her away hard enough, she would "adjust" and be all right. "If I had followed that advice, that kid would have committed suicide. I'm very glad I didn't," Elizabeth says.

Nate himself convinced his mother that Dr. Smith (not her real name) was wrong. The child, who was always quiet and shy in school, went in one day and told the psychiatrist, "All you're doing is trying to read my mind and you're a lousy mind reader. I'm not coming back here anymore because you don't know what I'm talking about."

After this showdown, Elizabeth says, "I went to see Dr. Smith a couple of times myself and I finally came to the same conclusion: 'She's not dealing with my child. There's no sense going on with it.' "

She took Nate to Dr. Jones (not his real name), a psychologist who had worked extensively with homosexuals. This time, Elizabeth remembers gratefully, "it clicked, God bless him! I credit Dr. Jones with a lot of the help that Nate got outside the house. . . . Dr. Jones's attitude is: 'We can't do anything about a lot of the problems, but we do have some options as to how to work with him.' "

First, Dr. Jones set out to develop a relationship with Nate. Like other adolescents, Nate had complained to his mother that she wasn't allowing him to be independent enough. To build Nate's confidence in him, Dr. Jones decided that Nate's therapy should not include his parents. "It was between Dr. Jones and Nate, and that's it."

That's the way Nate wanted it, she explains. "Nate is a very private person. 'It's my body, it's my life, and I'm going to handle it.' Though of course"—she laughs ruefully—" 'if I can't handle it, it's your fault.' " In spite of the peculiarities of his situation, Nate *was* an adolescent with the usual adolescent attitudes.

Dr. Jones referred the adult Rowes to another doctor in his group of psychologists. It helped to have a doctor on hand, not only for Elizabeth herself but for other members of the family who couldn't understand what was going on. Elizabeth's parents had been agitated since the bat mitzvah was canceled.

> When I explained to them why we were having to call the whole thing off, they expressed hurt to [Nate]. They did not understand. . . . So one time when they were up here, I asked them, "Would you like to talk to Nate's psychologist?" And they did. They had their questions, and they were answered as much as the doctor could answer them.

Elizabeth's mother and father both eventually accepted the situation, as have some but not all of the other members of the family.

Oddly enough, the member of the family who found it easiest to accept the change from Judy to Nate was little brother James, three years younger. Later a close friend, Mary Samuelson, told Elizabeth that James would come over to play with her daughter and then would leave, saying that his brother was waiting. "My brother's out there," nine-year-old James would say. "I have to go."

"That's funny," Mary thought. "He only has a sister." She decided James had an imaginary playmate. Not until later, when Elizabeth told her what was happening at the time, did Mary realize that James had simply accepted what Nate told him.

With those outside the family and the inner circle of friends, communication about Nate's problems came harder. Elizabeth remembers the first time she told a casual acquaintance. "What a beautiful daughter you have!" another mother commented to her one day when she was picking Nate up from Hebrew school. With what she describes as a funny feeling in the pit of her stomach, Elizabeth said in a thin voice that sounded not at all like her usual rich alto, "Judy feels she is a male, not a female." The mother looked startled and shooed her own child quickly out the door.

Nate came in for his share of difficulties with other children, of course. He didn't report many of them, but Elizabeth learned that day after day on the school bus one particularly obnoxious little girl used to say, "Let's strip Judy and see if she's really a girl or a boy."

"Once I was able to tell people, there was a feeling of relief," Elizabeth recalls. "I think talking about things helps, even if other people don't always understand."

Counseling helped too. Elizabeth learned that when Nate accused her of "tying him to her apron strings" or "trying to hold him back," he was possibly projecting his own fears of not being able to let go.

"I mean, Nate was just a kid!" Elizabeth exclaims. "He couldn't see that we were doing everything we could." From sessions with her own therapist, Elizabeth gained assurance that she was proceeding correctly with her "special child." With this basic and necessary reinforcement, she redoubled her efforts to find medical aid for Nate's problems. Was he truly a transsexual, a male trapped in a female body? If so, what could be done for him?

"We were batting our heads against the wall, trying to get help. Not too many people want to deal with a thirteen-, fourteen-, fifteen-year-old child who says, 'I want to change genders,' or 'I am not the right gender.'" Two years after Nate had first shocked his parents on the eve of his bat mitzvah, Elizabeth had still found no medical help for her child. Nor did she really know what medical help was required.

In those two years Nate had not softened his stand at all. He dressed as a male, let his classmates and teachers know that he regarded himself as male, and put in a formal request that all his school records be altered to reflect the change.

The principal of the Hebrew school that Nate attended after regular school was surprisingly understanding. "He was a man from Israel," Elizabeth says.

> His whole cultural background was Mediterranean, very different from ours. I didn't know what to expect. But I walked in there, and I explained to him what was happening with Nate. His reply was, "What a turmoil that child is going through!"

I fell in love with the man right then and there. Someone understood! And he dealt beautifully with the situation.

The teachers at Nate's exclusive private high school were more difficult to convince. They asked to talk to Nate's psychologist and to know more about the situation. Elizabeth made the arrangements.

When Nate, by now a determined fourteen, heard about it, he said, "I want to be there." Faced with Nate's insistence on being present at the conference between his doctor and his teachers, Elizabeth decided to be there too. Victor Rowe was far from convinced that Elizabeth was treating Nate's problems sensibly, but he reluctantly joined forces with his wife and his child.

> My husband and I said [to Nate], "If you're going to be there, we're going to be there." Not the whole faculty, but a nice cross section was there. Dr. Jones went in first and talked to them about the transsexual phenomenon. Then Nate and my husband and I went in, and Dr. Jones was there, and Nate fielded the questions that were put to him.
>
> One of the advisers for the high school said, "Wouldn't it be easier, just getting along with other kids, so that you don't have to undergo problems with the other kids, to let them call you 'she' and say 'Judy' and just let them think that?"
>
> Nate's answer was, "How can it be easier, not being what you know you are? You can take things if you know who you are, and if you don't have to try to pretend to be something else."
>
> I'll never forget, one of the men teachers, a big man, had tears in his eyes. And he said, "Nate, we will support you in any way we can."

In spite of himself, Victor was impressed, as he was impressed with a paper Nate wrote for school that year. In it, Nate coined the term "masheep" to describe most people. The main point of the paper was, as his mother recalled it, that "we are machines, and we do everything everyone else does just like sheep do. Sheep will follow the lead sheep, just go without even thinking. Society makes most people masheep, and if you do not follow along, society can't accept you." Whatever his reservations about his child, Victor Rowe knew Nate was not a "masheep."

The school agreed to change Nate's name officially in his records. With his mother's help, Nate also went to court and had his name changed legally. Incongruous as it may have seemed for someone who was—and still is—just a little over five feet tall and "maybe soaking wet weighs one hundred pounds," on the records he was no longer Judith Rowe, female, but Nathan Rowe, male.

As Nate moved from the ninth grade into the tenth, he had a clear sense of who he was. He was at last beginning to develop friendships with kids his age. He was seeing a therapist he liked and trusted. Although they had made no medical progress on Nate's condition, things were better for the Rowes than they had been for a while.

Elizabeth was terribly concerned therefore when, in May of Nate's tenth-grade year, Victor came home with a bombshell. His company wanted him to transfer from Philadelphia to Dallas, with a big raise and promotion. What did the family think? James, a sweet, steady, twelve-year-old, was willing. In spite of his mother's fears, Nate too agreed cheerfully. Nate didn't want to hold his dad back. If it was best for his dad, he was ready to go. So they went.

Nate absolutely refused to enter a public school. When they were unable to find a private school which was comparable to his school in Philadelphia, Victor suggested that Nate might take college entrance exams and try to get into a university instead. Eagerly Nate agreed. He scored in the ninety-ninth percentile on both the verbal and the quantitative sides of the SAT. At the age of fifteen, Nate Rowe was accepted as a freshman at an excellent small college in Texas.

More and more Victor Rowe began to acknowledge that Elizabeth had been right to pay attention, without distrust or prejudice, to what her child had told her. The summer elapsed before the family could join him in Dallas. During the solitary evenings in a strange city, Victor thought admiringly of the way his wife had handled the most difficult problem any of them had ever faced. She had been right to listen, to observe, to try to see the real child under the child that they thought they had.

One lonely night he happened to catch a public television interview with a cerebral palsy victim, confined to a wheelchair, who nevertheless had gone on to get a doctorate in psychology. This

young woman was describing her life, and what she said hit Victor
hard.

He told Elizabeth about it later.

> Her parents were told they shouldn't even keep her alive,
> should just let her die. But they fought to help her get an
> education.
>
> When she was going to college, she was trying to fill a
> cigarette lighter, and she caught on fire. And then too the
> doctor said, "Let her die. What do you want to save this
> pathetic thing for?" And again, her parents had to fight to
> keep her alive. . . .
>
> And she was talking about life, and she said, "I view
> myself as a normal human being trapped in this deformed
> body. But *I* am normal."

That clicked with Victor. He realized that Nate had been saying the
same thing. Nate too was normal inside, but trapped in an outward
body that didn't belong to him.

Victor remembered, alone in a hotel room in the hot Dallas night,
all those nights that Elizabeth had spent talking to Nate, trying to
convince him that help could be found. In his mind, he replayed the
scene many times. She would be asleep when all of a sudden, at
eleven or twelve o'clock at night, would come the call, "Ma!" And
she would get up and go into Nate's room. And the voices would go
on, an hour, two hours, till at last Victor fell asleep, still hearing
them.

Even now, in his mind, he could recall the sound of her voice,
calm and caring, the energy of her responses, the passion of her
concern. In the secret recesses of his heart, he had always believed
men were stronger than women. But she had been stronger then.
He shuddered to remember the callousness of his own remarks to
her when, exhausted, she would at last come in to lie down beside
him. He had resented his child, had felt that she was choosing the
child over the father.

But, he defended himself in his internal monologue, it was not all
selfishness on his part. He didn't like to see what a nervous wreck
she was becoming. She was always calm with Nate, but Victor saw
her when she wasn't, when she was dragged out from her nightly

vigil. He had thought that she should quit indulging such silly fancies in the child.

But she had been right. Elizabeth, he realized now, had determinedly and reverently observed the central command of Judaism: Choose life, whatever its form. His own attitude had been: "I am the father. Do what I say, whether you feel you should or not." Her attitude had been: "Everyone is a living human being, with special needs. No one's needs are wrong just because they're not like mine."

Brooding over that awful time three years earlier, he marveled all the more at his wife's endurance, her perception, her wisdom. Where had these things come from? He couldn't understand it.

Elizabeth herself says that help came from God. "From whence cometh my help?" the psalmist cried over two thousand years ago. "My help cometh from God, who made heaven and earth." If God had given her a "special child," God would help her to handle his creation. She firmly believes that the strength to pay attention to the strange things that her child told her came from God, the same God who had sent a dream at thirteen to prepare her. "I definitely believe that's where it came from. I don't know any other way I could have dealt with it."

The attitudes of Elizabeth and Victor illustrate the male and female ethics described by Carol Gilligan in her book. Victor, Elizabeth says, depends on scientific authority and the written word. He wants to do the just and fair thing, but, like a doubting Thomas, he needed proof that what Nate said was true. Once he began to get medical confirmation of his child's condition, he was entirely supportive and helpful.

Elizabeth, on the other hand, put her child's feelings first. She operated throughout on faith. And faith, her personal faith—not the temple, not the rabbi, but *faith* tempered by the understanding and acceptance of others that her traditional Jewish parents had taught her—was the rock that sustained her.

Not only had God sent her strength when she needed it. He had also given her the insight to see that by paying attention to her child, she was obeying his will. When at last, in the fall of 1977, Elizabeth and Victor talked it all out in their new Dallas home, she told him that she had been conscious throughout of staying on the side of life as it is. "I'll tell you," she said. "When you're pregnant, you carry a baby for nine months. You don't know if it's going to be a male or a female, and you don't care. Your concern is with the baby.

"Okay. We called our baby 'she' and 'Judy.' Now it's 'he' and 'Nathan.' But I still have my child, and I don't care what you call it. It's my child, and that's the most important thing."

TAKING ACTION

The move to Dallas proved fortuitous in the beginning for Nate and his family. With Victor more solidly in their camp, Elizabeth and Nate consulted the head of the psychiatry department at a major university. At first they met with discouragement. The "big man" took one look at small Nate with his delicate, refined features, and said, "You are too feminine-looking. You are *not* a transsexual."

"That has nothing to do with the situation," Elizabeth says. By now the Rowes had read enough to have become lay experts on Nate's condition. Nate suffers from a disorder called "gender dysphoria"—severe unhappiness with one's genetic sex and maladjustment because of it. Probably, medical experts and transsexuals alike agree, the condition is caused by an imbalance in the male sex hormones in the developing fetus rather than by social or psychological factors after birth. Stress on the pregnant woman is sometimes cited for the condition, which currently drives about one thousand Americans a year to seek surgery. Transsexuals have the physiques of one sex and the psyches of another. Appearance is less reliable as a guide than the feelings of the victim, but only rigorous psychiatric screening can identify the true gender dysphoric. The two top places in the country for this kind of testing, the Rowes learned, were Stanford and Johns Hopkins.

The Rowes decided to put Nate's case to the test. Although Nate had come to Texas legally a male, he still functioned as a female. Monthly periods were agony, a reminder, Elizabeth says, that "this is not who I am and I don't want it." His severe depressions interfered with his academic work, which otherwise remained excellent. Something had to be done.

The Dallas doctor put them in touch with a doctor at Johns Hopkins. Nate made the telephone call himself to set up an appointment, in August of 1978, with the doctor whose books he'd pored over and whose help he believed would set things right for him.

The family traveled to Baltimore. For a full day and a half, they submitted themselves to tests and questioning. "A whole battery of people" questioned Elizabeth, questioned Victor, but mostly talked to Nate. Elizabeth describes the conclusion of that ordeal, when they walked into the doctor's office:

> Dr. Brown [not his real name] referred to Nate immediately as our son, and he said he does endorse treatment for Nate, limited treatment. [He recommended hormone injections, a hysterectomy, and breast removal.] He told Nate, "I do *not* want you to try to have a penis constructed. It's not successful." And he told us that they had dealt a lot with veterans, biological males, who come back wounded, and there is nothing they can do.
>
> He said, "Someday, maybe in your lifetime, they will be able to do it, and I want them to have fresh tissue to work with. So don't do it. If anyone advises it, leave them immediately."

At this point, Elizabeth worried aloud, as mothers will, about the chances for her child's happiness.

> My thoughts were, "What kind of life is ahead for this person?" Because when you and I sit and talk about a child growing up, we assume the child's going to find some mate, be it male or female, a mate to share life with. What is ahead for this child?

Dr. Brown understood her concern and gave her an answer that she thinks of as "very beautiful."

> He said, "Just remember, the most important sex organ we have is our brain, and the largest sex organ we have is our skin. If you can accept this, you will realize that any person can have a sex life."

"I accept that," says Elizabeth. After having seen in Nate himself the extent to which the psyche dominates one's sexuality, she found the doctor's answer comforting and credible. Nate could have a full

SECOND BIRTH

life, she hoped. "If Nate can find someone that he can be happy with
and have companionship with, that's all we ask. Some transsexuals
do marry, adopt children, and if he can do this, fine. I don't care, just
so he can find *someone*." As always, Elizabeth is willing to accommodate the manifold forms of life.

She was to need this affirmative attitude as the Rowe family, now
united, went on to the next stage in coping with Nate's problems,
the stage which involved taking the action that the doctor had recommended. Back in Dallas, Nate himself once again took the lead in
finding an endocrinologist to give him the hormone treatments.
Some doctors refused outright. Others were sympathetic until they
were told that Nate had a blood condition which could cause heavy
bleeding. After that, as Elizabeth says, "they didn't want to put a
needle anywhere near him." But the boy, by now sixteen years old,
persisted.

"Things were not working out in Dallas" in Nate's search, so
Elizabeth and her son returned to Philadelphia. Nate enrolled in a
local college. Victor, always slower than Elizabeth to respond to
Nate's needs, stayed in Dallas. Again the family was split.

After numerous calls, Nate located a reputable Philadelphia doctor who was interested. "The doctor himself got on the phone and
asked Nate a whole battery of questions. When he found out that he
had been to Johns Hopkins, had been through all this stuff, that he
had been living as a male for a couple of years by that time, the
doctor said, yes, he would work with Nate."

Dr. Green [not his real name] prescribed hormones that deepened Nate's voice, stopped the menstruation, and put hair on his
face. The psychological change in Nate was immediately apparent.
Always so quiet in school, he became much more assertive. When a
teacher gave his class the writing assignment "What does it mean to
be masculine or feminine?" Nate wrote *two* papers. One took, Elizabeth remembers, "an extreme male chauvinist point of view: women
belong in the home, they're good for nothing but taking care of a
home and raising children. The other was from an extreme feminist
point of view, right down the line."

On the whole, however, Nate became a convincing male. Just how
convincing is indicated in a little anecdote he shared with his
mother. In a class discussion on male chauvinism, the professor, a
male, who later became Nate's good friend, said jokingly, "Of

course men are superior. That's why God made men first." Without missing a beat, Nate popped up with "Well, he was only practicing, you know." And the professor said, a little more heatedly, one gathers, "You're a traitor to your sex, young man." If he had only known!

Assignments and conversations of this kind helped Nate to clarify his feelings about his own sexuality. Unlike most of the mothers in this book, Elizabeth does not deplore the social climate of the times in which Nate grew up. In his crisis, she thinks, the liberality of the period was an asset. As she sees it, his problems were not caused by his environment but by something in him: "There is no why. It just happens, the same as left-handedness happens in some people, color blindness in some people." But the emphasis in the sixties and seventies on trusting one's feelings gave Nate the freedom to speak out and to get help for himself.

And the medical advances of the late seventies allowed Nate to have the surgery the doctor at Johns Hopkins had recommended. He had his spleen removed to correct the blood condition, then went back to school and again pulled all A's. Eight months later, Nate had his breasts removed by a plastic surgeon, and a complete hysterectomy by a gynecologist.

Nate had made all the arrangements himself and had gotten Blue Cross approval for the surgery. In his eagerness for independence, he actually requested that his parents not be there the day he was operated upon or come to visit him afterward. ("But, being parents, we were there all day, of course," Elizabeth says, laughing.) Before the hysterectomy, the gynecologist told the hospital staff, "This is a young person who knows who he is. His head's together. If there's any problem, it's your problem. Don't put it on him." And Nate's cool stoicism won admiration from doctors and staff alike.

AN EXPECTANT MOTHER

After the operation, Elizabeth understood that Nate wanted to be in control of his own life. Victor, who had rejoined his family, encouraged her. With the good sense and tact she has always exercised with her special child, she began to detach herself from Nate. She no longer needed to be "mother in the middle," and in fact could take great pride in her son's independence.

"When your children are growing up," she says, "you tell them, 'Figure out what you believe in, and go for it.' You teach them to be independent thinkers, and yet in the back of your mind you're saying, 'Think independently, but think as I do.' It can be very hard when they do it. Well, Nate has done it."

Nate transferred to another, larger college as a second-semester sophomore on a full scholarship which he had arranged himself. His grades, as always, were excellent. Away from home for the first time in his life, he lived on campus, and thrived in the laissez-faire atmosphere of the dorm. "He was very, very happy," Elizabeth says. His academic record was superb, and he made good friends of both sexes.

Two years later, in his senior year of college, Nate developed a neurological problem which causes bad backaches and also affects his ability to learn. The change in him was dramatic. "When his mind is working clearly," his mother says, "he's as sharp as ever. Other times this person, with a four-point average, can't read. . . . He said, 'I sat there for five minutes trying to determine, do I want a 3 or an E?' He couldn't differentiate between them."

Once again, the Rowes have been looking for help everywhere, from the Mayo Clinic down. The doctors, who have diagnosed the illness as everything from psychological problems (now ruled out) to epilepsy (also ruled out), have confessed they don't know what is wrong with Nate.

A European neurologist has told them of studies done abroad which show that neurological dysfunctions of the kind Nate is experiencing are common among gender dysphorics. This doctor theorizes that the neurological problem and the gender-identity problem may both be traced to the time before birth when the brain was developing in the mother's uterus.

Nate was forced to return home and to give up some of the independence he so desperately wants. His mother, who had been planning to go back to college for a master's degree in early childhood education, has had to postpone her project. "When you are dealing with ongoing problems like this," she says, "you can't take time out and be very selfish and do it." Instead she has taken a flexible part-time job, so that if, as sometimes happens, Nate can't manage alone, she is there to help.

Both mother and son regret the step backward. Elizabeth is "still hoping" to get her degree. Nate's problems, she says, "have made me more determined than ever to work with people, especially children, because I feel I have even more to offer them now." The time will come when she recognizes that this dream is anything but "selfish," and that her needs count as much as Nate's.

In the meantime, she has tried to respect Nate's desire for independence in the living arrangement in the family home. Nate has a separate apartment, including a separate, if somewhat makeshift, kitchen. A strict vegetarian who not only refuses to eat meat but also refuses to wear animal products, Nate observes the Jewish dietary laws with the utmost punctiliousness. As Elizabeth says, "I keep kosher, but I am not kosher enough for him."

Several years after his sex-change operation, Nate has decided that he is no more male than he had been female. "Now he considers himself asexual," Elizabeth says. "He knows he is not a female. He could never have lived as a female. Yet he also knows he is not a normal male. He says he is a human being; that's how he classifies himself."

In accordance with his mother's instructions to act on what you believe, Nate has insisted that both his birth certificate and his driver's license be corrected to reflect his sexual ambiguity. His birth certificate has "female" crossed out and "asexual" written over it. "That took some doing," Elizabeth laughs.

The driver's license was even tougher. When Nate filled out the application, he left the "male or female" line blank. Seeing his name, a Public Safety clerk automatically marked "male." "But Nate is a scrapper," Elizabeth says.

> He said, "I will not sign it," and he went in and talked to the manager of the Secretary of State's office and said, "I am not a male. You are asking me to sign a fraudulent statement."
> And they said, "Well, are you female?" and he said no.
> And they said, "Well, you have to be one or the other."
> And he said, "I'm neither."

His driver's license is issued to "Nathan Rowe, male." Neatly printed over the word "male" is the cryptic remark, "Applicant claims this is not true."

Like his mother, Nate is strongly motivated to serve others. As a volunteer, he has worked with mentally impaired adults and as a teacher's aide on several occasions. Once Victor protested, somewhat unnecessarily in view of Nathan's academic prowess, that Nate should be concentrating on his own grades instead of trying to help others. "What good is having a four-point average in psychology," said Nate, "if you don't know how to work with people?"

Elizabeth glows with pride when she tells this. Obviously she believes that she does indeed have a "special child." "Oh, he has a beautiful way. There's a Jewish term for what I think Nate is—a *tzadik*, a very righteous person. He sees things you don't expect."

And she tells of a remark he made to his favorite teacher in college.

> They were talking about roles, men and women, one time. And Nate said that God's a hermaphrodite. He said, "Well, if you look in the Bible, it says, 'God created man and woman, he created them in his image.' Therefore he must be both."

If Elizabeth has a special child, there is no question that Nate has a special mother. She met the shock of her child's astounding revelation head-on. She paid attention to her child when no one else would, and made enormous efforts to see "Nate" instead of "Judy."

Her faith, her ability to understand, and her respect for her child's individuality gradually won her husband to her side. However, though Victor understands Nate's situation intellectually, emotionally he still sometimes resents Nate's continuing need for his mother's attention. Nevertheless, the whole Rowe family has taken intelligent, prolonged action to help Nate.

If Nate, for physical reasons, has not yet reached detachment, Elizabeth knows his strength and does all she can to foster his independence. The time is coming when Elizabeth too will have the autonomy she needs to pursue her own life, and the connection with Nate will move to a new level.

Motherhood has conferred a wisdom on Elizabeth: Life in all its rich eccentricity is to be embraced, to be chosen. Through her child she is conscious of having received a gift herself. "I was given the awareness to know that you don't pray, 'Let this pass.' You don't pray, 'Make him better.' You pray, 'Give me strength, give me understanding.' "

What has she learned from her experiences? "I've learned that human beings are remarkable creatures—what we can go through, what we can take, and still come out with humor. It's fantastic! We're marvelous creatures, and I consider it miraculous that we are as we are."

Laughter comes easily to warm, motherly Elizabeth, and she can't resist telling the time son James described her as an expectant mother. He had gone to the amusement park with a friend and the friend's family. "You've seen the signs," Elizabeth says, "that say people with pacemakers or expectant mothers should not go on this ride? Well, James said, 'Gee, my mom couldn't go on this ride.'

"And his friend's mother looked very serious and said, 'James, does your mother wear a pacemaker?' And he said, 'No.'

"So then I guess she looked shocked—I mean, James was fourteen at the time, which means Nate was seventeen or so—and said, 'James, is your mother pregnant?' And he said, 'No.'

"And she says, 'Well, why can't she go on here?'

"And James says, 'Well, it says expectant mothers, and with kids like us, my mother expects anything, anytime!' "

Stage Three

ACTION

Turning from feelings to action; looking for help
from family, friends, and experts

6

Taking Arms Against a Sea of Troubles

The time comes when a mother must act. After she has survived the shock of her child's unexpected behavior, after she has paid scrupulous and open-minded attention to his real nature and the situation he's in, a mother wants to _do something._

Suzanne White expresses this maternal assertiveness. Faced with her youngest daughter's anorexia nervosa, Suzanne's impulse was to act. "I was never angry, none of this 'Why did this happen to me?' kind of stuff, not at all. I just felt that it was something we dealt with, we go from day to day, we do the best we can.

"And I always had a very positive attitude. I never felt, in spite of all you read, that this was going to get Meg. No way. I mean, I wouldn't _let_ it happen!"

In the most basic way, concerned motherhood demands activity. Few women can face a child's danger or unhappiness without resisting with all their strength, without trying, as Hamlet says, "to take arms against a sea of troubles, And by opposing end them." And, no matter how big the sea or how inappropriate her small sword, no mother expects to fail.

In fact, many mothers in a crisis receive a rush of adrenaline that allows them to do the seemingly impossible. A mother lifts the front end of an automobile to free a trapped child. Another eludes the firemen and runs back into a burning building. Already in these pages, we have seen Rosemary Dixon go to New York, collect Polly, and in a couple of days have her installed in the best psychiatric clinic in the country. We've seen Sharon Marsh restore her son's life after a drug overdose, and later oppose the law to protect him, stepping between him and two burly police officers and screaming, "You can't take him! He's sick!" And we have watched while Elizabeth Rowe challenged her husband, her rabbi, her parents, the courts, and a series of medical men to protect Nate's right to life on his own terms. These women will not *permit* tragedy to strike their children; they will defy heaven and earth to prevent it.

Yet such defiance, heroic as it is, may not be effective. Tragedy does strike. The mother lifts the car from the child, but the child is dead. The mother rushes into the burning house, and mother and child both perish in the flames. Polly Dixon killed herself at the age of twenty-six. Today, Russell Marsh still struggles unsuccessfully with his dreadful addictions. Nate Rowe has solved one problem only to be brought low by another.

Fully half of the mothers in this study felt that their best efforts for their children had not succeeded. Why not? That's hard to say. Two families, equally concerned; two mothers, equally striving; two children, equally valued—and one child at last becomes happy, independent, and productive, while the other doesn't. Luck? Fate? A kind of cosmic unfairness? Because it isn't fair. But then, as mothers often tell their children, no one ever said that life had to be fair.

It may be nearly impossible to see why a mother's actions aren't effective. But when what she does *works,* as it worked for Suzanne White, it's surprisingly easy to see why. Perhaps the most important initial step a woman can take, when she sees her child drowning in a sea of troubles, is to *get help at once.* An alarmed mother might be wise to act like the potential victim of a rapist, and to scream for help from every quarter—help for the child, help for herself.

SCREAMING FOR HELP

Some women go for help to their clergymen. When Margaret Bentley learned that her daughter Nan was a lesbian, she went at once to her parish priest. Nan demanded immediate and complete acceptance of her homosexuality from her parents. Father Terence (not his real name), a knowledgeable and understanding man, helped Margaret to avoid alienating her child. "I felt that I wanted to tell her exactly how I felt," Margaret says, "so I wrote her a letter."

> It took me three months. I was going to mail it, then I thought, "I'd better call Father." I wanted to be sure that it wasn't a negative thing to be doing.
> So he asked me if I would mind reading it to him, and I read it to him. It was very hard to read, because I really poured my heart out. I told her that I loved her, and that I knew she felt that way, but that obviously she was keeping score [on how I reacted].
> Then Father said, "That was a wonderful letter, but you didn't write this for her. You wrote that for yourself. So you keep it, and you read it when you want to."

For months, Father Terence provided "a wonderful help" for Margaret.

Margaret's experience with the clergy is not typical of the women in this study. Ministers, priests, and rabbis were rarely capable of the kind of thoughtful support that Father Terence supplied to Margaret. Sometimes, it is true, they offered help with practical matters. For example, when Janet and Marshall Crocker's small grandson died, their minister suggested that a newspaper story might prevent Janet's having to repeat the details over and over to well-meaning friends. A simple expedient that Janet hadn't thought of, this obituary saved Janet hours of painful recapitulation.

What is remarkable in the stories of these mothers, however, is not how much real help they got from their churches but how little. Most of these women, in spite of strong personal religious feelings, found their clergymen to be aloof, tactless, uninterested, unsympathetic, uninformed, or misguided—all in all, a peculiarly inadequate source of strength.

Neither Myra de Shazo nor Jean Brooks felt she could talk to her minister about the criminal charges her son faced. Myra's minister was new and Jean's just "not the kind of man you could talk to."

Nor does a talk with the minister, even when it is possible, always help. Judy Fielding was frantic about her son Jerry's alcoholism and desperately afraid he might be schizophrenic. She and her husband made an appointment to talk with their minister. "We went in, and we talked for an hour and a half, and the next Sunday after church he didn't even remember our name. So that kind of turned me off. I don't mean *kind of*—it did!"

When she was concerned about her daughter Kris's sexual standards, Rebecca Winslow believed the attitude of her Episcopal minister contributed to the problem. Kris was attending a sex course, led by the clergyman, called *Joie de Vivre*. "It was exactly what I expected," Rebecca says, in her crisp New England manner. "It provided no moral guidelines whatsoever." Rebecca visited the last session, during which the minister allowed the audience to raise questions for discussion.

> And I got up and said, "At no point in the whole course could I see where there was any discussion of what is right and what is wrong. What is the moral way [for young people to behave sexually]?"
>
> His response to my question was, "I imagine you were one of those girls who always did what her mother told her."
>
> Well, I was, and proud of it. . . . My daughter knew exactly where I stood. I think she agreed with me, because Kris was in my opinion a very moral person and still is.

And several years later, the day before Kris's wedding, the same minister suggested to the young couple, "Why don't you two just go off and live together?"

Ministers are, after all, only people. They have biases of upbringing and personality. They make mistakes. When a mother places all her trust in any single source of help, the consequences can be fatal.

When sixteen-year-old Joe ran away from home, Patricia Wentworth turned to her minister. Joe had worked in the church and knew the pastor well, and during Joe's absence Reverend Lucas "saved my life," Patricia says. "He was down at our house every other day."

After several months Joe was found and brought home. Patricia asked the minister to determine whether he believed Joe needed psychological counseling. Early the following morning after Joe arrived, before she had really had a chance to talk with him herself, Reverend Lucas came to talk to Joe. "I went down and ironed," Patricia recalls. "I didn't talk to them at all. . . . I stayed right out of it."

After a couple of hours the pastor left without speaking to Patricia again. Later Reverend Lucas called Patricia. "There's not a darn thing wrong with that kid," he told her, "except that he has ants in his pants. He doesn't need any help."

"So I felt," Patricia says, "that I probably could relax with this youngster. The minister knew him so well."

Several years later, with no warning, Joe killed himself. Patricia looked back to the running away and its aftermath as a place where she went wrong in her handling of her son. "I think now, maybe we should have gone for professional help anyway. That's one thing that if I had it to do over, I'd do differently. I'd be more thorough about investigation, try to really *see* the kid. I'd have had someone else's good judgment as well as the minister's."

Patricia blames herself rather than her minister for this neglect of Joe's psychological welfare. She did not allow the mistake that she believes was made with Joe to come between her and the church. It's true that for a time after Joe's death she couldn't go to church, but only because she broke down in the service. "Church has always been emotional for me; it means a great deal to me." But she maintained a close connection with the pastor, who visited her regularly. "He'd come and see me and we would just talk really and say a little prayer and he'd leave. And then I'd cry." Today Patricia is back in church as always.

Most of these women claim to have received great strength during times of trouble from their personal faith; only one of them identifies herself as an agnostic. Most of them have bonds with a specific church. Only a handful, however, got a lucky break and found a member of the clergy who was especially helpful. Apparently the clergymen involved were not by temperament or by training uniformly equipped to help families in trouble.

Doctors too were a mixed bag, though in general they were considered more helpful than clergymen by these mothers. After Joe's suicide, Patricia fell into a serious depression. She couldn't sleep. Her hands and wrists became painfully swollen and discolored from a bout with arthritis which she believes was largely psychosomatic. Finally she was "just numb" with exhaustion and grief. "I spent a great deal of time in my bed. I'd get up and get a meal and go back to bed."

She consulted a doctor for her physical problems and got more help than she had expected because he understood her feelings. "He was more than sympathetic. He had lost a child too, a youngster who died at eleven, and so he knew what it was. He just had real empathy for me, and that's what I needed."

Patricia was trying to pick up the pieces of her life after a child's untimely death. When counseling became necessary for the problems of a living child, many of these mothers found family therapy to be more helpful than other kinds of psychiatric services. Karen and Rex Matthews arranged for family therapy following their daughter Elisa's diagnosis as a manic-depressive. As soon as Elisa was released from a month-long hospital stay, Karen, Rex, their son Ron, and Elisa began bimonthly sessions with a therapist. Ostensibly the therapy was for the purpose of helping the family adjust to Elisa's illness, but its benefits turned out to be wider-ranging.

Essentially it brought the whole family into more open and honest communication with each other. "I found that a wonderful way for us to talk," says Karen. "Things that we didn't say to each other we found we were saying in the therapy. It was a very comfortable little circle. It was beautiful." The Matthews family continued the therapy until the time came for Elisa, who was now working and doing fine, to leave home.

Even Elisa's decision to get out on her own the family took up in therapy. "I was balking a little bit," Karen says. "I thought, 'Oh, gosh, you know, she's not really well enough. What if something happened to her, if we're not around to see that everything's okay?'"

Rex, on the other hand, encouraged the girl to become independent. "He said, 'Yes, I'd like to see her go on and get out,'" Karen recalls, "and I thought, 'Oh, he's being so harsh about this. We can't really push this girl out of the nest yet.' But he said, 'Oh, yes, we can. We should.' "

Family therapy brought the issue out into the open. The therapist suggested that if Elisa were not allowed to become independent when she wanted to, she might never take the chance again and she might never know whether she could manage on her own. Although Karen's desire to protect Elisa was natural, the therapist thought Rex was right.

And he was. "He is smarter than I am," Karen laughs. "He realized it would be very bad for us to coddle her." At the time of the interview, Elisa had "a darling apartment," a very nice roommate, and had been completely independent of her parents for almost two years.

One of the advantages of family therapy, according to Karen, is that all the children in the family, troubled or not, "realize that help is there if you need it." Many children don't know that, just as some mothers find it hard to ask for help, either for themselves or for their children, especially when the help needed is psychological rather than medical. It's one thing to rush to the hospital for a ruptured appendix, something entirely different to consult a therapist about a broken heart. Ask Martha Pauley.

Martha had five daughters, the youngest only a baby, when Walter, her husband of eighteen years, died, leaving her impecunious and heartbroken. For a couple of years, she struggled along, crying only in private, "trying to figure where I was going to get nickels," coping with the state of single parenthood that as a good Irish Catholic she had never expected to face. Desperately she attempted to abide by the tradition in her family of the stiff upper lip. "I grew up," she says, "with 'You can handle it' and 'Nerves, forget it' and 'Pull yourself together.' "

But the inner toll was great. She lost more and more weight, became more and more debilitated. "I realized finally that 'I can't handle this, I just cannot. I've got to see a psychologist or psychiatrist or somebody.' And I also thought, 'Sometime maybe the girls will need someone, and they'll know that I went first.' "

She made an appointment, and then delivered the bombshell at the family dinner table.

My mother nearly hit the ceiling, as close to hitting the
ceiling as she's likely ever to do, including in heaven. She
said, "You don't need a psychiatrist or psychologist. Just
pull yourself together. You're doing fine."

I said, "Mother, I can't. There's nothing left for me. I—I
cannot do this by myself."

Jenny, who was eight, was passing something, potatoes
or something, and she stopped and said, "Are you crazy,
Mama?"

And I said, "Not yet, but if I don't go, I will be."

Martha's mother came to her later and said sternly, "That was the
most foolish thing you've done, in a lot of foolish things. Nobody
ever went to a psychologist or a psychiatrist in our family."

"Well, now one's going," Martha told her, "and I want the girls to
understand. The reason I'm going is that I'm afraid all these ugly
things I'm thinking are written across my forehead."

Martha was in therapy for about a year, a year during which she
assessed her own and her family's prospects and came to realize that
"we might not go down the drain after all." Just as important, to her
mind, were the consequences for her children. Some years later her
oldest daughter, who had gone into the convent, decided she
wanted to leave. With the authority of her own experience, Martha
suggested that psychological therapy would make the transition
from convent life to life in the world less difficult. In this case, Mama
was the pioneer.

Like doctors and ministers, teachers were unpredictable in their
ability or willingness to lend a hand to the concerned mothers in this
study. Elizabeth Rowe believes that Nate's teachers in both high
school and college supported the boy during his trauma and helped
him greatly to understand the complex subject of human sexuality.
Joy Baron found sympathetic teachers and administrators who saw
to it that her daughter was not punished by loss of academic credit
when she became pregnant at fourteen.

Other mothers were less happy with the teachers their children
had. An indifferent or insensitive school counselor discouraged
Kate Barnes in her initial efforts to find help for her daughter
Debby, insisting that the only problem Debby had was Kate's med-
dling concern. Ellen Kincaid greatly resented the fact that her

daughter Trudy's first lesbian lover was a professor at the university Trudy was attending. She believed, justly, that this professor abused the bond between teacher and student.

As the incidents above indicate, a mother cannot be sure that the assistance she wants from the social institutions of religion, medicine, or education will be available or effective. These service professions, from which some mothers expected to get direction and support, ran the gamut from extreme helpfulness to dangerous incompetence.

SUZANNE AND "A TEAM EFFORT"

No mother has a guarantee that the action she takes to help her child will work. The odds, based on the experience of the mothers in this study, are fifty-fifty. Only half of the focal children, in their mothers' assessment, have come through the straits of untraditional behavior and reached the shores of responsible maturity. Taking arms against a sea of troubles doesn't, even for the best-intentioned mother, guarantee victory.

For that reason, tracing the many skirmishes in Suzanne White's four-year battle with her daughter Meg's anorexia is a pleasure. What Suzanne did worked. Through a combination of Suzanne's intuition, information, and determination, the alliance of her husband Bruce, the support of Meg's siblings, the assistance of good doctors, and of course Meg's own strong spirit, the White family succeeded where others have failed.

And all of those forces mattered. "I really feel," Suzanne says, "that the reason Meg came out of it was—well, it was kind of a team effort. Because basically we're a close family, and we weren't going to let anything happen to that kid."

Anorexia is a disease particularly associated with young, white, upper-middle-class females. It does on occasion strike young men, and recent studies show it to encompass all socioeconomic levels and all ages, though 97 percent of its victims are white. The typical anorexic, however, is like Meg White: an adolescent girl, not the oldest child, in an upper-middle-class family, a girl by nature intelligent, aspiring, eager to please, "a perfect child."

Among girls like these, eating disorders have reached epidemic proportions in America. According to Dr. Steven Levenkron, who specializes in eating disorders, the two most common are *anorexia nervosa,* in which food intake is so rigidly limited by the sufferer that she in effect starves herself; and *anorexic bulimia,* in which orgies of eating are usually followed by self-induced vomiting. Anorexia often leads to bulimia, when the young victim can no longer resist her own hunger and comes to see vomiting as an "easy" way to avoid gaining weight. Both are pathological responses to the commonly held belief in this country that "thin is beautiful."

American females are always dieting, but an ordinary dieter is not anorexic. Anorexia is diagnosed only after the dieter has lost at least 20 percent of her normal, healthy weight and cannot, or will not, stop losing. She will probably have suffered radical declines in body temperature, blood pressure, and other physiological functions. Menstruation frequently stops altogether.

Equally important in diagnosis, Levenkron reports, is her psychological state. Obsessed with eating (or not eating), she will devote much of her thought and energy to weight control and exercise. She often turns away from her friends, feeling that they are immature or undisciplined. If she becomes bulimic, she may not have time for friends or activities in her rigorous regime; hours may be spent in alternately eating enormous amounts of food and then throwing it all up. The anorexic literally loses her sense of proportion about her own body, and will see herself as deplorably "fat" when in fact she looks like a concentration camp victim.

At least one in every two hundred and fifty women is anorexic, perhaps as many as one in every hundred. Anorexia generally begins between the ages of thirteen and twenty-two, and it may continue in an individual indefinitely. A very conservative estimate holds that at least 3 percent of the female college population has anorexia. Medical experts have said that nearly a third of all women may be bulimic to some extent. Other studies indicate that a third of the female college population suffers from some form of disordered eating.

What gives these figures a horrible significance is the low recovery rate for anorexics, perhaps only around 30 percent, and a mortality rate as high as 10 to 15 percent. Many anorexics simply never recover, and eventually they die of slow starvation. As Suzanne White says, "Untreated anorexia is something that you could have all your life"—though "all your life" might not be very long.

Suzanne is a tall, rangy woman in her mid-fifties, her strong face bare of makeup and her brown hair pulled back in a careless ponytail on this pleasant October morning. She had rushed home for the interview from a pottery class she teaches twice a week, and she still wears, over her tan corduroy slacks and beige sweater, the man's denim shirt that is her version of a painter's smock.

"Home" is a comfortable, sprawling, two-story house in Montgomery, Alabama, where her husband Bruce practices law. The house, like her attire, reflects Suzanne's casual, informal nature. Her brown eyes are humorous, her wide mouth smiles readily. This is a woman easy with people, comfortable with herself, a woman who would yell for help when she needed it. And she needed it when Meg, the youngest of her four children, was sixteen.

At that time Suzanne herself was forty-six, a vital, energetic woman who had two children in college, another ready to go, and a high school junior. "Meg was a very bright, bubbly, gregarious, quite pretty young lady," her mother says, "with loads of friends and lots of interests." The family was close and warm. Until the time of Meg's anorexia, the most difficult time Suzanne had had as a mother was the high school career of her oldest child and only son, Ted. Today Ted is a serious and well-liked young businessman, "a very handsome, nice guy." But his mother despaired of him when he was in high school.

Now she realizes that she overreacted to Ted's problems. "He was a normal rotten kid, smoking pot and all that kind of stuff, but I didn't cope with him very well at all. I used to scream a lot and he really got to me. I used to say, when he was fifteen and sixteen, that I wished we could take the thirteen-year-old boy the minute he says, 'I don't want to kiss you good night,' and hand him to somebody till he's twenty-two and he's starting to kiss you good night again."

But Suzanne learned a lot "practicing" on the first three children, particularly on Ted. She wanted to create an atmosphere in the home that allowed her children to be open about their feelings and behavior, in part because she had not had that in her own childhood. "My mother was an incredible lady, but she was the original ostrich.

She used to hide everything, all her feelings. She was brought up not to discuss certain things. You don't discuss sex, you don't discuss money, you don't discuss feelings. There was an awful lot we didn't discuss."

One night when she and her parents were sitting at the kitchen table, Suzanne remembers, she asked some question about sex, and her father started to answer her in some detail. "Ed," her mother gasped in a shocked whisper, "don't talk about that in the kitchen!"

> Even when she was dying she couldn't talk about [her feelings]. I would sit on the side of the bed, and she just would say, "This is so terrible for you girls to go through." But I said, "Hey, we're yours, you know."
>
> But she would turn away. She was dying and she would not talk about it. She would never talk about anything that was too close to her or that upset her.

Suzanne refused to allow this sort of retreat in her own family. She herself changed. "I've come a long way from the very private person of many years ago; I've decided that the very private person kind of hurts herself. I think that part of growth and relationship is sharing."

By the time Meg, the baby of the family, was in high school the home atmosphere was relaxed, loving, and humorous. After her bad experiences with Ted, Suzanne had learned even to discipline with some lightness. "I still said the same things, 'Clean your room' and 'Be accountable,' but it was my way of doing it."

And she could handle serious cautionary advice gracefully. After the herpes problem surfaced, for example, she would leave a note on the kitchen chalkboard when her college-age son was out late: "I understand So-and-So has herpes." She got his attention, without a sermon.

She tried to let her children know that they could talk to her about anything, even drugs. "They've all tried pot, I guess, I don't know. They talk about it, and they said if I'd like to try it, they'd be happy to get me some, you know. Children are a riot."

This good humor was a deliberate strategy that Suzanne used. "I mean, put the cute cartoons on the bulletin board, and all those little extras that mommies try to do to keep some semblance of levity in a home. I tried to do it, and I think possibly some of that permeated the whole four years we've put in with Meg and her anorexia."

Witty, ebullient Meg seemed perfectly at home in her family. As the youngest she came in for a good deal of teasing, but she gave back as good as she got. One of her nicknames in the family was, in fact, "the Mouth." Meg laughed too when they joked that her mouth would make her a fortune someday. "You watch," Suzanne liked to predict, "Meg's going to be the anchorwoman on the six o'clock news."

Another family joke hit a little closer to home and may have started all the trouble. At sixteen, Meg was five feet seven and weighed a hundred and forty pounds. Her older sister, who was a little hefty herself, began calling her "Thunder Thighs." That hurt, her mother says, and Meg decided to do something about it. "It all started out very innocently. She kind of dieted, but she wasn't starving herself; she was eating pretty well."

Then Suzanne realized that the dieting had gotten out of hand.

> All of a sudden, I really looked at her one night. I'll never forget it. She was getting ready to go to a school dance, the annual dance for fathers and daughters. She asked me if she could wear one of my dresses. So she had the dress on, and I looked at her, and my child looked too thin.
>
> So I said, "Hop on the scale for me." And she weighed a hundred seventeen, which should have been all right, but it looked wrong. It wasn't healthy-looking.
>
> I told her, "You're getting too thin, and let's kind of cool it a little bit on the diet. You look wonderful right now."

Suzanne took her daughter to see the family doctor for a physical examination and dieting advice, and Meg told him she wanted to maintain her weight at one hundred fifteen. "Let's do it," he approved. "Two more pounds, and that's it."

"He was very upbeat and positive," Suzanne says, "but I was worried because I was seeing some psychological manifestations that I was not too happy about too. . . . I noticed that she was pulling away from her friends, was a little bit irritated by them, kind of drawing back."

This was in February. In March, Meg went back to see Dr. Schickel (not his real name). She was down to one hundred and six, and hardly eating at all. Suzanne sounded the alarm. "I think Meg has anorexia," she told the doctor.

"No," he reassured her, "she's in a gray area, somewhere almost there, but she really doesn't have it yet."

"Who cares," Suzanne demands, remembering that afternoon, "whether it's gray, white, or purple? She had anorexia, and he was trying to be kind to me, because I think he thought I was going to be a hysterical mother. Well, I'm not a hysterical mother. I just had a very gut feeling about what I was dealing with." She shrugs, flashing her wry, lopsided grin. "Let's face it. Mothers are much smarter than doctors."

"IT WAS WE"

In late March, the whole family went to Bermuda. Meg was behaving oddly. "She's been the most popular little thing we've had in our house since Day One. Now this bubbly, outgoing, popular lady didn't want to see her friends, could hardly wait to go to Bermuda just to get away from it all. This was not Meg."

But the real shock came the first day on the beach, when Meg appeared in her "little bitty bikini," her mother says, and "she looked like something from Ethiopia. That's when I flipped. I really flipped. She wasn't eating *anything*, and the rest of the kids in the family were bugging me about it. You know, 'What are we going to do about Meg? She's not eating at all.' "

Suzanne sat up all night that night, "just worrying and worrying, and finally in the middle of the night just crying and crying. I was so upset, and I knew we were really in trouble."

She corrects herself. "I've been speaking in the *I*, but I should be speaking in the *we*, because Bruce and I shared all of it. He was with me all the way on this. We *both* sat up that night in Bermuda, and we really just brainstormed every aspect of it, how to do it, how to deal with her, where are we going to go now? We realized that we had a terrible problem."

As we have noticed, many of the women in this study dealt with at least the initial stages of a child's problems without any support at all from their husbands. In some marriages, communication between husband and wife was virtually nonexistent. As one woman, Betty Carver, remarked of the supreme disenchantment she felt with marriage when her sons took up drugs, "The basic communication between a husband and wife is, 'Please pass the salt, please pass the sugar.' It's not any more than that. He doesn't know what I'm thinking and I don't have any idea what he's thinking." These women have often lost the ability to get their husbands even to recognize family problems, much less to help solve them.

It wasn't that way for the Whites. "Bruce saw it all the way along the line just as I did," Suzanne says. "It really was *we*. He's very emotional also, so he was upset by it too. But we were able to—if I were to name the thing in our marriage that we have really teamed the best on, other than creating our children, it would probably be this.

"And, interestingly enough, it was good for our marriage, because we really hung in there together and we really talked a lot."

After that first horrible night, Suzanne and Bruce talked to Meg. Her friend Milly was supposed to come to stay with them in Bermuda for a week. They told Meg that if she couldn't start eating something other than the lettuce she was subsisting on, they would cancel Milly's visit and the whole family would return to Montgomery so that she could see the doctor.

"That really kind of jolted her a little bit," Suzanne says. That her mother and father, who were such "cool" parents, were not being the least bit cool at this point, frightened Meg. What frightened her even more was that, shortly after the family left Bermuda, she stopped having her periods. "She started to realize she had a problem. Before that, you know, she was perfectly fine, nothing wrong with *her*. But it got to a point where it went from diet into something very chemical. All of a sudden she stopped being a normal dieting teenager, and almost overnight—it's weird—she looked like a very sick young lady."

Back in Montgomery, Suzanne took Meg back to Dr. Schickel, who acknowledged that the "gray area" was pretty black by this time. "If I hadn't been kind of a Jewish mother throughout the whole thing it might have gotten much worse. Meg knew we were with her, but the psychological state an anorexic is in is so bizarre. You can't understand it. They don't understand it themselves."

Suzanne began doing some reading, and discovered that the experts on anorexia agree that psychological counseling is necessary for the recovery of the anorexic. She was anxious that Meg begin psychotherapy before the disease became entrenched. When the sufferer has lived with anorexia long enough, she becomes much harder to treat. The illness creates patterns of behavior and thought that become intrinsic to her personality; Levenkron describes the chronic anorexic as solitary, hopeless about her condition, and cynical about the prospect of help. Once the disease is chronic, even the recommended treatment of hospitalization, intravenous feeding, and intensive and prolonged psychotherapy may not cure the patient.

"It's terrifying," Suzanne says. "To me it's inexcusable that an anorexic be untreated. I have run into mothers whose child has been anorexic for five years and they haven't gotten the child into psychological treatment. The father thought it wasn't necessary, and all these kinds of wacky, dumb things, when you can *see* it, you can pinpoint what's happening. It's so dangerous, so bizarre. It's terrifying for the patient and terrifying for the family."

But Meg didn't want help and she kept what was happening to her to herself. She made "the typical anorexic response," according to her mother—"I don't have it. I'm fine. I'm just on a diet."

Suzanne and Bruce didn't allow themselves to become hysterical, though Suzanne admits that "I spent most of the time with my stomach in knots, watching, and realizing how powerless a parent is. Anorexia is bigger than the doctor, and it's bigger than the parent, and it's certainly bigger than the patient. It just makes you feel helpless."

Dr. Schickel advised them not to impose counseling on Meg before she was ready for it. Knowing how rebellious teenagers can be, they recognized the wisdom of this, and decided to hold off until Meg acknowledged her need for help. "We were really very understanding," Suzanne says, "and tried to work with her, once we knew what we had." Whatever happened, they were ready to go into action.

SHARING HELPS

Suzanne, as she mentioned earlier, believes very strongly in the efficacy of open human relationships, of sharing feelings and problems with others. What bothered her most during the early stages of Meg's anorexia was the way in which Meg, her most popular child, cut herself off from her friends. So when June came, in spite of Meg's problems the family decided to go on with a raft trip down the Colorado River that they had planned some time earlier. This decision turned out to be a lucky break for the Whites, when Meg received some help from an unexpected quarter.

"There were thirty people in two boats—six couples and all their kids—for eight days and seven nights," Suzanne remembers. "We were from all over the country. The parents knew each other, but not all the kids did." Meg was put into a completely new group of people. "Of course, she looked awful," her mother says, "but the kids loved her anyway, because she was a nifty lady." From these totally "objective observers" Meg was willing to listen to the truth about herself. "They said, 'You're a cute kid, but you need to put on some weight.' "

One of the women on the trip, an old friend of Suzanne and Bruce, had had anorexia as a girl, before anybody knew what anorexia was. She watched Meg for a while and then pulled her aside, saying, "Meg, the same thing happened to me."

"She told her all the funny stories," Suzanne says gratefully, "the things people tried to do to get her to eat. Her mother used to pay her dates to take her out and buy her hamburgers, and then she'd go home and throw them all up. She made it an okay thing to admit that you had anorexia."

When the Whites got back to Montgomery, Meg approached her mother. She sat down at the kitchen table with Suzanne one day, and said, "I would like to get out of Montgomery, Mother, really go *away* to school."

> "Well, Meg," I said, "let's consider your pattern. You wanted to leave parochial school after the ninth grade and go to a public high school. You wanted to go there so badly, and you seemed to love it for the last two years. Now you

want to leave it, to go North to boarding school. Don't you
think you're running away from something?"

And she looked at me with her big, beautiful blue eyes,
and she said, "Yeah, I am."

And I said, "Well, would you like to talk to somebody
about it?"

And she said, "I sure would."

And I said, "Fine, I'll just do a little checking and see
what we can do." And that was the beginning of psychological help for Meg.

Meg went into therapy. After her counselor had seen her several
times, he asked Suzanne and Bruce to come in without her. "She's a
textbook case of anorexia," he told them. "I'm glad I've got her
early, but it's going to be at least two years before she gets through
this—*at least* two years. Be patient and ask the other members of the
family to be patient."

It was fortunate that Suzanne and Bruce had worked to create an
atmosphere of cheerful, open, loving support among their children,
because for the next three years all the patience and understanding
that the family could muster was necessary to deal with Meg.
"There's a lot about an anorexic personality that drives you ba-
nanas," Suzanne says. "As a mother, I had to be understanding, her
father had to be understanding, and so did her brother and her
sisters."

All the children helped Meg in different ways. Ted, the oldest
child and the only boy, was least affected. He was away from home
and caught up in his own life, and, though he was concerned, he was
perhaps naturally less involved than Meg's sisters. But "he thought
she was cute and funny," Suzanne says, and that gave Meg a feeling
of worth that anorexics often lack.

The oldest girl, Nancy, approached the situation scientifically.
She was taking a biology class in college, and she took to looking up
nutritional information in the library and passing it on to her sister
in regular phone conversations. "She would call and say, 'Now,
Meg, you should be having so many calories, and your electrolytes
should be this and that,' just talk to her about it clinically. And Meg
would listen to her, and try to understand what was going on with
her body."

The child who was most upset was Laurie, two years older than Meg. It was Laurie who had nicknamed Meg "Thunder Thighs," and when she realized how sick Meg really was, she felt guilty, concerned—and terrified. Laurie had gone from a weight of one hundred fifty to about one hundred twenty and was very thin. In her freshman year at college, she saw anorexia everywhere in her school; someone had told her that one sorority alone had eighteen anorexic girls. "To come home and find it in her own home was just terrifying to her," Suzanne says. "She just freaked when she saw Meg."

Later Laurie told her mother that she had been frightened of becoming anorexic herself. "She told herself, 'I'm too smart to be an anorexic,' but it was too close for comfort, and she was scared to death." Laurie desperately wanted to help Meg, but she also wanted Meg to get well *immediately*. "She kind of gave me the business," Suzanne laughs, "as if I were going to make this child well overnight, when we all knew that wasn't possible."

"ALL BLOW AND NO SHOW"

If Laurie felt responsible and involved with Meg's anorexia, Bruce White did too. When the Whites had reached the stage of asking themselves why the disease had afflicted their beloved youngest daughter, they found out that a child's relationship with her father may be a factor. Has the father been too hard on her? Has he lacked understanding in his treatment of her? Bruce, an introspective and serious man, took this discovery to heart.

Bruce always had more trouble in dealing with Meg than with the other children, Suzanne says, because she is so much like him. Suzanne, on the other hand, thought Meg "the perfect child. Oh, she was kind of a slob now and then, but she still was an awfully nice child. It was her spirit that bugged Bruce, but the spirit was what I married him for. So I found her easy to handle, whereas he found her tough."

Meg is a clone of Bruce when he was a kid. When I met my husband, he was a bright, vivacious, crazy, wild, fun-loving nut. He has since evolved into a quiet, gentle, loving, dear, sweet, conservative husband.

When I see this clone, female version, bopping around, I just giggle. I *adore* her, because she's exactly like her father.

Now, Father thinks she is a spoiled, unbridled, nutty kid who should behave herself better. He can't understand the messy room, any of these little foibles of hers. . . . He felt that she needed some extra discipline, that she was too much of a flibbertigibbet. He was awfully tough on her. . . .

[Anorexics] really want to please their dad. I mean, every daughter loves her father to death. And Meg really wasn't pleasing Bruce very much.

Bruce was "shattered," Suzanne claims, when he realized the part his disapproval might have had in Meg's eating disorder. He told her, "You know, I feel very badly for my part in this." He consciously tried to ease up on Meg and to let her know how much he cared for her.

Suzanne wondered about her own responsibility. An accomplished potter and a successful free-lance commercial artist and designer, she especially worried about her own role as "the achieving mother whom the kids feel they can never [measure up to]." But she tried not to feel guilty.

I think parents feel guilty about too much as it is. . . . I cannot apologize for being an achiever. I have had goals that reached outside my family, I've had lots of interests, but any child should be able to take that in stride. I can't be guilty for who I am.

After she had thought about the matter of parental responsibility at length, Suzanne reassured Bruce. "Look," she said, "the mother has a role in it and the father has a role in it. But it's such a complicated disease, let's not blame ourselves. We've got too much else to do, without blame."

They read and read, learned more about the mysterious force that had their daughter in thrall. They learned that the position of the anorexic in the family is important. Rarely is an anorexic the first-born child; almost never is she in the family spotlight. She is cooperative and agreeable at home, obedient and successful at school. She is also, or feels herself to be, powerless.

Meg, her mother says, was

> the perfect child, really a textbook case [for anorexia]. She came in on time, she did as she was told, we didn't really have to tell her to do too much, because she just did it.
>
> I think she had heard so much discipline and rules and guidelines and stuff with the three older ones that just by osmosis they sifted down to her. She was just a good kid.

Suzanne felt better able to help Meg as she and Bruce became knowledgeable about Meg's illness. The anorexic personality, seduced by circumstances into powerlessness in the family, wants to gain a greater sense of control. "Meg probably didn't feel she had it at our house." Her response was to control her eating rigorously; her fanatically controlled body became the bulwark behind which her whole personality retreated.

Anorexia also halted Meg's growth into adulthood, an effect that Suzanne believes Meg desired passionately. "When you're an anorexic, you are frightened to lose your family. You pretend that you would like to be independent, to be away from home, to do something on your own, but really you're terrified of it."

When Suzanne read about the typical anorexic's fear of independence, it struck a chord in her. She remembered the difficulty she'd had years ago getting Meg off to nursery school. "She wanted to go to nursery school the worst way, but I'll never forget the first day. She just hung on to my hand with such fierce strength and wouldn't let go. And I realized that my little Meg, who was three then, was all blow and no show. And she's still kind of all blow and no show." Anorexia allows a fearful person, "all blow and no show," to remain a child in the bosom of the family, with more power and more parental attention than she has ever had.

As the Whites learned more about Meg's anorexia, Meg slowly began to bring her self-starvation under control. For two years, she continued sessions twice a week with her therapist. Slowly her weight came up. She had been a day student in a local college. Now, a college sophomore, she felt confident enough to take a dorm room in a college a little farther away.

Although she did not welcome it, Suzanne was prepared for the next installment of Meg's illness. When Meg came home for Christmas her first semester away, Suzanne knew at once something was wrong. Meg was in an obviously overwrought state, but it took her a while to get around to telling her mother that she had been bingeing on food and then forcing herself to throw up. She wanted to eat so much, but then she got desperately afraid of being "fat." She'd hit on vomiting as a solution, and now she couldn't help but want to throw up everything she ate.

"All the time I'm eating," she told her mother tearfully, "I'm preoccupied, I'm wondering, 'Will I be going upstairs to upchuck?' It's so awful!"

Suzanne was ready. "Meg," she said, "you think you've caught something brand new, but this is not a separate thing. It's an extension of—well, really another phase of your anorexia."

"Are you sure?" Meg asked, looking at Suzanne hopefully through the tears in her big eyes.

"I'm positive," Suzanne answered. "This is something that's very normal. It happens a lot of the time with anorexic kids."

Meg seemed reassured. The bulimia continued for about a year. That summer, when Meg was at home, after Meg would throw up, she wouldn't clean up the mess. Suzanne recognized that her daughter was sending a message to her: "It's still happening, and I want you to know it."

As a mother she became concerned with the reaction of Laurie, Meg's older sister, who was also at home for the summer. "Laurie would come down, and she'd say, 'Do you realize she's doing that?' I mean, she'd just be in a rage.

"And I'd say, 'Yes.'

" 'Well, why don't you do something about it?'

" 'Laurie, there really isn't a lot we can do right now. It's all part of the process.' I think that frightened Laurie as much as anything, all the bulimic stuff that year."

To protect Laurie, Suzanne consulted Meg's psychologist. "Be quite adamant," he told her. "Tell Meg, 'If you're going to get sick, you're going to get sick. But for God's sake, *you* clean it up. I don't want to find it around. *You* do it.' " And although Suzanne understood that Meg was in her own way just keeping her mother informed, she took his advice.

In a year's time, the bulimia disappeared, and Meg told Suzanne,

"I don't even think about it anymore." The family had seen her through the most difficult year of the second phase of her illness.

"A COMPLETE WOMAN"

But all of this was not easy for Suzanne White. It's true that Suzanne was remarkably capable, as well as remarkably lucky, in taking action against the physical and mental devastation that threatened her youngest child. In her humorous way, Suzanne dismisses any claims to maternal grandeur. "Oh, I'm great on the spot all right. I really operate well under pressure. I can get the kid to the hospital for the cast and the stitches. I'm just marvelous, and then I go home and shake for two days, while the 'what-ifs' work on me for a while."

Suzanne was "on the spot" with Meg's anorexia. She didn't allow herself to be traumatized by the shock of the disease itself. With her husband, she enlisted intelligent support from her children and from good doctors. Immediate, responsible, consistent action saved her child.

Suzanne didn't have to deal with the additional trauma experienced by another mother, Agnes Price, of Tulsa, and her anorexic daughter Phoebe. For Agnes, a staunch Baptist and a religious fundamentalist, the first shock was not the greatest shock she would have during the years the family grappled with the complexities of Phoebe's illness. That came later, just as Phoebe was emerging from the bulimic stage, when in fact her complete recovery looked like a sure thing. If Agnes had not understood the psychological nuances of anorexia very well at that point, she herself would have been devastated. As it was, she was deeply wounded during what she describes as "the worst week of my life."

If anorexia allows a return to childhood, to a secure, important place in the bosom of the family, the anorexic also returns to sexual immaturity, a state which Agnes thinks Phoebe unconsciously sought. A lovely girl with a mature figure and a winning personality, Phoebe at sixteen was attracting a lot of attention from boys. She was not ready for sexual experience, but because of the relaxed sexual code of the time, she got a great deal of sexual pressure.

"Phoebe was unable to deal with it," Agnes says. When she stopped eating, physiologically she became a child again. Her voluptuous figure turned childish. Boys lost sexual interest and were willing to be friends again. Menstruation, the unwelcome sign of adult femininity, stopped.

As Phoebe recovered from anorexia and her eating became more nearly normal, her periods resumed. At the end of the bulimic stage, she looked womanly for the first time in several years. At home for the summer, with a filing job in a city government office, she dressed to the nines every day for work. She spent her evenings running around with her friends, particularly her boyfriend Randy, described by her mother as "a darling boy she'd been going out with for about a couple of years."

One day when Phoebe came home from work, Agnes was sitting on the sofa reading the paper. She looked up as Phoebe walked in the door. Without warning a thought came into her mind: "Phoebe, you look pregnant."

Throughout the whole weekend, she watched her daughter unobtrusively. She tried to talk herself out of the idea that had come to her unbidden. "She's just gaining weight because of the bulimia," she told herself. But she couldn't quite get rid of the feeling. "My tummy jumped all weekend," Agnes says. "You know, mothers know these things."

Monday morning when Phoebe came down for breakfast she told her mother, "I don't have to work today. Randy's coming. We're going to go fishing, probably stay all day."

Fishing, Agnes thought; interesting. Randy came and they left.

As Agnes went through the motions of her housework, she began to figure the whole thing out. "I just knew Phoebe had gone somewhere to have an abortion. Randy is a responsible boy. He'd gone with her to do it."

Sure enough, early in the afternoon Phoebe came in. "Are you home already?" Agnes called.

She lay down on the couch and said, "Terrible cramps, terrible cramps. I'm having a terrible period, Mother, a terrible period."

So, knowing what I know about such things, I said, "Well, if you're having such a terrible period, I suggest you don't use a Tampax." I thought, "If they haven't told her that, wherever she's been, I'm going to tell her, and just act dumb for a while."

"No, no, no," she said. "I'm not. I'm just using pads."

At some point later on that afternoon, I found a belt in the wastebasket in my bathroom, not even wrapped—a hospital belt, just like I had when I had my babies.

And I started to shake, and I shook, and I shook, and I thought, "Oh, my God! I can't believe it." But in the next breath, I was relieved to know what was going on. . . . Even if it's horrible, you want to know what happened.

Agnes took the belt in her hand and went into the den, where Phoebe lay on the couch. "Why don't you tell me about it?" she said to her daughter.

Phoebe burst out crying. "I didn't want you to know," she sobbed.

"Well, Phoebe," Agnes said, putting her hand on the girl's shoulder, "I do know. Obviously you wanted me to know, or you wouldn't have left this thing unwrapped in my bathroom. I really would have liked to know beforehand, so we could have at least discussed the alternatives to having an abortion."

I really was feeling like kind of a poopy mother at this point, because she hadn't shared this with me. I think if I had been pregnant back in 1950 or '51, I would have run right to my mother for counsel or guidance.

She just said, "Mother, I couldn't tell you. I did not want to hurt you, because I know how you feel about sex before marriage and about abortion." She was protecting me. I have always been dead set against abortion.

"I really have no guilt about this," Phoebe told her mother. "In my own mind, that was the only thing I could do. And in a way I'm glad it happened."

"What in the world do you mean?" Agnes exclaimed.

"Well," Phoebe said, "this isn't something Randy and I do. This is a fluke. But now at least I know I can get pregnant."

"Oh, my God," Agnes thought, "it's this anorexia, no periods. She has been worried whether she'd ever be able to have a child."

And I certainly wasn't going to kill the kid for having an
abortion. She had done what she thought was best, and
that was her decision. It certainly wouldn't be my decision,
but I understood it.

She thought anorexia was going to ruin her forever, and
now she knows it hasn't. She can get pregnant. She's—you
know, she's a complete woman.

Phoebe pleaded with her mother not to tell her father. Larry Price
is a deacon in the Baptist Church and a man of firm moral convic-
tions. "I cannot have Dad ever know this," she cried. "He would just
be so terribly hurt. I don't think he could handle it."

"Honey," Agnes said, "I share everything with your father. We
talk about everything. I have never in all the years we've been
married not told him everything I feel. He would be as disappointed
as I am, but he certainly isn't going to think any the less of you for
one thing that's happened in your life."

"Please don't. Please, for me, Mother, will you not do it? Don't
tell him."

So I sat there with her, and I just sort of mulled it over,
because I wasn't going to make a promise I couldn't keep
or wasn't comfortable with. And I instantly weighed everything and decided I would not tell Larry.

He might say to himself that he would be big about it,
and not think any the less of her. But he's always been
more critical of her, more demanding of her, than of Barbara. This would not be a good thing for him to know.

So I promised her. I said, "I promise you, I will not tell
your dad."

And I made her promise me to talk to her psychologist
and to our Baptist minister. "You're going to have a lot to
work out on this," I said. "You may not think so now,
because you're so relieved. But you're going to have a little
tussle with your head."

I've never told Larry. I had the worst week of my life after
that. I was so torn and so wrenched, I was just shattered,
you know, but I really understood where she was coming
from.

Agnes had not promised silence anywhere else, however, and she guessed where Phoebe had gotten some of her ideas. Several days later, while Phoebe was out, Agnes walked into the bedroom Phoebe shared with Barbara, her older sister. Barbara was sitting cross-legged on her bed, doing her nails.

"Barbara," Agnes announced, "I know everything."

"What do you know?" Barbara asked.

"A mother knows everything."

"Oh, boy," Barbara said affectionately. "There she is again, the all-knowing mother who knows—even before it comes into my mind, my mother knows I'm going to do it. What do you know, Mother?"

"I know the counsel you gave Phoebe, and I don't like it."

Barbara blushed a slow deep blush, but she stood her ground. "She thinks I'm some old fogy out of the hinterlands, I think," Agnes says, "but we talked about it. I just let her know, for her own benefit, that if she should ever get pregnant, she might have the gumption to go through with it and put the baby up for adoption. And I let her know that I would expect her to come to me."

"I guess somewhere along the line I've fouled up," she told Barbara, "because I haven't made it clear that it isn't the end of the world to me if somebody gets pregnant. It happens all the time. I guess where I was hurt is that you didn't think I was a big enough person to see Phoebe through something like this."

THE THREE R'S: REALISTIC, RESOURCEFUL, RESPONSIBLE

Few mothers would think that Agnes "fouled up." On the contrary, her attitude toward Phoebe's abortion was one more instance of her instinctive fidelity, throughout the battle with anorexia, to what we might call the three R's of proper action.

First of all, she was realistic. She learned of the abortion when it was a fait accompli, and she didn't waste her energy on useless recriminations. Assessing the situation realistically, Agnes focused on the most important issues: she persuaded Phoebe to seek counseling for the feelings she would have to face; and she let Barbara know that she too could count on her mother in an unwanted pregnancy.

Next, Agnes was resourceful. She paid attention to her intuition and the uncanny foresight it gave her of Phoebe's behavior. But she had also prepared herself intellectually to understand the kinds of fears and anxieties that lay behind Phoebe's pregnancy and her subsequent decision to have an abortion. Moving emotionally and intellectually beyond her own biases, she was able to empathize with her child.

Finally, she was responsible. She merited Phoebe's trust in her when she agreed to protect her daughter's confidences. She was responsible to her own point of view, carefully reiterating her position on abortion to her daughters. But she did not hound Phoebe or usurp Phoebe's right to make a decision which she herself would not make. She respected Phoebe's autonomy and treated Phoebe herself as a responsible person.

The most effective action that a mother can take is realistic, resourceful, and responsible. Though action with these qualities may not always work, action without them almost never works. Like Agnes, Suzanne White, from beginning to end of Meg's battle with anorexia, acted effectively and consistently. She took up the right arms and was victorious against a sea of troubles.

From the start Suzanne was realistic in her attitude toward Meg's illness. She recognized it immediately as anorexia, and rejected the nonsense of "gray areas" that the doctor offered as a panacea. In this respect she was very unlike Gloria Tipton, another mother of an anorexic daughter. Mary Tipton certainly sounds anorexic as her mother describes her: her weight is extremely low, she has hospitalized herself for treatment, and, twenty years old when her mother was interviewed, she has not had a menstrual period since she was fifteen.

Yet Gloria insists that Mary is not a "classic anorexic" and claims that Mary lacks the emotional problems of a real anorexic. To say Mary is anorexic, she protests, would be "like somebody wants to say she's *schizophrenic* or something. It's not as much emotional [with Mary] as it is basically not liking fat and wanting to stay thin." Yet Mary Tipton throws constant temper tantrums and subjects her family to wild mood swings and childish, manipulative behavior.

Gloria is allowing herself an unhealthy semantic nit-picking, which could be a dangerous evasion of the realities of her daughter's state.

Suzanne White was also, from beginning to end, resourceful. With energy and forthrightness, she enlisted the help of her husband, her children, and medical and psychological experts for Meg. She and all the Whites made a genuine, sustained effort to understand what was going on in their family.

Again there is a sharp contrast between her resourcefulness and Gloria Tipton's lack of it. Gloria has sought medical help for Mary, taking her first to her pediatrician and then successively to a general internist, a gynecologist, and an endocrinologist. But Mary has not gotten the ongoing psychological counseling that Meg got, twice a week for two years or more, and that experts on the disease agree is necessary to full recovery. Somehow Mary had the will to check herself into the hospital and to attempt to combat the illness on her own, without the all-out "team effort" the White family made on Meg's behalf.

Nor has Gloria Tipton done any reading on the subject of her daughter's illness. "I probably just wasn't going to admit that Mary had anorexia," she says, with a shrug and a defensive laugh. "I think way down deep, I maybe just think, 'She's our daughter.'

"I don't know, it's interesting, isn't it, that I don't [want to know more about it]? I've read enough to know that she's got, well, touches of anorexia, for sure." For whatever reason, Gloria has apparently been incapable of taking realistic, resourceful, responsible action to help Mary.

Lucky Meg! At the time of the interview, she is a senior in a college in Cleveland, a long way from Montgomery. Independent and active, in some ways she's twenty going on sixteen, moving backward in order to experience the adolescence she missed the first time around because of her years with anorexia. "When she comes home, it's just like a bomb hit the house, an explosion," Suzanne sighs. "She wears me out—*totally.*"

She makes a mess in the kitchen, hogs the girls' bathroom, "borrows" her sisters' things, and is generally "such a sloppy slob," Suzanne says, that Nancy and Laurie would like to wring her neck. Laurie, in particular, who's never been long on patience with Meg, expostulates, "Mother, she's had no training!"

And when Meg leaves, like a typical adolescent she is apt to take

some of Nancy's and Laurie's clothes with her, a charming misde-
meanor which makes them crazy.

In other ways, however, Meg is quite mature. Like her mother, she
believes in sharing the experiences of her life with those around her.
Recently she wrote her autobiography, including a full account of
the years with anorexia, for a college class. Meg has also served as a
volunteer counselor to other young people with anorexia.

Suzanne approves of her daughter's candor, of what she calls "the
evolution from the private person to the public person." "If you
don't want to be lonely," she says, "you have to give. . . . It's okay
to share a lot, and okay to receive sharing. We all need each other,
and anybody who says she can do anything by herself is nuts."

And she would like to help other parents with anorexic children.
"There's so much of it now, and too many parents are hiding it. I
think we have to be very honest and candid about it. I'd like people
to know that it's happened in our family, so that they can come to me
if they're frightened or something."

But where Meg herself is concerned, her mother has reached the
stage of wholesome detachment. "I worry a lot about her, and I
think I'll probably always worry about her, just because of what she's
been through. I live with it day and night, but I don't dwell on it."

She has turned Meg's life, and Meg's illness, over to her. "I just
treat her like a normal person.

"I admire my children's independence," she concludes. "I admire
Meg's. If I were just twenty, as she is, I wouldn't have the courage
she has to go all the way to Cleveland and get myself into some
school and find myself a place to live—she's not even living in the
dorm."

She grins. "Now, mind you, she's screwed up some, gotten her
bank accounts all messed up and so on.

"But still, she's proving something to herself. She told me that.
She has to do it. She said, 'I can do it, Mother, I know I can. Trust
me!' "

Like her mother, Meg is ready for action.

7

When Action Doesn't Work

A G-RATED MOTHER IN AN R-RATED WORLD

Some actions that a mother takes are not as wise as they might be. Patty Ingram, at forty-four one of the youngest of the mothers here, admitted with chagrin that she had frequently behaved unrealistically in trying to handle the adolescent problems of her son Charles. She seemed uncertain whether to laugh or cry as she described the heavy-handed moralistic stance of some of her less successful attempts.

When she caught Charles smoking marijuana, for example, instead of, as Suzanne White learned to do, seeing it as a natural youthful curiosity, she took it as a personal insult. "The problem doesn't lie in the fact that he smokes pot, because I don't think he smokes a lot, I really don't. The problem lies in the fact that we have asked him not to do it, because it is illegal. We have asked him not to drink, and we don't like it when he drinks, because it is illegal. But [what we want] doesn't matter to him. He's going to do it because he still wants to do it."

Patty had Charles write a report on how detrimental marijuana was to his health. He wrote the report, but didn't alter his habits. Patty's next step was to patrol to catch Charles and his friends smoking again. "I would get in my car, and I would roam, just like a policeman would, at their break time or after school."

Unable to catch the boys at it, finally she called the police and asked them to patrol. Before long, she got a telephone call: "Your son is at the police station; he has been picked up for possession of marijuana."

Patty and her husband went down to get Charles out. Having engineered the whole thing, Patty then threw a scene in the station house. "I guess I always say what I feel. I said, 'This is a disgrace to our family. You are the only person in our family . . . that has ever been picked up by the police and taken to the police station.' "

When the family got home, Patty was "in a terrible state."

> It was such a shameful thing. I'm a very proud person and I have always tried to be good, and this boy—this boy was not being good, had not been good for years. . . .
>
>   I can't even remember what I said to him, but I remember I began to beat him with my fists. . . . My husband had to put his arms around me and forcibly pull me away from this child, because I couldn't stop it.

Little wonder that, in all "the yelling and screaming" that have gone on in the Ingram household, Charles told his parents, "The more you push me, the more you demand of me, the less I want to do," and himself resolved at the ripe age of sixteen never to marry or to have children.

At the time of the interview, Patty had begun to see how unrealistic her actions as a mother had often been. "I've only just in the last few months realized that it isn't such a terrible thing to have a child who does these things." She acknowledges her part in Charles's ongoing bad behavior. "If I can just not magnify [his problems], if I can just not anticipate and already know what my son is going to do before he does it, it will help a lot."

Rightly or wrongly, she believes that she gets back from Charles the distrust and hostility she has given out. "If I had been able to raise him in a more understanding way, his behavior now would not be as it is." Ruefully she recalls a comment from her husband, who in a moment of disloyalty to Patty summed up the problem succinctly when he told their children, "It's too bad you live in an R-rated world, and you have a G-rated mother."

ANN ASSAILS THE MOONIES

Patty knows she has a lot to learn. Ann Rourke, older than Patty and the mother of seven children, has a much firmer grasp than Patty on the predictable problems of adolescence. One look at her tells you that. With her tanned face and her trim, compact body, Ann is a handsome, vital woman. Born Ann O'Malley, married for twenty-eight years to Tom Rourke, manager of a large importing firm, Ann is the best of the Baltimore Irish. Everything about her says no nonsense, from her short, curly, salt-and-paprika hair to the direct gaze of her piercing blue eyes to her casual gabardine slacks, tweed jacket, and loafers. A woman, one would say, uniquely fitted to handle whatever life dished out.

But what has happened to Bob, the fourth of her seven children, has her stymied. Since 1979, Bob has been a full-time member of the Reverend Sun Myung Moon's Unification Church. For several years, Ann tried desperately and unsuccessfully to free Bob from what she considers a state of criminal bondage. Today, though she still tries to persuade Bob to leave, she has come to realize that that is all she can do at this point. She hopes and prays that Bob will free himself.

Statistically, this seems unlikely. Psychologists who have worked with former cult members report that about three-fourths of these members needed outside help in getting out of their respective cults. The longer they stayed in, the more difficult getting out and the more threatening life in the outside world became. Almost three-fourths of those who left the cult needed some kind of deprogramming once they were out, according to Willa Appel in *Cults in America.*

It is far more likely that Ann must continue to cope with the greatest loss, short of a child's death, that a mother can face. To Ann, the Bob that she knew for his first eighteen years has been swallowed up by an automaton. Some mothers might, in fact, find it almost as easy to accept the death of a child as to accept, as Ann must, that child's strange zombie-like state. Bob is alive, she hears from him regularly, but she hardly recognizes the son she knew in the person he has become. Heart, mind, and soul, as far as his mother can tell, Bob is controlled by his cult.

No one hearing Ann outline her gargantuan efforts in Bob's behalf can see them as anything other than the maneuvers of a desperate and loving mother, or fault her for them. But Ann herself believes that she failed Bob by exercising what she refers to as "bad judgment." She describes her son as a "victim" of forces beyond his control, and points to a series of "mistakes" she made, as well as to a constant run of bad luck. And it's true that, if things went incredibly right for Suzanne in her dealings with Meg's anorexia, things went incredibly wrong for Ann when Bob became a Moonie.

Yet Ann was hardly a naive young mother, inexperienced in dealing with the psychological problems of her young. With three older children, she had become proficient at mothering by the time Bob came along. Her first real maternal trial had come when her daughter Lisa, the firstborn, after her first year at college had a psychological breakdown brought on, as Ann describes it, by Lisa's overwhelming sense of responsibility as the oldest child.

Ann handled Lisa's difficulties very well, she thinks. "Boy, I mean, I just moved." She found a place for Lisa in an excellent psychiatric hospital, and she and her husband Tom drove all night to get Lisa immediate medical attention. "That turned out very well," Ann says proudly, "and to this day Lisa is just great. She's really a very effective person. It was something she had to go through, and I thank God she's through it and has it out of her system." This experience with Lisa gave Ann self-confidence as a mother.

Her experience with Bob is a different story. Her self-confidence rapidly evaporated in the face of her difficulties with her son and in her dealings with the Unification Church. Improperly schooled in Moonie methods, desperate to act, Ann and Tom Rourke came up against a wealthy, powerful, ruthless organization whose effective conversion techniques resemble, according to Appel, the classic brainwashing strategies of Chinese Communists. The Rourkes were dreadfully outmatched. They acted quickly, impulsively, and, Ann declares, unwisely. Looking back at their efforts in the clear light of hindsight, she claims that the action she took in Bob's behalf was not as realistic, as resourceful, or as responsible as it should have been.

Nor did it work. Bob's phone calls home today are carefully monitored by other cult members, and his irrational, "programmed" remarks drive Ann sometimes to despair that he will ever liberate himself. Nevertheless, she keeps trying to talk sensibly to him, as these calls are the only regular contact she has with her son. Bob has been promised "furloughs," but none has ever materialized. He has not been home for a visit since he went into the Unification Church in 1979, three months after he graduated from high school.

To his mother he has become a stranger. "We're really dealing with *two* Bobs, not one," she says, her bright blue eyes flashing with indignation and grief, "the Bob before the cult and the Bob as he is now. Before Bob went into the cult, he was really a delightful person. . . . I can remember when he was growing up, and things would be going wrong, the kids and all their problems, I would sometimes think, 'Well, at least I have Bob.' "

ANN AND "THE OLD BOB"

The most important quality of the old Bob was his idealism. Even in high school, Ann says, "he took everything about his life seriously. He knew that he had something special, having life itself, and he was going to do something special with his life. . . .

"He was an idealist. He did papers in high school about the injustices of the world, the starvation, and he became interested in nutrition. . . . He wanted to do something *good,* so he was thinking about being a doctor specializing in diet, getting the right foods to people, going to South America or India, that sort of thing.

"But he was interested in everything."

Ann had a very good relationship with her idealistic son. She liked his independence and encouraged it, as she encouraged it in all of her children. But she was happy also that Bob confided in her. "He would go to a movie, and he would be so excited about what the movie was saying that he'd come home and literally follow me around the house and tell me everything about it, try to arouse my interest, and offer to go back and see it with me so he could point some of these things out."

She shakes her head in amusement, remembering Bob at eighteen. "If anything, he talked *too* much. . . . But he really was fun. I enjoyed him. I truly liked him. I liked to be around him.

"Oh, he was stubborn, and like all of us Rourkes he had a temper. When he lost his temper, he'd go off and really think about it, and"

—Ann chuckles—"decide where you were wrong. Then he'd come back and explain it to you." She throws her head back and laughs. "And you'd better understand how you were wrong! Oh, he was a great kid."

Bob had seen his older brothers stay in college without purpose or much enthusiasm in order to avoid conscription during the Vietnam War years. He wanted something more positive for his life. "He was searching, all the time searching for what he wanted to do."

Finally he decided that instead of going on to college without a purpose, he would take a year off and take a bike trip around the United States with a friend. "He spent the last year of high school getting ready," Ann recalls. "He worked and paid for a Japanese bike. He bought camping equipment, everything scientific for weight; he had really thought the whole thing through." Just before departure time, his friend had a serious car accident and couldn't go, but that didn't deter Bob. He would go on his own.

Trusting her son, Ann didn't interfere with his plans in any way. He was to leave for his year-long excursion the day after the rest of the family had gone to their lake cottage for a brief visit. The family said goodbye to Bob at dawn that late-August morning on the porch of their house in Baltimore.

"It was a tearful farewell," Ann recalls. "Bob was crying. He really loved his family, and it was an emotional thing. It was a big, first departure, breaking away." Though she didn't realize it at the time, it was the last time she was to see "the old Bob."

A MOTHER'S FEELINGS

Ann wanted Bob to be independent and happy in his own purposes. She would not have held him back for anything. Nevertheless, as she lay on the raft in the sun at the lake, watching her younger children cavort in the water, she could not rid herself of a sense of disaster that was totally out of line both with her sunny disposition and with her cheerful expectations for Bob's upcoming trip. She had the bleak feeling that something had already gone horribly wrong. "I felt the way I feel after a death, when something is gone and you can't get it back."

After supper that night, sitting out on the porch of their cottage in the cool lake breeze, Ann felt her heart grow heavy with fear and dread. As the night grew late and one by one the lights in the cabins around them winked out, the darkness in her mind grew. At last she could no longer keep her feelings to herself. She told her friend and lake neighbor Kathleen Murray how anxious she felt for her nine-teen-year-old son.

Kathy said, "He doesn't leave until tomorrow morning, Ann. Call him up and tell him not to go."

"Oh, sure," Ann said. "What am I supposed to say?" She parodied the imaginary conversation. " 'Oh, Bob, you know that trip you've been planning for a year? Well, I have a terrible feeling about it. Don't go.' 'Okay, Mom, anything you say.'

"You know, how can you tell a kid not to go?" Kathy laughed, and after a minute Ann chuckled too. But her "tremendous feeling of loss" continued. "I just couldn't get over it."

The Rourkes were at the lake for a week. When they came home, Bob was gone, but Ann could not shake her fears for him. One morning she came downstairs and said to her son Martin, Bob's senior by two years, "Martin, I had a horrible dream last night. I dreamed Bob joined the Moonies."

Martin and Bob were very close, "both very liberal and going to save the world and the poor." But Martin was a smart-aleck twenty: "He had the answers to the world, and mothers were just to be tolerated, you know."

He looked at Ann condescendingly when she told him her dream and said, "You can worry about a lot of things, Mother, but"—"I can just see him and hear him to this day," Ann says—"that isn't one of them."

Ann tried to put the dream out of her mind.

But, she later learned, her dream was uncannily accurate. Even as Martin was scoffing at her fears, his younger brother was neatly rolling up his sleeping bag in a Moonie house several hundred miles away and preparing to go downstairs for the first "lecture" of the day.

FROM ONE "FAMILY" TO ANOTHER

As Ann pieced the story together later, on his travels Bob had gotten as far as Boston. He was wandering around the Boston Common alone, seeing what he could see, feeling light and happy on his own and, at the same time, a little at loose ends. When a young man came up to him, "just real friendly and smiley and nice," struck up a conversation about biking, and then invited him home to dinner with "the family," Bob accepted gratefully. Life was as exciting as he'd hoped it might be! He followed the young man across the street to a big old five-story house on Beacon Hill, where a lot of other "smiley, happy" young people were waiting.

"It really wasn't Bob's fault," Ann says. "He was definitely trapped. From that evening, he was never on his own again."

Ann attributes Bob's spiritual seduction by the Unification Church to some of the virtues he'd acquired in the bosom of his biological family: his religious training, the idealism which his mother had encouraged, above all the innate innocence which was a product of his middle-class upbringing. Some 80 percent of Moon's American converts are either Catholic or Jewish, she says, and Bob was a perfect target for the Moonies. "They go after kids that have been educated, mostly upper-middle-class. They want kids that make good appearances. Basically, they come from families that have had some kind of a religious background that maybe they're not quite satisfied with. They're idealistic, and a lot of them are not streetwise."

A poor ghetto kid, she reasons, might be suspicious when invited to dinner with "the family." "He'd ask, 'What do you want?'" Streetwise kids learn that they have to pay somehow for what they get. Not Bob. "Not a suspicious bone in his body," his mother sighs, "just 'Aren't they wonderful people? They're having me to dinner and they really love me.'"

Ann blames herself now for not having prepared Bob better for the world. "If there's anything I'd do differently now, it's to prepare him for what's really out there." In her own naiveté, she just never thought that a cult could be a problem.

But she thinks that by and large she was a good mother, fostering solid values and independence in her children. "I think I'm liberal, but I don't like to see destructive rebellion and flouting of all the rules. . . . I believe in working within the system to change the system." Describing herself as independent, she recalls that quality in "the old Bob" too. "I think that both of us were very independent. He certainly was independent in his thoughts and ideas. I didn't see any dependency. I saw enjoyment in being able to share. I've always encouraged independence in each of the kids, and I've liked it in myself." The Moonies, on the other hand, work to create neurotic dependence in their followers.

At that first dinner, Bob's new friends learned he didn't have a place to stay in Boston. They invited him to leave with them later that night for a three-day "retreat" at their farm in the country. Bob thought he had found exactly the kind of people he had been looking for, spiritual people who could help him discover the secret to a good life. Excitedly he called home to tell his own family about it.

For Ann, already in shock from the feelings which warned her that Bob was in danger, that phone call was a nightmare, the incarnation of the dream Martin had scoffed at. "Bob was already beginning to sound strange. I knew that he was scared. I said, 'Bob, they're not Moonies, are they? You're not with Moonies!' And he said, 'Nooo!'

"And then finally he admitted they were. 'Well, they're Moonies, I guess.' He had to acknowledge that they were Moonies, but he had no idea what Moonies were.

"And I can remember just total panic, and I just was telling him to get out of there, to get away from 'em, walk away. I hadn't done any study, but I just had a really strong reaction. 'Get the heck out of there!' "

Since that awful moment, Ann has made herself something of an expert on Moonie tactics. Vividly, she empathizes with her son as she describes the way the Moonies brainwashed the idealistic boy in the house on Beacon Hill and during the three-day retreat at the farm.

Once Bob accepted the invitation from the nice young man "to come to dinner and meet the family"—"Bob, I'm sure, thought he was going to meet *his* family"—the first step was a process known as "love-bombing." "Everybody just thinks you're terrific and wants to know all about you and is so interested in [whatever you're interested in]. Of course, they originally snared him with the great interest they all had in bicycle trips. They'll say anything you want. You really get a feeling of love."

The next step is a lecture. "You're bombarded with this folderol that you can't make heads nor tails of. I've sat through these lectures; I *know*. You can't really follow the person, where he's going; all you know is that he's going to give you an ideal world, and if you move now, you can be part of it. And, of course, from that evening, Bob was ensnared."

Ann sees her son as a victim, similar to a prisoner of the Vietcong, at the mercy of mind manipulators. "They take you out to this farm, that's the next thing, and they keep you up nights. They allow you very little sleep, two or three hours in a weekend, in a bedroll with about twenty other people sleeping near you, or right on top of you practically, so that you never get a good night's rest."

The Moonies also attacked through junk food. Bob was a health-food addict who had tried to rid his system of sugars and caffeine, so he was extremely vulnerable. "The last thing you have at night is cocoa and brownies. They really plan this out, you know. When you do go to sleep, it's a very fitful sleep because of all the caffeine. Then at four or five in the morning, it's 'Rise and shine, there's so much to do, it's a wonderful day,' and they get him out on the field for these wild physical things, the constant, constant, constant, constant motion.

"And they're brought in for another lecture, and they're lectured all day, with breaks for these wild games, and a planned junk snack. So that when they're listening to the lectures, they just can't even put up any resistance. They may even be saying no and avoiding the subject or not wanting to make decisions, but they're just pounded and pounded until their defenses are down, till they don't even know what they're doing."

Meanwhile, back in Baltimore, Ann too was completely traumatized, "just overcome with fear." Like her son, she was suffering from sleeplessness. "In the beginning," she remembers, "I slept not at all. My nights were filled with terror. I was taking aspirin, all the bufferins, Sominex, everything, and really, it was just impossible. It was a hellish time, to get up and wander and do something, try to psych myself into sleep. But these problems would butt in and I couldn't do anything. I would fall asleep perhaps about four in the morning."

To her horror, Ann, a devout cradle Catholic, discovered that she couldn't really pray for Bob. When she tried, all she could do was to repeat the "Our Father" and the "Hail Mary" and other prayers of her childhood. If she tried a more personal supplication, she would find herself "shaking a fist at the Lord and saying, 'What are you doing? What is going on? I can't stand this,' really taking it out on him, you know."

Fortunately, Tom Rourke, Bob's father, normally a cheerful, hearty businessman, was as horrified with what had happened to Bob as Ann was. But the children had always been chiefly Ann's concern, and this situation was no exception. "Tom just gave me the green light," Ann says. " 'Go ahead and do what you have to do; you figure it out and we'll do it.' "

She looks grim as she remembers her state of mind during those early weeks. "If Tom had not supported me, I can't imagine how I would have felt—probably that he didn't love his child as much as I did, and therefore I would have to act on my own. I mean, thoughts go through your mind like 'If I have to leave him, I will.' " During the long dark nights in which she lay awake, angry and terrified, in spite of Tom's concerned support Ann was lonelier than she had ever been in her life. "I felt it was all up to me."

One sleepless night, when Tom was working late and the children were in bed, Ann was doing laundry in the basement when the phone rang. Amanda Ellard, a woman from her church, was calling. Amanda's son had been taken in by the Moonies, and had subsequently been kidnapped and deprogrammed by the Ellard family. One of Bob's friends had asked her to help Ann. Amanda wanted to be sure Ann understood what the Rourkes were up against.

"You've got to act *now,*" she told Ann, "this minute. You've got to learn everything you can right this instant. I'm coming over to bring you some literature, and I want you to read it right now."

"And she came," Ann says. "And it was dark, and we were sitting down in that dismal basement, and she was telling me how horrid this was, and what a dangerous situation Bob was in, and we must do something immediately. It was so frightening, I just wanted to do what I had to do—lay down my life, sell the house to get the money. I've got to get my kid out of there, you know, and whatever I have to do I'll do, *anything.*"

THE COILS OF THE MONSTER

Ann began reading everything she could get her hands on about the membership and power of cults in general and of the Unification Church in particular. Reverend Moon's was no penny-ante operation in 1979, and is richer and more powerful today. The Unification Church claims to have thirty-seven thousand members in the United States, and the United States government has estimated its real estate holdings to be worth more than two hundred million dollars. Bob was in the hands of a leviathan. Ann decided she wanted to see the monster in action for herself.

In October, a month after Bob had gone to live with the Moonies in Boston, Ann went to Boston also. She told Bob she was coming on business for the American Association of University Women, but she really planned to talk to some former Moonies in Cambridge who could help her make a plan for Bob's release.

Bob invited her to come out to the Moonie house for dinner, and she agreed. Quite by accident, however, as she was on the way to one of her own meetings she ran into her son on the Boston Common.

> I was going down into the subway when I heard "Mother!" And I turned around and there was Bob, and I nearly died. He was there with three other Moonies. They were wandering through the streets trying to raise funds. . . .
> Suddenly there he was, with his hair cut off, right to the roots, and he had two black eyes, which didn't help.

Seeing the black eyes made Ann feel sick and frightened. Bob tried to allay her fears, telling her he got the black eyes in a particularly lively volleyball game at the Moonie farm. Ann was doubtful. She suspected that he was lying to protect her feelings. Later Bob confided to his brother Martin that he had been beaten up in a slum area where he'd been sent to solicit money.

"But he was so happy to see me," she says. "I could read it in his face, 'Oh, my God, Mom! Mom!' " Ann thinks now that she should have taken advantage of the chance that Bob's delight in seeing a member of his family gave her. She likes to believe that, if she had it to do over, she would talk to her son forthrightly and passionately, and trust her own abilities to persuade him to leave. "Now," she says, "I know I could do that."

It may not have worked. The Moonies, Ann explains, try to set up doubts about the converts' families by bringing out family problems and by disputing all parental authority. "It's them on the inside and us on the outside, even their parents. Their parents are only their physical parents, but Moon and his wife are their spiritual parents." The natural parents are seen as agents of evil, "and if we do anything to try and get them out of there, we are working for Satan." There is also the fear of retribution against members of the family, Ann says. "If you leave the cult, your family will die, your brothers will die."

She pauses a moment, thinking how to be fair. "And besides that, you know, they may *buy* it. They become—Bob still, to this day, is in definite psychological bonds, chains."

Seeing the invisible chains on her once independent son convinced Ann that she must carry out the plan she had already embarked on of contacting the ex-Moonies in the Boston area. At their advice, she was deceiving Bob, distrusting his ability to resist the Moonie propaganda, making plans to get him out without his knowledge or cooperation.

She was also, she says, making rash decisions which came out of her fear and shock. "I was just using such bad judgment," she says, "turning myself over to others, and saying, 'What should I do?' And [they all said] this was the best thing, to pretend like you support him, and that you're going to let him do his own thing, and just deceive him. Then he'll keep in contact with me and I'll know where he is so we can go get him."

Ann spent the next two days with Bob and his cult members. She tried to pay attention to what was really going on in this strange life her lively, intelligent son had fallen into. She went out to the farm, attended a whole day of lectures, sang the songs, played the games. "I saw their whole operation and how they do it. It's just absolutely incredible."

But she was very conscious the entire weekend of the ambiguity of her position. To deceive Bob, she was pretending to be sympathetic to thinking and attitudes that in truth made her feel almost physically ill. At one point one of the Moonie leaders put his arm around Ann and told her he was glad to see her having such a wonderful time. "We'd love to have you join us for good," he said, looking at her earnestly.

"But I have a husband and six other children," Ann responded. He waved his arms expansively. "They can all come!"

Remembering this, Ann laughs till tears come in her eyes at the thought of the whole Rourke family turning into Moonies. "That just cracked me up. I did try subtly to point out to Bob some of the ridiculous things they were saying." Bob's unwillingness to listen convinced her that the kidnapping advocates were right. She went back to Baltimore to make plans to kidnap her own son.

The first delegate she selected was his brother Martin. If she couldn't influence Bob to see that he had become a pawn of the Moonies, perhaps Martin, to whom he was so close intellectually, would have better luck. Martin might even be able to persuade him to leave the cult voluntarily in order to regain his intellectual freedom. Dreaming of the two boys suddenly appearing together on the Rourke doorstep, Ann and Tom sent Martin to get Bob and to bring him back home. Martin left college for a weekend in late October and went to "visit" his brother.

Sunday night he called home to reassure his parents. "Mother," he said, "you have absolutely nothing to worry about. He's with a group of good Christian people. In fact, I've promised to go back at Christmas, when the semester is over, and do a week's workshop with him."

Ann shudders in horror at the chance she took with Martin. Instead of Martin's counteracting the Moonie influence, he had been indoctrinated by them just as Bob had. "That plays right into their hands, because they get older brothers and other family members that way." Nor did Martin change his mind; at Christmas he came home, ready to go back to Boston for a weeklong retreat.

"Don't go, don't you dare go," his mother implored. "You won't come out." Belligerently, Martin insisted that he was indeed going to go back. "That was the worst Christmas of my life," Ann says. Desperately she gave Martin reading material and pleaded with him not to go. He was sulky and surly, but, for some reason—she still doesn't know why—he didn't.

Ann's next step, which she now considers the single biggest mistake she made, was to hire an organization called Freedom of Mind to kidnap Bob. She had learned about Freedom of Mind from a support group she had been attending for the parents of cult members. With her predilection for "working within the system," she liked what she considered the careful legality of the way they operated. Before they would move in to abduct a cult member who had reached legal majority, Freedom of Mind insisted that the parents go to court and have themselves declared the legal guardians because their child was *non compos mentis*. Then, with a court order in hand, Freedom of Mind was ready to move.

Ready, that is, if they had been paid. Before anything, however, they had to have their money—fifteen thousand dollars in advance. With seven children to raise and educate, the Rourkes didn't have that kind of money lying around. They did what thousands of other families have done in similar circumstances: they borrowed.

Needless to say, all these arrangements had to be carried out in absolute secrecy, so that no hint of danger from his family would get back to Bob himself. Ann had to deceive her children about what was happening. "The kids were so upset about Bob, and always trying to talk to him. He was calling home frequently, because I think from the start he was screaming to get out of there, but he didn't know how. They were angry because [as far as they could tell] we weren't doing anything. Here were their parents just sitting on their hands."

Martin especially could not figure out why his mother was so concerned to keep him from returning to the Moonie retreat in Boston as he had promised, but at the same time didn't seem to be doing anything to get Bob home. "That was the most stressful time in my life," Ann says. "I couldn't undergo any more stress, no matter what the circumstances were, it was as awful as that."

If Ann faults herself for being too slow at the beginning, now she thinks she was moving too quickly, too rashly. Freedom of Mind urged haste: "Time is of the essence. You've got to move." "So we couldn't sit back and talk to a bunch of people, or ask, 'What do you think about this?' We had to *go.*"

In the rush and confusion, Ann didn't realize that the court order wasn't worth much. Some states recognize them, others don't, and the Moonies are smart enough never to leave new recruits in one state for any length of time. Without a valid court order, Ann herself and her agents could be arrested for what they were about to do.

"I WANT TO GO TO JAIL"

At first Ann didn't understand how subtle and powerful Bob's bondage was. She thought that if she could free her son physically, she could also free him psychologically. But freedom of body doesn't mean freedom of mind, and in fact the whole Freedom of Mind experience became a black joke for the Rourkes before it was over.

The court order was good in Boston, but just before the Freedom of Mind "thugs," as Ann calls them, went into action, Bob called home, in the middle of the night as usual. He was at an airport, about to take off for Utah, where he was going to be for a while. "So we thought, 'Well, what are the laws in Utah?' And we started the whole process again, and pretty soon he was in Kansas City, and he was in Denver, never for long in any of these places. Finally he got to Portland, and he was going to be there for a while, he thought. They never knew for sure, but he might."

So the Rourkes' kidnap maneuver would be executed in Portland, which involved an additional three thousand dollars or so in plane fare, hotels, and surveillance for the Freedom of Mind operation. A Sunday near the end of January was set as Emancipation Day. Tom went to Portland on Saturday morning, but to allay Bob's suspicion Ann waited behind in Baltimore for the usual Saturday-night phone call. Yes, Bob told his mother when he called, the Moonies were in retreat, but they would be back in Portland Sunday night. Sunday morning she flew to Portland to meet Tom and the Freedom of Mind group.

She wasn't really thinking rationally. "I was just absolutely so scared that I went in disguise," Ann laughs. "I wore a huge hat with a big brim down over my face all the time, and I insisted Tom wear the hood on his jacket up."

"You know," she continues, "I was just doing what I was told. I was so terrified. We were making bad judgments. . . . And it was just incredible how everything worked against us."

They had no trouble in finding the Moonie headquarters. "We had the place staked out, I had the address, I even had the phone number, but they didn't come back. They didn't come back all night. . . . At three or four in the morning, the Freedom guys said, 'Well, I guess they're not coming. There's not a sign of life.' "

For the next three nights, they did the stakeout, and the Moonie group still didn't return. With the expenses, this fruitless vigil was costing the Rourkes a thousand dollars a day. "Freedom of Mind kept saying, 'We might as well leave, and then we'll come back.' Come back? And fly everybody out at four hundred dollars each?" Soon, however, the Rourkes saw there was no point in keeping Freedom of Mind around. They dismissed their three kidnappers, and Tom went back to Baltimore.

Ann stayed. "I said, 'I'm not going home. I'm just so near. I'm not going to let go.' I should have, as it turned out."

Through contacts in her support group in Baltimore, she linked up with parents of ex-Moonies who volunteered to help her. She hired a van, in which she and her new group drove from shopping center to shopping center to look for Moonies. She also hired a private detective with a truck, and the truck and the van drove around for four days searching, communicating with each other through their CBs.

Ann describes herself as "mentally paralyzed" during that whole difficult week, with only a saving sense of humor to keep her sane. "The situation was so ridiculous. We were sitting at the hotel the next Saturday afternoon"—by now they had been on the mission a week—"waiting for Tom to call after he had received Bob's weekly call. Nobody was to touch the phone. And the phone rang, and I went straight up in the air, and I ran and fell down. I was flat out." She laughs at the recollection. "I did sprain a toe. I could hardly move, and it was my husband, and Bob was going to be back that night."

They hid in front of the Moonie house and waited all night. Nothing. They staked out the house again the following night. Nothing. Then Bob called his father in Baltimore again and said they were in Salem, but they were going back to Portland for one night, then on to Seattle. Ann knew it *had* to be that Monday night. She and her troops drove around Salem looking for the Moonie group, then came back to Portland.

Desperately, Ann decided to phone the Moonie house, pretending to be in Baltimore. "I called from the roadside, the number that I had, and said, 'Dad says you're going to move,' so I verified that he was in the house."

At last the Moonies appeared, Ann says. "I was with this huge guy, one of the parents, and the Moonies started to come out. I was supposed to be standing in front of the place with my arms around this guy, like we were lovers. . . . And Bob walked right by me [without seeing me]."

"There he is," Ann whispered. Ann's group grabbed Bob and stuck him in the back of the van. "He immediately started screaming his head off . . . and all the Moonies in the place came out, twenty-eight in all."

Ann's small group of five was outnumbered more than five to one. "That was where we were really stupid. I don't know why I let them talk me into it."

With strong feelings on both sides, an impassioned fracas ensued. "There was beating, there was hitting, there was throwing." Trying to free Bob, Ann's group struck symbolic blows for the freedom of their own children from this cult from which they as parents had suffered so much. The Moonies, who might, ironically, have been those children, saw the parents as allies of Satan. In resisting, "they're fighting Satan," as Ann puts it. "They think if they are captured, they are going to be lost forever."

In the confusion, Bob escaped without ever realizing his mother was on the scene. As the melee subsided, Ann climbed into the van to confront her captive son.

> I started screaming, "Where is he? Where is he?" And the van owner said, "Shut up! Don't you hear those sirens? They've called the police."
>
> And I said, "But where is Bob?" and he said, "Will you be quiet? They're going to come and throw us in jail!"
>
> "WHERE IS MY SON?" I said. And he said, "We've got to get out of here!"

"I'm not leaving," Ann said. "Let me out of this van. I'm going back in there."

"Something just exploded," she explains. "I was going to go right in and say, 'Damn it, come home.' I'd had enough.

"So [the group] said, 'Well, by damn, if you're going to do it, we're going to do it.' So back we all went." They pushed open the front door of the Moonie house and walked in.

When I walked in, Bob was totally stunned. He thought he had just talked to me in Baltimore. He said, "Mother, I was just saying this morning how great my family was, that they supported me."

And I said, "Bob, this is how much I want to get you out of here." I could hardly talk. I was drained.

Things looked bad. Police were everywhere. Ann's court order, invalid in Oregon, meant nothing to them. "This state trooper treated me like the scum of the earth," Ann says. "He had pointed black patent-leather shoes, and slicked-back hair, a nasty little person with authority."

Law-abiding Ann, who wanted to work within the system, remained consistent. If she was outside the law, she was ready to pay the penalty. With fire in her eyes, she faced the trooper. "Arrest me," she said defiantly. "I want you to arrest me. I want to go to jail. And put my son in a jail cell next to me. I'd rather see him in court than not see him at all."

Ann did not get her wish. Though the Moonies threatened to press charges, they never did. Ann thinks Bob wouldn't go for it: "There was that much of him left at the time. I know he would not let them sue his parents."

"LETTING GO"

"When I came back home from the failed kidnap attempt," Ann remembers, "it was like a death. It was just wipeout." She didn't know if she would ever hear from Bob again, but "I was beyond thinking about it. I was even beyond being able to react to friends' sympathy."

She smiles reflectively. "You know what I did? I made an appointment and had a massage and a facial. It became absolutely essential to me to do that. I mean, I had to be good to this body. I had to make some kind of truce with this tired body."

Another kind of truce was in order also. When Ann's birthday rolled around in February, she got her birthday call from Bob as usual. "He wanted me to know he still loved me and knew I still loved him and all of that."

The kidnap attempt had impressed Bob after all. In the early spring, Bob got disgusted with his life with the Moonies, and just walked out. He started across country toward Baltimore, penniless and on foot. But after six or seven months under Moonie control, he couldn't survive on his own. He got as far as Montana and broke down and called his "spiritual father." The Moonies picked him up, took him back to Boston, and reprogrammed him.

He has since tried several other times to come home "legally" by getting permission from his "spiritual leaders" to visit his family. Ann learned just how strong a hold the cult had gained over her son on one such occasion, in October of 1981, when he wanted to come for his brother's wedding. From Bob's comments to her, she describes the way the scenario went:

> He went back to his leaders and said, "I'm going home for my brother's wedding." . . . And they tell him, "Bob, it's your decision. If you want to go home, fine; it's up to you."
>
> So then he works out all the plans from his end, and he believes them, and then he goes back and says, "I'm going home on such and such a date."
>
> "Well, that's fine, but you know there's so much going on here, Bob, and we did have plans for you, and you know it is really going to put a crimp in our plans, and it isn't going to be very pleasing to the Father." The Father is Moon.

Instead, Bob was sent to Korea. The week that his brother was marrying the girl of his choice in their church in Baltimore, Bob too took a bride. In a mammoth ceremony for six thousand couples, he was married, at the age of twenty-one, to a Japanese woman whom he had never met before. "He had no idea he was going to be part of that group," Ann says, "because we talked about it. [When he asked to come home], they thought, 'We've heard that old thing before, off to Korea with you, and we'll marry *you*.' "

The Moon leaders had told Bob to expect his parents to be dismayed that he was marrying an Oriental. In this way, they set him up to disdain any protest from his family as "racism"—"I mean, 'That's how narrow your parents are,' " Ann says sarcastically, presenting their argument. "I think he wanted this blowup about the race, so that he could say, 'Yeah, they were right.' "

He called from Korea well after midnight on the eve of the multiple marriage, and asked to speak to his father, who could probably be counted on to be more incendiary than Ann. But Tom was recovering from surgery, so Ann refused to wake him. Reluctantly Bob agreed to talk to his mother. "He told me he was going to be married to a wonderful girl, and he repeated in a very dull voice, 'I've never been so happy in my life,' three times."

"When did you meet her?" Ann asked.

"This morning."

Ann was too stunned to respond much at all.

Two days later Bob called again, asking to speak to Martin. Again Ann intercepted the call, and this time she managed to make her argument to her son. "I was strong. It was daylight. When I get these calls at night—and all the bad news with Bob is always at night —I am so drained before I even start. So I was glad to have that opportunity in the daylight and really let him know how I felt."

Bob began with the question of "racism": He said very proudly, "I got to choose the race I would marry. How did Dad react to the fact that she was Japanese?"

"So I really set him straight," Ann says. "I said that we would accept anyone of any race if we knew she was his choice and not someone he was told to marry. And I said, 'Bob, you know, you tell me that you're totally in love with someone who's totally wonderful —and you hadn't known her for even twelve hours! That's not even possible.'

"And when I was coming back like this, he could hardly say anything. A few times he tried to get authoritative and nasty, threatening to hang up, but I wasn't afraid. I think maybe that was the first time I let go. I really am letting go."

She has seen Bob only once since the kidnapping attempt, when she traveled to a Moonie complex in Washington for a visit. Bob calls on birthdays, and keeps in touch with his brothers, especially Martin.

Oddly enough, it encourages Ann that he has to keep going to Moonie seminars. "That only happens to those that they have to *keep* brainwashing," she explains, remembering Bob's stubborn character. She hopes that means there's enough of "the old Bob" left to free himself one day.

But she's not terribly optimistic, because she sees an ongoing deterioration in her son.

"He doesn't know what he's doing. I cannot believe, when I ask him what he's doing, how little he knows about it. He'll start out with 'We raise money for drug addiction centers and helping the poor,' and then I'll say, 'What centers have you helped? Have you seen any of them? How do you know how the money is being spent? All you know is, you bring it in and it goes someplace. Show me.' "

The old Bob, Ann knows, would have risen to the challenge, but the new Bob can't. "He gets very uncomfortable with that.

"It's the same thing when I ask him to tell me about the Divine Principle, which is what they believe everything is. His response is always 'You know, I'd like to have you talk to So-and-So.' " She tosses her head angrily. "I mean, this was a bright kid."

When his brother Martin went out to see him recently, he went armed with some books to discuss. Martin came back and told Ann, "Mother, he can't read!" "Bob was an *avid* reader," Ann remembers, "but he just can't concentrate anymore."

Tears come to her eyes. Recollections of "the old Bob" hurt. "For the last five or six years, I've tried not to think or talk about the way he was. That's when it gets painful."

Ann is teaching herself to "let go"—to let go of her memories, to let go of her son.

"WHOSE CHILDREN ARE THESE?"

What has enabled Ann to learn to let Bob go? First of all, she became increasingly aware that Bob was not her only responsibility. She also had responsibilities to her other children and to her husband. During Bob's first months in the Unification Church, Ann was so desperate to get her son out that in a way the rest of the family got lost in the shuffle. She felt ready to sell the house, give up the car, go into debt, lay everything else in her life on the line.

In this state of desperation, acting out of a mother's loving concern, she lost her sense of priorities. Foolishly she risked one son for another, when she dispatched Martin to save Bob. She was even willing to leave her husband if need be.

"I was so consumed with this," she remembers, "that if one of the children asked me what we were going to have for dinner, I'd get upset [and yell], 'Don't you understand? Bob's in terrible danger.' "

But losing a brother to the Moonies was hard on the Rourke children also. Hardest hit, Ann thinks, was Janie, just younger than Bob. "I think probably of all the kids she's suffered the most, and she's been a long time really dealing with it." Like many younger sisters, Janie adored her big brother. "She trusted him . . . and they were such good friends. She was friends with his friends. And you know, you've been rejected when your brother goes off to a very strange thing." Janie had to have counseling.

The oldest son, Fred, "just blocked it out," Ann thinks. It was Fred's wedding for which Bob planned his aborted trip home. Fred tried to be cool when Bob didn't come after all, but Ann knows his surface poise hides deep feelings. He has told his mother, "I don't think I can handle the emotion."

Hank, the youngest son, who was fourteen when Bob became a Moonie, reacted differently. "If there's anyone who feels shame, it's Hank," his mother says. At his age, he "really feels the embarrassment of having a brother who's a Moonie."

None of her children could afford to lose their mother as well as their brother, a fact Ann was at first reluctant to take into account. "It was practically like somebody had to slap me in the face and bring me back to my senses." The "somebody" was her friend Kathy, who finally exploded to Ann one day, "My God, woman, you've got other children!"

She also had a husband who needed attention. At first Tom supported Ann totally in her efforts to free Bob. Positive, robust, outgoing, he called members of his family and asked for their prayers. He learned all he could about cults. He cooperated with his wife's financial arrangements for their son's liberation.

Confronting a major problem together actually strengthened Ann and Tom's marriage. Although Ann was more active in their efforts to free Bob, Ann says that "it helped enormously that he supported me from the beginning in what I was saying. You know, it was a terrible mistake to go out and spend all that money and go through all of that without reflection, but at that point, if he hadn't agreed and thought it was best to support what I did, it could have been really destructive."

But as the years passed with Bob farther away from the family than ever, Tom Rourke became terribly tired. Social and business drinking had always been a fact of his life, but at some point Ann realized her husband had crossed the fine line that separates the controlled drinker from the problem drinker.

Then he had to have two serious operations. A beneficent effect was that his drinking stopped. But, as surgery took some of his physical vigor, he felt less positive about the possibility of freeing Bob. Worried about his family's financial well-being, he regretted all the money that he and Ann had spent in vain attempts to get Bob home.

Eventually, as Ann puts it, where their Moonie son was concerned Tom "reached a cutoff point." When she offered him a newspaper clipping about Bob's "wedding" with twelve thousand people, Tom pushed it away. "I don't want to look at it," he said.

Worried about her husband, Ann does not insist that Tom be involved in the efforts that she continues. She still does her reading and she still seeks out others who are experienced in dealing with cults. But these days, though she regularly attends meetings of a support group for the families of cult members, she goes alone.

Ann's need to continue to search for solutions, to continue to talk about her son's problems, is more persistent than Tom's. Her powers of psychological endurance amaze her husband. In fact, the mothers in this study almost always had a greater need and ability to talk the problems out than the fathers did. They maintained an open communication with their children in difficult circumstances, and continued to express as well as they could their love, their hopes, and their fears. Many mothers felt, as one of them put it, "If I say it again, I might get it right."

But Ann, recognizing her husband's diminished strength after his illness, has begun protecting Tom from "the new Bob." The last time Bob called, she didn't call Tom to the phone. "I just thought, 'I'm not even going to subject him to it.' There is a limit when you just can't talk about it anymore."

If her responsibility for the other members in her family has helped Ann to restore proportion to her responsibility for Bob, the

renewal of her spiritual faith has helped her even more. Like many
of these mothers, Ann, a strong Catholic, has always had a high
degree of spiritual awareness. Her bad dreams, her powerful sense
of loss, alerted her, at the time Bob joined the cult, to dangers she
could feel but not yet see. She trusted those feelings. "Why am I
given this power," she asked herself, "if I can't do anything with it?"

But she couldn't. She was not able to save her son from the evil
that she knew had befallen him. She grew frantic in her anger with
God. Her prayers accused God of failing her. Then she discovered
she could no longer pray. "When I knelt down to pray, I'd get torn
up and hysterical."

Frustrated, she had reached a spiritual impasse, especially as she
also had a fanatical idea that, as she puts it, "everything depended
on me. It was all up to me."

Finally, just before the trip to Washington when she last saw Bob,
she visited a prayer group at her church. Afterward, she told the
speaker of her difficulty in praying. "I told him that I had to pray,
you know, and then God would help me. I said, 'That's been my
philosophy all my life, that God helps those who help themselves,
and I've got to do everything I can.'

"And he said, 'Nowhere in Scripture does it say that God helps
those who help themselves. What it does say is that God helps those
who ask for his help.'

"I thought, 'What? You mean that it's not up to me?' " A burden
was lifted from Ann's shoulders. "And that was two years ago and
it's been a growing process ever since, leading up to letting go and
trusting that somebody else will take care of this because I can't."

Ann mentions "letting go" frequently, echoing perhaps unconsciously the words of the hymn: "Let go and let God have his
wonderful way." Letting go for Ann does not mean giving up. Ann
has not given up on Bob. "I've never stopped learning, I've never
stopped talking to him, I've never stopped trying to do what's logical."

For Ann, letting go means discarding some of her own useless or
outworn concepts. She has let go of her fears, fears of her own
incompetence, fears of the Moonies. "At this point, I know that I
could walk right in among the biggest group of Moonies and not
have one shred of fear . . . because I know they're not the most
powerful thing on earth." She no longer needs to go to "authori-

ties" like Freedom of Mind to buoy her confidence that she is doing the right thing. Instead she trusts her own judgment. "I don't have to run to somebody like a novice and say, 'What do I do in this situation?'"

Ann has let go of self-protective concealment. She has learned to be open with others about her problems, and "I always feel better. It's very therapeutic to talk something out, even if you don't get a solution" right away. People have a way of remembering and letting her know, she says, "if they come across anything that they think can be helpful." Other seemingly unrelated fears, such as the dreadful fears of old age and death that were beginning to plague Ann, have vanished as well.

She attributes this courage in large part to the prayer group to which she still belongs. "How can I go over and pray and say, 'I want this to happen,' and then live a life of fear?" Even more she credits her fearlessness to the power of God. "It's not a mental decision, not to *seem* to be afraid. It grows in you. I mean, you can't decide you're not going to be afraid. You just become that way as a result of where you've gone through your heart. And that's God."

Ann has not won her battle with the Unification Church. Bob is still a Moonie. His mother, remembering the bright promise he had at nineteen, his eagerness to make a difference in the world, deplores the waste, the outrage of the life he has settled for.

But Ann herself is not a loser. She sees that the "terrible, terrible" suffering she has gone through on Bob's account has brought her "an enormous amount of good." Her marriage has been tested and found solid, and the family is strong. She has gained good friendships and worldly wisdom and spiritual faith.

Nor does Ann think that her child is lost. She realizes that nothing will free Bob as long as the strongest chains are in his own mind, but she recalls the stubborn independence he once had. It may return. She dreams of a day that "he will walk out on his own. And it will be *his* choice."

The action she took for Bob didn't work. But Ann has avoided despair by turning her son over to another force, that source of all good action in the world whom St. Augustine called "the Unmoved Mover." She tells a little story that illustrates how she feels:

I think of a bishop I heard speak one time. . . . He was talking to the group about how, as a young parish priest, he couldn't sleep nights. The people were coming to him all the time with their problems, and he was trying to handle them.

And he said, "One night I was lying there, wide awake. This woman had come to me a couple of hours before with her story. It was a terrible story, and I had to do something.

"And I raised my eyes to heaven, and I said, 'Look, God, whose children are these, your children or my children?

" 'They're your children, you take care of them.' "

And he said, "I went to sleep, and I've been sleeping ever since."

And, you know, I know what he was talking about.

Stage Four

DETACHMENT

Recognizing the limits of responsibility; letting go

8

Detachment for Survival

THINGS DON'T HAVE TO MAKE SENSE

For the most part, the women interviewed in this study began their careers as mothers subscribing to one of the myths of child development described by Jerome Kagan. American parents, Dr. Kagan says, think that with a combination of love and discipline from his parents, a child will grow up to be a happy, independent, productive adult.

According to this view, both parents are important in a child's growth, but especially mothers. Striving American mothers like those presented here tend to follow popular belief in what Kagan calls the "mysterious force" of mother love, the idea that a good, loving mother will ipso facto create a strong, healthy child.

It's easy to see why women in our society find comfort in such simple, democratic, mechanistic, logical views of human growth. If these theories are valid, the world is fair and things make sense. Do your duty as a mother and reap the rewards. In an orderly world in which parents set children once and for all on the right road, in which maternal love guarantees a child's "salvation," to use Kagan's word, goodness would be rewarded and badness punished.

The only trouble is, according to Kagan, that these theories aren't valid. The interviews with these mothers sustained Kagan's objection. The women whose stories are recounted in these pages had learned through experience that the simplistic formulas for child-rearing carry no guarantees.

These were "good" mothers. All of these women insisted, with complete justification, that they loved their children and had done their conscientious, earnest, enlightened best as mothers.

Nor were their children "bad." Not a single one of the women interviewed would admit to having a "bad" child. Many of them considered their children "perfect."

Yet bad things had happened to these good people, things for which the theories didn't allow, things that didn't make sense. Factors other than family life had influenced the children definitively. The world hadn't played fair.

Ann Rourke is a case in point. Ann had reared her son Bob to be compassionate, independent, and productive. At nineteen, he exemplified intellectual, physical, and spiritual virtues. Ann was a good mother and Bob a good child. Yet before he turned twenty, Bob had lost control of his life. Why? And what could be done about it?

Ann did a lot of wheel-spinning as she tried to answer these questions. The only reasonable answer to the "why" seemed to be the answer mothers sometimes give their children: Who ever said that the world is fair? Things just happen. What makes sense is that things don't make sense.

As for seeing to it that Bob regain control of his life, at length Ann realized she couldn't do it. It wasn't her life; it was Bob's life. It was up to Bob to handle it. She had to cultivate the art of detachment.

Detachment, the fourth stage in the process a mother goes through in coping with a child's untraditional behavior, begins when a woman recognizes that *her child is not herself.* She is responsible for herself, but her responsibility for another person has recognizable limits. Her child behaves in ways that the mother can never entirely predict, for reasons that she can never entirely comprehend. The child is a separate person, answerable to the laws of his own nature. As a mother, she can neither control nor make sense of the vagaries of her child's life. "It's not all up to me," Ann Rourke put it. "They're God's children too."

At the stage of detachment, a mother recognizes that she has gone as far as she can in understanding her child and helping him to find resources for his own development. She acknowledges the limits of her responsibility for the child.

Clearly some parents must always bear more responsibility than others. Ruthanne Mowbray, for example, has learned from doctors that her daughter Beth, who suffers from serious mental illness, will always be her charge. Beth can enjoy some independence—she has a home of her own near her parents—but she will probably never be competent to take complete care of herself. The other Mowbray children have promised to care for Beth after the death of Ruthanne and her husband. Family responsibility for Beth will end only with Beth's death. A mother in Ruthanne's situation must struggle to find emotional detachment rather than physical or financial detachment. She must carve out areas of her life that are personally satisfying to her and that have nothing to do with her child. The satisfactions thus gained will give her strength in her life with the child.

Other mothers can aspire to physical, financial, and emotional detachment. Ideally, the mother and the child's father will agree about the treatment of the child. If they can't agree entirely, they work out a more or less satisfactory compromise. Then, lovingly but firmly, the mother frees her child from her definition of his life. She turns his life over to him to do with as he will.

Some of her old certainties about the world itself may vanish at the same time. These outmoded ideas are replaced, in the mother who copes best, with new skills in living: a willingness to entertain contradictions; an ability to tolerate disorder; an appreciation for the pleasures of the present; an optimism about life even though she admits she can't always make sense of it.

At her highest, such a woman comes to give the world the same loving detachment she has learned to give her child. She cannot know the meaning of it. She cannot impose her sense of order on it. She can only concentrate on living well in it, facing with equanimity the inconsistencies, paradoxes, and ambiguities of child-rearing and of life.

She lets go. Letting go involves taking risks, just as helping a child does. A mother who will lay her marriage and her life on the line for her child's sake will eventually take the risk of granting the child responsibility for his own life. Hard as it is, this detachment is essential for two reasons: the mother's emotional survival and the child's mature independence. In the remainder of this chapter, various women show through their stories the impact that detachment has on their emotional health. Chapter 9 contains the experiences of mothers who used detachment as a strategy to help their children reach mature responsibility for their own lives.

"MY LITTLE HAND"

Women can unconsciously exploit "mother love," relying on the company of their children to fortify themselves against life. When her family was young, Bonnie Scott had a bout with agoraphobia, the exotic and crippling fear of open spaces that sometimes afflicts women who then feel compelled to cloister themselves in the security of their homes. "It was really a full-blown case," Bonnie says, as she recalls the pounding of her heart, the dryness of her mouth during a typical attack. "Your eyes cross, your legs wobble, and all you can think is, 'I've got to get out of here. Where's the door, where's the door?' "

At first she couldn't bear to leave the house without her husband in attendance, and he had to go with her to the grocery and on her other errands. "I couldn't stand to go out and about alone." As she got better, Bonnie found she could function when she had one of her children along, particularly her daughter Joan. The time came, however, for Joan to go to school. "I thought, 'There goes my little hand.' She was like my crutch to go out shopping and everything. Now she was going to go to first grade and I was alone. How would I ever shop again? So that's the first time I got help."

Nothing is more beautiful to Western eyes than the sight of a loving mother and child. We pay reverence to it in religion, art, and literature. We smile with approval at the sight of a Bonnie and Joan walking hand in hand through the shopping mall. We assume that the mother is directing and protecting the child. Few of us would realize, as Bonnie herself did, the extent to which the mother may be sheltering herself from a demanding adult world behind the form of a little girl.

Bonnie and Joan developed a symbiotic relationship, a close association in which each partner satisfies the needs of the other. Symbiosis can be healthy or unhealthy. Her dependence on Joan was, Bonnie came to see, unhealthy. It kept her from correcting her inadequacy for independent adult life. The "little hand" became an extension of Bonnie's own personality. Bonnie was incomplete without Joan, and Joan was shackled by her mother's needs. For her own survival, as well as for the child's sake, Bonnie had to let Joan go.

Many mothers are tempted into symbiosis with their children. After all, in the womb the child is an extension of the mother. But the most loving mother must eventually detach herself, at first physically and then psychologically, from her child in order to see the world—and the child—through adult eyes. Without detachment, a mother relinquishes her adulthood and can develop, detrimentally, a child's-eye view of events. Instead of providing her child with adult perceptions and a model of mature independence, she follows her child's lead.

A mother who lacks her own point of view deprives her child of a valuable counter-perspective to his own that he needs to grow up. Betty Carver, for example, has adopted many of the attitudes of her children as if they were her own. Disappointed in her relationship with her husband, with whom for years she has had, she says, "no communication," she got caught in the cross fire between him and their three children. "I felt that I was a football. I was knocked back and forth between my husband and the kids, always."

Eventually her sympathies lay closer to the children than to her conservative husband. She didn't mind when her boys let their hair grow, started a rock band, and dressed the part. She admired their ability to make money with their music, and wasn't much worried about the drugs readily available in the milieu. When they became vegetarians, she bought protein powder for them to be sure they didn't suffer nutritionally. Her role as a mother was support, not leadership. She saw them as pioneers. "It was unconventional behavior," she says, "especially then, but I think in their own minds, they always had it together."

Most important, when two of her children joined off-center religious groups, Betty refused to label the groups as cults, though they had the earmarks of cults, or to see them as threatening. She herself took up the study of the occult. Today lectures, courses, and faith groups in parapsychology and reincarnation are her central spiritual interest, to which she freely acknowledges her children "led her." Although she also continues to go to Methodist church services with her husband, she dissociates herself from him in matters of faith. With apparent pride she allies herself instead with her children. "There's a kind of network out there of people who meditate and who believe in the fringe of things. . . .

"My children believe all of this, and so it's three of them and me against my husband, who doesn't believe this."

With her open-minded interest in the ideas of her children, Betty has been an easy convert. In fact, she has consistently taken her children's views as her own. She doesn't represent an alternative perspective on issues, and her husband's position in the family is weakened. But Betty's family has been lucky; none of her children's actions has led to tragic consequences.

Other families with such a pattern have not been so fortunate, especially in an earlier decade, when parents and society were less capable of seeing and responding to the symptoms of serious problems. A mother who through ignorance or denial is insufficiently objective may have to cope with her child's permanent disability or death.

When young Paul Morrison experimented with drugs in the sixties, his mother Margot did the best she could for him with the information available to her at the time. Still, trying to understand what was going on with the boy, she might have identified too closely with him. She blamed the men in his family, the Vietnam War, his role as the youngest child, everyone and everything but Paul himself.

As time passed, Margot learned that Paul was heavily addicted. She was frightened. As she recognized his passivity and dependence, she had a recurrent nightmare. Night after night in dreams, "I would be hunting for Paul, looking for Paul, trying to find Paul." Paul was always missing, and it was her responsibility to find him and protect him.

Even after Paul died at the age of nineteen of a drug overdose, Margot continued to feel protective of her son. Taking a less than objective view of the events leading up to Paul's death, she describes Paul himself as a victim, nearly blameless. "He went out and made contact with these guys. They somehow talked him into it, and they went to a house on Record Street. Then they gave him an overdose and never took him to the hospital. . . . He was murdered."

In her version, Margot overlooks Paul's habitual drug use, his search for drugs, his responsibility for knowing and controlling what he put into his body. Instead she pins the blame on the young men, themselves addicts, who were with him when he died. She makes the kinds of excuses for Paul, in fact, that an irresponsible boy might make for himself.

Such unrealistic partisanship with a child can make a mother's independent emotional survival uncertain. After Paul's death, Margot had the strength that her husband lacked to go to the morgue to identify her son's body. When she came home, however, she fell apart. She dealt with her devastation by trying to forget she had ever had a son. "I destroyed, threw away, or hid all his pictures. Anytime his name was brought up, I must have looked absolutely stricken, because it was immediately dropped. *For eight years* I was not able to talk about him. I literally tried to block him out for eight years."

Most parents of suicides recover slowly, like Margot in seven or eight years. Recovery for her began with the realization that she was angry with Paul. She felt that by dying he had rejected her, after all her efforts to take care of him. She had desperately tried to please him, to make him happy. Her whole life, she saw during her soul-searching, had been devoted to pleasing others—her mother, her father, her husband, her children. She had never really developed her own point of view toward life.

After an eight-year hiatus in the process of coping with her child's drug addiction and death, Margot finally moved into the stage of detachment. As she slowly, very slowly, detached herself from a feeling of total responsibility for Paul, she became able to face Paul's death as the consummation of his life, not of hers. She decided she really only had to please one person—herself. "I thought, 'Gee, Margot, you know, you really can't please Paul Sr., you certainly can't please Paul Jr., you'd better forget about trying to please all these people, because you can't do it. You'd better start taking care of yourself."

Margot had always loved music and had played the cello in her college orchestra. As part of her emotional recovery, she got out her cello, took some brush-up lessons, and practiced for hours. She went on to join a chamber group, with whom she still plays. Making harmonious sounds is one way for her of "taking care of herself."

PULLING THE STINGER OUT

Detachment doesn't just happen. Many of these women see the stage of detachment as a choice which one makes more or less consciously. Elizabeth Rowe, describing the attitude of detachment she was eventually able to reach about her son Nate's transsexualism, uses the analogy of a bee sting. "When a bee stings you," she says, "the bee flies off. It's out of the picture. You have your choice. You can leave the stinger in. It will fester and become infected. You will be in pain, and you can become very ill from it.

"Or, after the bee stings you, you can remove the stinger. It will still hurt for a while."

Then, one day, the familiar pain won't be there. "You will remember that you were stung by a bee and that it hurt. But you will have healed, and the pain will be gone."

Yet pulling the stinger out, detaching herself from the source of pain, is difficult for a mother. " 'You have to solve them—you made them.' That's the way my mother always put it to us," Jean Brooks remembers. " 'You've made your bed, now you have to lie in it.' That's easy to say, and I believe it, but boy, is it hard to follow."

However, several years after her son Tom was imprisoned for criminal assault and theft, Jean, who once was in so much pain that she couldn't bring herself to attend his trial, has achieved a "shaky" but determined detachment from Tom's problems. At the time of the interview Tom was out of prison and trying to pick up the strands of his life. Jean seems to be counseling herself as she describes her present relationship to her son. "He still has lots of problems, let's face it. We've handled it by turning them over to him. They're not our problems. He's thirty-two years old."

Jean says she is still tempted constantly to tell Tom what to do. "But I have to be quiet because this is *his* life. . . . My telling him isn't going to do it."

Like the bee in Elizabeth's story, Tom is following instincts of his own. "He listens to what we say, but then he does what he wants to do anyway."

So Jean is ready to extract the festering stinger. "I've had enough. I want to go off on my own and forget."

Mothers and children tend to cling to each other. Sometimes another person can tactfully force the issue of detachment. Susan Howard attributes her detachment in part to her husband Ralph. When their son Stan went through the second of two divorces, Stan's ex-wife decided to follow her new lover from Michigan to Washington. She wasn't ready to marry again, but she wanted to live with him and see how it worked out. She took Stan's young daughter Maria, Susan's only grandchild, with her.

The divorce hit Stan hard. He loved his wife, and hadn't known that she was unhappy. And he adored his daughter. He didn't have the money to see Maria often, and he worried about her constantly, often to his mother. Susan was sick about the whole situation.

Both Susan and Stan turned to Ralph, who was concerned and sympathetic. "My husband is more likely to reveal his feelings than most men," Susan says warmly. "He's very loving and very sensitive to other people." The grandparents corresponded faithfully with Maria's mother and with Stan. They paid for plane tickets, had the child with them part of the summer, did what they could to help out.

But eventually they realized that they could not effect a permanent solution. Ralph told Susan, "We really don't have a choice, except to keep communicating. So we can't afford to sit here and do nothing but talk about this every evening that we're together or every morning at the breakfast table. We have to go on living our own lives, too."

Because Ralph had already shown his concern and sympathy, Susan was open to his suggestion. If Ralph had previously been less involved, she might have felt differently. But Susan knew Ralph cared. She trusted his judgment. Thus Ralph was able to force an adult perspective on their place in the tangle of Stan's life. He and Susan could not impose their ideas about order and family solidarity on a generation with attitudes which were different from theirs. They could not make sense of a world where a child had to be portioned out to those who loved her. It was Stan's problem, not theirs. Emotionally, they had to accept that. They had to let go.

Sometimes the child himself forces the issue of detachment. A parent's suffering doesn't really help a child, and may, in fact, harm him by adding to his burden of guilt. Ron Matthews knew what his parents had gone through with his sister Elisa's manic-depression. He had attended the bimonthly family therapy sessions they had arranged to help the family cope with Elisa's illness. When he drifted into alcoholism, the last thing in the world he wanted was to see his parents unhappy on his account. At a certain point, the most unselfish action a parent can take is to let go of suffering and to practice detachment.

At least, that's what Ron implied to his mother Karen, though he called detachment "non-association."

"I want you to develop non-association where I'm concerned," he told her. "I don't want your happiness to depend upon what I do with my life."

A week or so later Karen reported her progress to her son. "I'm trying this non-association bit," she said, "but it's real hard, Ron, it really is."

"Well, just practice, Mom," Ron told her, with a big grin. "Just practice."

Soon she was doing better with it. "There is no way I can practice complete non-association," she said in the interview. "It's difficult. But I could use a little bit of his non-association. I just decided, 'To heck with this kid!' . . . I don't give up on him, ever! But I'm not going to let it destroy my life."

Time, many mothers agree, is the great aid to detachment. Most bee stings will quit hurting of their own volition if enough time goes by. But removing the stinger will speed the process up. As Karen says, "I *chose* to quit suffering so much."

LUCY AND THE "BIG MISTAKE"

"Why did you ever have me?" David Carpenter asked his mother Lucy not long before he died. "Surely you can see by now it was a big mistake."

Mothers give their children life. But suppose a child hates the life his mother has given him. Suppose he wants to die. Can his mother change his mind? And if she fails, must she bear forever the guilt of his death? What was Lucy Carpenter's "big mistake"? David's life? His death? Or neither? What responsibility does a mother have for a child who comes to feel, as David did, that life is not worth living?

Lucy Carpenter sighs as she straightens her shoulders and crosses her trim, silky legs. From the waves of her carefully coiffed blond hair to the soles of her black patent pumps, impeccable, pretty Lucy is a lady. Though she is wearing hose, dress pumps, and a printed silk dress with a blue linen jacket on this scorching July day, she appears to be cool and composed. In spite of her delicate beauty, she perfectly fits her husband's description of her: "an organized, competent, self-sufficient, get-it-all-together lady."

But as she talks about David, her composure leaves her. "A horror show" is a phrase Lucy uses frequently, and indeed much of the family life Lucy describes in the interview has been a horror show. From time to time as she talks, she dabs unobtrusively at tears with a lacy handkerchief, but at one point her feelings overflow. The tape is stopped while Lucy cries. And cries.

She has removed the stinger, but she still feels the pain. She is so sorry, so sorry, that David's life turned out as it did. But what more could she do? She has forced herself to let go of her guilt for David's suicide at twenty-six. "In a positive way, you can overcome these feelings. Basically, you know, you're just a human being. You can only do so much. We can't be God."

A manic-depressive, David had often, since his first serious bout of depression at the age of sixteen, questioned whether his miserable life had any value for himself or for anyone else. In the journal he was keeping at the time of his death, he described his desperate feelings of hopelessness:

> I am handicapped. Many people are. But this handicap is difficult to accept because it is elusive. I can't put my finger on it. . . . I feel lost. If I could get some kind of sign that there is a chance. Some kind of look into the person I really am. I do not feel like a person, more like a question mark. . . .
>
> But it doesn't matter. I have little or no control over this melodrama. I'm the man in the middle who never gets the ball. It keeps sailing over my head, coming close, within

reach at times, but forever eluding me. When I do think I'll get the ball, the game is called suddenly without explanation. Just like that.

I sit around this house like a piece of furniture waiting to be polished. I've had it! FUCK THIS SHIT! Excuse me, I must take my lithium.

What "kind of sign" would it have taken to make David feel "like a person" instead of "a question mark"? Nothing, short of a miracle, that Lucy can imagine. She did all she could for David—maybe even more, she thinks, than she should have done—but it was never enough. She no longer reproaches herself for his death. "David gave us ten years to help him. There are many cases where the suicide comes without any warning and then I don't know how you deal with it. He gave me enough time to be rid of guilt."

Lucy couldn't bring herself to read her son's journal until several years after his death. But she was never unaware of David's feelings. Almost from birth, David was especially close to his mother. The youngest of the three sons of Lucy and Frank Carpenter, David was sickly and accident-prone as a baby, needing extra attention from his mother. Over the years David came to adore Lucy, seeing in her sweetness, her fragile blond prettiness, her infinite goodness to him, all that a woman ought to be. In an earlier journal he wrote, "Mom was her usual fantastic self. I doubt I will ever run into a person like her. She is incredible, indescribable. Nuff said, you get the general idea."

On the other hand, David never had much love for his father. Frank Carpenter, a high school teacher in Orlando, Florida, was an adequate parent to his two oldest sons—Stan, the earnest, achieving image of his father, and Gene, gregarious and loving. But the family atmosphere was generally not very good. "As the children were growing up, Frank and I were not very compatible," Lucy says. "We argued a lot."

They argued, for example, about whether the boys should get an allowance. Frank worried a lot about money, and he thought allowances for his children were an unnecessary expenditure. Lucy disagreed. "I felt that, for chores and so on, they should have money of their own to make choices about. He would give them money if it was necessary, but if they wanted to go to the movies or to buy a candy bar or whatever, they always had to ask." Though she thought that the boys should have some independence through a regular allowance, Lucy let Frank have his way. If Frank was often insensitive to his sons' emotional needs, Lucy, who understood more, was too placatory in nature or too weak in will to stand up against him.

At one point when the oldest child, Stan, was about seven, he developed migraine headaches. He also began misbehaving in school, writing on his desk, causing problems with the other children. At the suggestion of Stan's teacher, Lucy took the child to a child psychologist. After several sessions, the psychologist discovered the problem: hunger, emotional hunger as well as actual hunger.

Lucy explains: "My husband has a hang-up, a complete hang-up, about money. I tried to budget our groceries so severely that I deprived Stan of food when he came home from school, and that food was love to him." Frank went with her to a couple of the sessions for Stan, and his interest helped to loosen the purse strings. "Before that he thought I was just spoiling Stan, giving him what he asked for."

Frank and Lucy played backgammon together, but the Carpenters didn't do a lot as a family. Frank himself had never been a part of a family. His own mother had died at the birth of Frank's younger sister. The children were farmed out to separate families, and Frank never saw his sister again. He couldn't grasp the first principle of family therapy, that a family is a *unit* which can create psychological health or psychological illness in the individual members. His way of handling family difficulties was to pretend they didn't exist.

Lucy recounts a significant incident that occurred when Gene, the middle son, was an adolescent which shows Frank's emotional irresponsibility to his family. Gene and a group of boys had experimented with a drug; they swallowed a powder for the relief of asthma which was not meant to be taken internally, and they had a bad reaction.

> We had a party that night, and at five o'clock in the morning, the phone rang. It was the hospital. Gene had been brought in by the police. He was hallucinating. . . .
> People were still there; we had played a lot of cards and

had done a lot of drinking, or they had. And Frank didn't
want anyone to know.

I was ready to say, "Go home, I'm going to the hospital,"
but my husband wouldn't let me. And I said, "Well, how
are you going to get rid of these people? Gene is at the
hospital, and I want to know what's going on!"

So I went upstairs and put my pajamas on and came
down and said, "Well, I'm going to bed," you know, hint-
ing loudly, "It's time to leave."

About forty-five minutes later they left—I thought they'd
never leave! Then I got dressed and went to the hospital.

I would have said, "Our son had a problem, and he's at
the hospital, and we have to go." But my husband just . . .
Maybe he really didn't want to go to the hospital and see
what was going on. I'm not even exactly sure.

Frank's own early years had left him with an incomprehension of
ordinary family life as well as a deathly fear of illness. Both of these
factors were to weigh heavily on his relationship with his youngest
son, toward whom many of his unresolved fears and hostilities were
directed.

After David's birth, Frank felt himself displaced in his wife's attention. He watched with anger and resentment as Lucy devoted, in his
opinion, too much time to the sickly, troublesome child. Frank accused her of pampering the little boy. She, in turn, tried to compensate David for his father's indifference toward him.

If Frank resented his child, David disliked his father. One morning
when he was about nine, he came to his mother frightened out of his
mind. He had had a painfully vivid dream that he was going to kill
his father. Lucy had been seeing a psychologist for her marital
problems, and she took David in with her. "The psychologist had a
session with him, and she said, 'He's a perfectly normal child. You
have nothing to worry about.' " But Lucy saw that David was terribly
concerned. "I think he was afraid that maybe he could kill his father."

As David grew up, Frank gradually cut himself off more and more
from the son who took so much of his wife's energy. When, beginning at about the age of fourteen, David developed increasingly
serious psychological problems, Frank's fear of illness and his long-

standing jealousy prevented him from seeing the boy objectively. He tried to deny as long as he could that his son's difficulties stemmed from anything other than David's bad behavior and Lucy's pampering of him. The gap in understanding between father and son widened, never to be closed again.

"GET HIM OUT OF YOUR BED!"

Events from that alienation between David and Frank Carpenter have already been described in Chapter 3. Frank refused to attend court-advised counseling sessions when David had a minor brush with the law at fourteen. In the next two years, David made two suicide attempts. In the second attempt, he slashed his wrists and required lengthy surgery. Frank came to the hospital *eight hours* after Lucy first called him. By that time, David was so angry at his father's apparent indifference that he refused to see him. During his son's subsequent hospitalization for psychiatric therapy, Frank showed little or no interest in his youngest child's progress.

Thus, by the time David was sixteen, a classic Freudian situation had developed in the Carpenter family. Lucy was cautioned by a hospital psychiatrist that concern for her son should not be allowed to displace her loyalty to her husband. "You must get David out of your bed," the psychiatrist told her symbolically and bluntly.

Lucy was caught in the middle between husband and son, placed in the position of trying to respond to their conflicting needs. David was volatile, desperate; Frank, angry and bitter. Neither respected the other. Frank regarded David as, his mother says, "a klutz. He just always felt that if something was going to go wrong, David would be instigating the whole thing." He steadily maintained that everything David did was a calculated bid for attention, and that as the boy's father he was simply refusing to be "manipulated."

Two weeks after David left the hospital, he was threatening suicide again—"always to me," Lucy says, "never to his father. He really didn't talk to him." Of course, Lucy called David's doctor. "If they say they're going to kill themselves, it's a valid threat." The doctor advised immediate hospitalization, but David refused to commit himself. Lucy had to get a court order, and put her adolescent son, his arm still in a cast from the suicide attempt, into a state hospital for the mentally disturbed.

She drove him out there alone. By the time she got home, David was already on the phone. "Get me out of here," he told her. "This is a horror show. I can't stand this place. If you'll get me out of here, I'll go willingly back to the other place." "The other place" was the private hospital he had just left, which was "like a country club in comparison," Lucy says.

Seeing this willingness to cooperate as a good sign, Lucy arranged the transfer. A few days later, she picked David up. Again she was alone. "Frank thought that this was a ploy, and that there was no reason that David couldn't just shape up, that he didn't really need all this attention."

In the private hospital, David began seeing a new psychiatrist, Dr. Abernathy (not his real name), who was much more optimistic than the earlier doctors had been. "In six months," he told Lucy, "David will look back on this as a bad dream. He's going to be just fine." David liked Dr. Abernathy very much, and the two quickly formed a close relationship, "almost a father-son relationship." Aware of the breach between David and Frank Carpenter, Abernathy took the liberty to warn Frank, "You'd better get involved with your son or he could kill himself."

David came home and continued to visit Abernathy regularly. For a while David was "all right," his mother says. "He was still depressed . . . but he was managing. He went back to school." An excellent student, David kept his grades up and read a lot. At home, he was withdrawn, spending hours alone in his room, but "he wasn't causing any actual disturbance." Lucy felt hopeful.

Then David quit eating. Without explaining, he decided that he wasn't going to eat at all. "That made me feel quite panicky," Lucy remembers. She called Dr. Abernathy, who said that "he felt he had done as much as he could." He referred her to another psychiatrist, Dr. Simpson (not his real name), who insisted that she hospitalize David immediately. "If he won't eat," Dr. Simpson told her, "we have to put him in the hospital so he can be monitored constantly." David spent the next three months in a clinic for psychiatric care.

Up until this point, Lucy had been in a state of shock. Now, with her troubled son under day-and-night surveillance, she began turning the matter over in her mind. She paid attention to what she knew of David's difficulties, to which as yet no one had given a name. Her own mother had been a manic-depressive, but her depressions had been easily controlled with an antidepressant. Because she responded to medication so well, she only suffered two or three serious depressions in Lucy's life with her, and was capable of going for eight or nine years at a time without taking medicine or lapsing into depression. Nevertheless, wasn't it possible there was some genetic connection between her mother's condition and what was happening to David? Could antidepressants have a beneficial effect on David as well?

"Absolutely not," Simpson told her. "He just needs therapy." The therapy continued. A year passed, and David didn't improve. He slept a lot, occasionally refused to go to school for weeks at a time, and was periodically extremely depressed.

At length, Lucy took him to another psychiatrist, Jim Massey (not his real name), who was experienced in chemical treatment of psychological illness. Dr. Massey, who was his doctor until David died, gave the agitated boy a series of tests. The unhappy home environment had contributed to David's illness, he told Lucy, but there was a chemical imbalance that justified experimental use of lithium.

Massey was also interested in the illness of Lucy's mother. He questioned Lucy closely about her recollections of the pattern it had taken, and she began to see similarities she had not recalled before. She remembered an occasion, shortly after Lucy's first child was born, when her mother had fallen into a serious depression while visiting Lucy's cousin in California.

> The cousin called me, and said, "Your mother's in a very bad state, very depressed, can't really function, and I'm going to send her home on the train. I'll pin her name and address to her coat and put it in her purse."
>
> I said, "My mother? She has to have someone put her name on her coat?" I couldn't conceive of this, but when I saw her, I understood. She was absolutely dependent upon me, almost to the point where she didn't want me to sleep at night. She wanted me to sit next to her so she could hold my hand. She was afraid to sit down and eat, she was afraid

to go to the bathroom by herself. . . . It was just horrible. She didn't leave me for a minute.

Antidepressants cleared up the condition in about a month.

Remembering this, Lucy found herself more hopeful about David than she had been in some time. Surely David was no worse than this, and now her mother's illness was nothing but a bad memory. Now that David had found a doctor who recognized the possibility of organic malfunction and was willing to try to correct it with medication, David might respond as well as his grandmother had before him.

And, in fact, with his new prescription, David did seem to improve dramatically. He took his final exams and finished high school with a high B average, an amazing feat for someone who'd spent half his high school time in and out of hospitals. The Carpenters took a new lease on life.

"We thought he was just marvelous," Lucy recalls. "He was happy and outgoing, he was going out with his friends again, and we thought, 'Well, my! This is wonderful. The medication's really working.' " Lucy was tremendously relieved that David's problems were apparently caused by something other than his family situation. He had an illness, an illness with a name, manic-depression. And this illness could be treated with a medicine, a magic pill which would give her child a normal life.

Lucy didn't realize that David was not always taking his lithium, and that his good spirits were largely attributable to his first full-blown manic stage, which was fast approaching.

AT THE MERCY OF MANIA

When school was out, David went to Nevada, on, Lucy discovered later, money he had borrowed without her knowledge. Then he and a friend went on down to Mexico. When he came home from his travels, Lucy picked him up at the airport. As she waited on one side of the metal detector, she saw David coming down the hallway, carrying a pillowcase full of things.

> He was very agitated with me. He yelled at me down the
> hall, "Come and help me!" as if I'm supposed to know
> what was going on. And I thought, "Oh, what now?" I
> could tell from the sound of his voice that things were not
> going to be too good.

The pillowcase contained a load of Mexican tourist junk. David had
decided that he was going into the import business. "I'm going to
sell these things," he told Lucy, "and I'm going to make a lot of
money."

The next day, he decided that, as an importer, he needed a good
car. He came down for breakfast and told his mother he was going to
get a loan and buy a Cadillac.

> He said, "I need a ride to the bank." I said, "Well, I don't
> have the car here." And then he hit me. I couldn't believe
> this was happening.
> I said, "David, what are you doing?" and then I started to
> cry, and he hit me again. And he said, "You're never good
> for anything. I need something now, and you're not follow-
> ing through for me."

He stormed off to the bank on foot. Quickly Lucy called the police
and explained the situation. At the officer's insistence, she called her
husband also. "And of course, Frank panicked, he absolutely panicked, when he heard that David had hit me." They got a court order
for David's commitment.

> The police picked him up right out in front of our house,
> and it was very traumatic, because they ordered him out of
> the car that he was in and frisked him and treated him just
> like a criminal. He was very angry.

Lucy understood even at the time that David himself wasn't to
blame, but was at the mercy of his mania. Although her mother had
never reached the manic stage and thus Lucy had never seen one of
these attacks, Lucy had done her homework on her son's illness.

> When they're in full-blown mania, they have absolutely no
> conscience. They can do anything, shoot and kill someone,
> and they always have an excuse in their own mind, why it
> should be so. And they are so good, and so convincing, and

so cunning when they're in this stage that they can practically talk the shirt right off your back. . . .

Their charm, their whole personality, is such that you
wouldn't believe there could be a thing wrong with them.

The hospital admissions staff thought David seemed perfectly
normal. They were reluctant to keep him, until one of the attendants
overheard David telling Lucy on the phone that he was going to sue
her for two hundred and fifty thousand dollars for having him
brought in.

They took him in, and then he broke furniture, he broke
the window, he caused all kinds of problems, and so they
had to put him on, I think, Haldol and Thorazine. When I
first went to see him, he couldn't even walk. He had had so
many injections that he couldn't even walk properly.

A week later, Lucy arranged David's transfer to the private psychiatric clinic where his doctor had patients. He spent one night, and
came home the next morning, having called a cab and walked right
out of the hospital.

Frank Carpenter hadn't gone to work yet that morning when
David walked in.

Frank told me, "This is all your fault. You've always been so
lenient with him. You took him out of a place where you
knew he was locked in and took him down where you knew
he could get out." And he blamed it all on me.

He wouldn't give David ten dollars to pay the cabdriver,
so David called a friend. She came over with the money,
and David took off.

They had to get another court order, and back David went to the
state hospital. He was there for five weeks, the length of time it took
him to "come down" from the manic stage.

Even in his hysterical state, he was deeply repentant about hitting
his mother. "I can't believe I did that," he told Lucy tearfully. "I just
can't believe I would ever do that." But he was still furious with his
father, and at first refused to see him. A social worker at the hospital
told Lucy, "He's dividing you and your husband. If he's ever going

to get better, you must be a unified front. Tell David that if your husband can't come to see him, you won't come to see him either."

Lucy did so. Threatened with his mother's absence, David quickly agreed to see Frank the once or twice Frank would agree to come; he too was still angry. Lucy went to see her son regularly, often taking him food, because he couldn't stand the food at the hospital. "I did pamper him, I admit. . . . My husband objected to some of it. He thought I was doing too much, that it wasn't good for him. But I said, 'I have to do what I feel,' and I did."

Eventually David came home and got a job, working at night on the waterfront in a shrimp-processing plant. The job seemed to be a good idea because David wanted independence and usefulness; he also had to help with the cost of his treatment. Their hospitalization insurance didn't cover David's horrendous medical expenses, and for practical as well as therapeutic reasons David needed to work.

As he couldn't be trusted to drive the family car, however, once again his mother found herself caught in the middle between husband and son. She took on a responsibility that ideally belonged to David himself, but she didn't know what else to do. She had to, or felt she had to, drive David back and forth to work. He worked the late shift, so she took him to work in the late afternoon and picked him up about one o'clock in the morning. She had an hour's drive each way, along a bad section of the Florida coast.

> My husband and I had a lot of arguments over this. He felt, again, I was being manipulated, I was pampering him, and I said, "No, I don't agree." I felt that he really needed me to go with him at that time. . . .
>
> I was more or less frightened all the time, but my husband objected to being wakened and having to go, so I went alone. And I felt, if I'm doing the right thing, something will look after me.

THE CYCLE OF SICKNESS

They followed this routine for over five years. Lucy felt that she was helping David to maintain some semblance of normality in his life, to hold a job, to have money of his own. He continued to take medication, but his mood changes were still violent. As one year turned into another, Lucy began to observe a regular seasonal change in her son.

His illness followed a cycle. In the fall he would be extremely depressed. About the beginning of December he would be coming out of the depression. By Christmas, he was well enough to go out with his friends who had come home from college for the holidays, though he couldn't drink; when he did, the lithium made him sick.

By January, he started the upswing, and early in February he hit the full manic stage. During this period he could be dangerous. At one point Lucy discovered he was selling marijuana, getting it from a source at the processing plant and passing it on to his friends. "David," she told him, "that's illegal. Don't you bring that in the house again. I can't monitor you all the time, but if I find it in the house, I'll call the police." He agreed, but Lucy worried. He had the irresponsibility of a much younger person. Dr. Massey told her that, as David moved into his middle twenties, he still had the temperament and attitudes of a teenager, that he had stopped growing psychologically at fifteen, with the onset of the disease.

Like any teenager, he wanted to drive the car himself. Once he demanded that she give him the keys. When Lucy refused, he pulled out a knife and threatened her with it. Terrified and trembling, the small woman stood her ground as her tall son towered over her menacingly. "I thought, 'I'm not going to let you go and kill somebody else.'" Just as she thought she would faint with fear, he threw the knife across the room, went out the back door, and began to hurl rocks through the front window into the house.

At times like this he would have to be hospitalized, often for several months. When, as sometimes happened, he went into the hospital voluntarily, Lucy never knew when he might decide to check himself out; he could be detained forcibly only when he had been committed by court order. She would come home in the middle of the afternoon and find David waiting for her, ranting and raving in a manic delusion.

Once he left the hospital in the middle of the night.

At one o'clock in the morning, the phone rang, and the nurse said, "David walked out tonight." And I thought,

"Oh, I don't know how I can stand it." I wondered where he was, and of course we were up all night. I couldn't sleep, worrying about him, until he called the next day.

Then we had another scene, and I had to call the police, and they came. Then he said, "Okay, I'll go back," and he went back [into the hospital]. But I wasn't sure that he wasn't going to become violent. This was always the fear when he was manic.

When he came out of the manic stage, it was back into another depression, which got gradually worse until fall, when he hit the low point again. The depressions triggered other kinds of fears in Lucy, fears about what David might do to himself.

David's older brothers were not living at home during this time. Once when Gene was home on a visit, he became as concerned as his mother about his younger brother.

David had bought a gun and was showing it to everyone. This you would probably say was a cry for help. But we had been going to a doctor all along, so I didn't know what else we could do.

But Gene took instant action. Gene and David had always been close and loving, and Gene, gentle and accepting like Lucy, had some influence with his younger brother. And he was not afraid of David, as both David's mother and father had come to be.

Gene got very upset, and took the gun from him. He took it back [to the shop] and made the man give him the money back for it, because he just felt that there was no way for David to be having a gun in the house.

David's medication relieved his condition less and less. He talked to Lucy often about the hopelessness that he was beginning to feel. "I'd be better off dead," he told her. "There's no doubt about it. What am I doing? I'm working in a factory. What am I really producing?" He felt as though life lived on these terms was a total waste. He continued to hang on because Lucy suggested to him that some drug which would stabilize his depressions might be discovered.

He did the best he could. It broke Lucy's heart to "watch him suffer as he did, when he really tried so hard."

He took his medicine, he really took his medication. I
didn't have to be on his back every night about "Did you do
this?" I knew he had to have some control over this if he
was ever going to get any better, and I felt he really tried.

It was very important for him to make some kind of a
contribution to life, that he was not able to do. This made
him very angry. It hurt me to know that he had really been
blessed with good looks, intelligence, a sense of humor,
personality, he had everything going for him, but he
couldn't put it together because of the extreme depression
that he went through.

Lucy did the best she could too. Once Frank Carpenter heard the
term "manic-depression" and had a legitimate illness rather than a
recalcitrant nature to blame for his son's condition, one might have
thought he would be more sympathetic. But habits of behavior are
hard to change. Things in the family got a little better but not much.
"I saw Frank's total acceptance of it as an illness," Lucy says, shaking
her head sadly, "only after David killed himself. He now feels that he
saw acceptance in himself at an earlier period than I saw it. I don't
think he ever really accepted it [until David died]. You don't always
see yourself as someone else sees you."

Whatever his feelings may have been during the last of the ten-
year ordeal the family had gone through, Frank was of virtually no
help to his son or to his wife. What did help Lucy was being able to
keep father and son apart. David went to work before his father
came home, and Frank would be in bed asleep by the time Lucy had
picked David up from the shrimp-processing plant. Often the two
didn't meet from Monday until Saturday.

With this routine, there wasn't as much stress involved. It
was mainly when we were all together in the house that I
was always afraid something might happen to set one or
the other off. I mean, anger and shouting and so on—that
was all very difficult for me, so I tried to keep things going
on an even keel if at all possible.

In addition to a routine that assured a modicum of peace in the
home, another help for Lucy was being able to talk to others about
David's illness. When she had questions, she called Dr. Massey. She

faithfully attended a parents' support group. "I'm quite up-front with people. I didn't see it as a stigma attached to our family or our life.

"I've always felt free . . . except when my husband said that I really talked too much. He thinks that women have a tendency to do this, and maybe they do. But in the long run oftentimes it's easier to get it off your chest."

She also, as she puts it, "gained strength from an outside force." Although the Carpenters are not church members and Lucy has little use for organized religion, she was sustained by a belief that she was being sheltered by "a God that is helpful and looking after me." Once, on the lonely drive to pick up David in the early morning, three young men threw rocks at her car. "A car could have come and forced me off the road, but I had faith that as long as I was doing what was necessary, nothing would happen to me."

But her strongest support was faith in herself, faith she had developed from an unlikely source. God works in mysterious ways His wonders to perform, and for Lucy, finding out that she was a better than adequate backgammon instructor gave her the strength of character she needed during this most difficult decade of her life.

> A friend of ours wanted me to teach some backgammon classes for her. I said, "I can't. I'm not a teacher. I don't have any background. I can't do it. I don't want to."
>
> I was always kind of shy. But when I found out that I could get up in front of a group of strangers, that not only could I teach but that I was a good teacher, this was the big change in my life. From then on, I gained a lot of confidence in myself. I felt that I could do most anything that I wanted to.

"IN THE STRINGS"

What she wanted to do most, of course, was to save her son. Dr. Massey told Lucy that David's was the worst case of manic-depression he had ever seen, almost entirely beyond the help of accepted medical procedure. The cycle of depression, mania, depression, had

ground her son under and exhausted his mother. Finally, in desperation, David agreed to have shock therapy. Anything to break the
cycle he was stuck in, he said. Lucy was guardedly optimistic about
the possibilities. "I saw what it did for my mother. Her first deep
depression—it was like a difference of night and day. . . . She
came out of her depression, and she was just fine."

David was not so fortunate. He had a terrible reaction to the first
treatment. "He said it was the worst experience of his life, but he
was going to go through with it because this was going to work."
After thirteen shock treatments, David was no better. "I saw no
difference," Lucy says. "The only difference was that he couldn't
remember what his name was. . . . And David was getting very
discouraged, because of course he had thought he was going to get
better."

Disillusioned with the shock therapy, David signed himself in as a
human guinea pig in an experimental lab in Miami, where research
with machines was being conducted. To prepare himself for the
research, he had to discontinue all medication. It was early spring,
and Lucy warned the doctors that he was due for another manic
period. As soon as he quit taking lithium, he immediately went into
an incredible manic high. The idea of using him for testing became
an absurdity; simply controlling him was the issue.

He called his mother and said, "Listen, you've got to get me out of
here. It's horrible." "You signed yourself in," Lucy told him. "You
said you would go along with the treatment." He didn't say any
more, but "he seemed kind of upset."

Lucy went to see him on her regular visiting day. "I met the social
worker, and she said, 'You can't see him; they put him into the
strings,' which means they tied him down to the bed, and they only
let him up to go to the bathroom. . . . He was in the strings for
about two days, and he said it was a horror show." Later he told
Lucy, "You can't understand what it's like, you feel like an animal. I
can't take much more of this."

David had to go back on lithium. He stayed in the experimental
hospital for two months, working with a social worker. Their sessions were videotaped for use by the staff. He was terribly depressed, because he had realized, as his mother says, that "whatever
was able to be done wasn't going to be that much different from

what he had gone through already. There was no miracle pill that he was going to be able to take."

He came home. He tried to live alone, getting an apartment near the shrimp plant where he worked. Lucy helped him move some of his things. "It lasted one day. He said, 'I can't do it. I have to come back home today. I can't manage the depression alone.' "

Only his job stood between David and complete despair. Then, in June, the processing plant laid off half its workers. The night shift was suspended and only the best workers were retained on another shift. David, whose performance at work had always been erratic because of his illness, lost his job. He hit the bottom.

For years, David had threatened suicide. In the journal he was keeping the last year of his life, he wrote:

> My only alternative is death. A nice violent death like a bullet in the brain, this diseased, this disgusting mass of pain and problems. . . . Death to my brain.
>
> I'm forever imprisoned in the darkest regions of my mind. . . . I wish I had a gun. . . .
>
> I live in my own world.
>
> All these people talking about school, their fine jobs and glorious plans and I'm just wallowing. It's tough.
>
> I can't handle being around anybody. I don't belong in this world.
>
> I feel old. Maybe it's because I never really lived.

MOTHER, MAY I?

That fall, the fall of 1980, David was as usual depressed, even, understandably, a little more depressed than in preceding falls. After his stay in the Miami hospital, he had lost faith in his medication and even in his doctor. From the end of the summer on, he grew more and more reluctant to see Dr. Massey. In October he flatly refused to go in, and "I couldn't make him," Lucy remembers. "I wasn't even sure that he was taking his medication. He was supposed to go for a monthly lab report on the lithium, but he would sit down and talk to me about it. He really didn't feel that there was

going to be any difference, ever, and what was going to happen to
him?"

Since he was not working, the mother and son had long days
together. Mostly David stayed in his room, playing his tapes over
and over. He had saved over eight thousand dollars, so money
wasn't a problem for him. A tall, slim, good-looking boy, he loved
clothes, dressing up, and going out. In previous falls, even in his
depressions he had gone shopping, seen a friend occasionally, and
worked. This fall he had lost interest in everything. Lucy taught an
occasional backgammon class, but mostly she was home, cooking,
cleaning as meticulously as ever, watching David.

They talked. "We talked about suicide a lot. He felt that he should
be able to do [what he wanted] with his life, live or not live, that it
was *his* life."

Lucy agreed with him in theory. "David," she told him, "I understand that you feel that you should have the say over what your
destiny should be."

"Then why shouldn't I kill myself," he asked her, "when I'm
suffering so? I'd like to just stick a gun in my mouth and pull the
trigger."

"Because life is not hopeless," Lucy said. "Life is just never hopeless. You never know when they will discover something that may
help you."

She felt that David was asking her for permission to take his own
life, permission she certainly wasn't going to give. "I'm a mother,"
she told him, "and how could I ever approve of my child taking his
own life? That's just not in the feelings that a mother would have. I
can understand that you are suffering, but as your mother I will
never give up hope that eventually something can be done for you."

As October moved into November and David's depression wors-
ened, this conversation was repeated many times, as it had been so
often repeated in other falls.

The week that David died didn't seem to Lucy at the time different
from any other week. He spent Monday in his room. When Lucy
came to his door to check on him, he told her he was writing a letter
to his closest friend. She didn't think too much about it; David liked
to write and was always writing something or other.

Monday night Lucy was watching television in the den. Frank

came in and said, "When will your show be over? I wanted to watch the football game."

"This is a movie, and it just started," Lucy said. "I think David is watching football on his set. Why don't you watch it with him?"

Somewhat awkwardly, Frank went to David's door and asked if he could watch the game with him. "Okay," David said. The television set was placed at one end of the room between the twin beds. David was sitting on one of the beds, and Frank sat down gingerly on the other. Suddenly Frank looked around to see David's eyes fixed on him. "You'd better not sit there," David said. "And I don't want you in this room when I'm not here."

Frank didn't stay for a quarrel. He had gotten afraid to cross David, so he left the room nervously. He came back into the den, where Lucy was engrossed in her show, sat for a minute, then went upstairs to bed without mentioning David's strange behavior to her. It wouldn't have seemed strange to her anyway, she says now. David loved his room, his retreat against the world, and certainly didn't want his father in it. "If David felt pretty good . . . he had far more understanding of his father and his father's mood. But when he was depressed, he wanted little or nothing to do with him."

Tuesday morning David walked to the post office and mailed his letter. He spent the rest of the day quietly in the house.

Wednesday afternoon David decided to go to see a woman, Janey Barnet, whom he had met in the hospital several years earlier. Janey too was a manic-depressive, a little older than David. She had been married, but her terrible depressions had destroyed her marriage. She had a little girl, Donna, whom David liked. He liked Janey too. "It was an off-on relationship," Lucy says, "not anything that much, but he liked her."

Lucy was glad to see him visiting a friend. "I thought, 'Gee, it's nice to see him going out.' I was grateful." She herself dropped him off at Janey's place on her way to teach a backgammon class. When Frank came home from the high school, the house was empty.

Frank had been puzzling over David's odd behavior on Monday night. David had seemed unusually protective of his room, Frank thought, rather than just hostile as usual to his father. Finding the house empty, Frank decided to investigate David's quarters.

He went up to the bedroom, put his hand under the mattress on the bed David had warned him away from, and found a gun. He pulled it out and examined it closely. A revolver, loaded. What Frank Carpenter did then is hard to understand. He put the gun back under the mattress, smoothed the spread down, and walked out. When Lucy came home, he didn't tell her what he'd found.

Later he would ask Lucy, "Didn't you realize how upset I was that night when you came in?"

"But my husband is a very moody person," she says, "and I didn't think too much about him being upset. He would often get angry with me, for nothing really that I had done. So I just didn't think much about it at the time."

Later she would ask Frank, "If you knew he had a gun, why didn't you take it?" "I was afraid to," he told her. "He had told me not to go in his room when he wasn't there, and I was afraid of what he might do if I confronted him. I was afraid he might shoot me." So, as the week moved toward its end, the gun lay ready in David's bed.

Thursday passed uneventfully. Thursday night, Bob, the friend to whom David had written the letter on Monday, called. They talked for quite a while, and David talked to Bob's girlfriend also.

Lucy realizes now that David was saying goodbye to all his friends, though at the time she didn't suspect it. Bob told her later that David had written him a fifty-two-page letter. He was afraid David meant to do himself harm, and the phone conversation was his way of trying to give David a reason to keep going.

Friday morning, when David came downstairs, Lucy asked him to do a favor for her. Saturday was her uncle's eightieth birthday, and she had decided to give him a couple of bottles of a good wine. David was interested in gourmet food and wine, and had a subscription to a food-and-wine magazine. She asked him to go out and buy her uncle's birthday gift, so she could give it to him the following day. David seemed pleased. He went to his room and pored over his magazines briefly, then he came downstairs and went out.

He came home about six. Lucy was in the kitchen preparing dinner. He handed her the bottles of wine he'd gotten and told her he'd had coffee with a friend while he was out. When she and Frank sat down to dinner, David didn't appear, "but he didn't follow the pattern of eating with us anyway, so that I didn't think too much about it."

After dinner, Frank and Lucy went into the den to watch television. About ten-thirty Frank dozed off in front of the set. Lucy let him sleep. Feeling wide awake herself, she picked up the stack of Christmas cards she'd been addressing earlier in the day and sat down at the kitchen table to work on them.

About eleven-thirty, David came in and sat down across from her. "Mom," he said, "what do you really think of me?"

"I just wasn't ready for that question," Lucy says. "It had not been a particularly good day for me. I felt he was seeking something that at the time I couldn't manage to give to him."

But she tried. "I described him . . . a fine human being with a lot of empathy and feeling for others. We had often talked about how angry he was because this had happened to his life." They raised the question again, the feeling that the world hadn't played fair with him. "Why him? Why did he get stuck with this illness? [If it was genetic,] why him and not his brothers?"

They talked about the other members of the family. "When you were younger," Lucy said, "I used to think you tried to manipulate Gene somewhat."

He became very angry at that. "You know how much I care about him!" he said.

"I'm not questioning your love for him," she said.

David reminded her that Stan had always picked on *him*. He thought Stan and his father were a lot alike, but that he and Gene were alike.

"I cannot stand my father," he said. "I cannot stand him." Lucy nodded sadly. She knew.

He didn't tell her that he loved her. She knew that too.

"But what do you really think of me?" David persisted.

As Lucy remembers this conversation, her face is full of pain. "I said, 'Well, I love you very much and I admire you as a person.' "

But she was frustrated. She couldn't hit the right note, couldn't discover what he wanted to hear. "And I finally said, 'What do you really want from me, David?'

"And he didn't say anything more. He went upstairs, and about half an hour later I heard a noise. And I went up, and I opened the door, and he had shot himself."

Lucy stood in the doorway of David's room for a minute. The gun lay on the floor and David's body was sprawled across one of the beds. "I didn't look at David exactly," she says, "but I knew. He had told me how he was going to do it when he did."

She went into the den, where Frank was still sleeping, and woke him up. By this time she was crying. "David is dead," she said. Frank went up into David's room. One of David's tapes was still running, and his father turned off the machine. Then he called the police.

THE BIRD LEAVES THE CAGE

His death threw the pattern of David's life into greater clarity for Frank Carpenter. Sympathetic at last, he was the one who suggested the form for the funeral service. The Carpenters have no religious affiliation, but Lucy's mother is a member of the Baha'i, a religious group founded in the nineteenth century, which emphasizes the spiritual unity of mankind. The Baha'i belief that the best part of David's life would continue in the members of his family pleased all of them, particularly Gene. Frank suggested that they have the service done by a Baha'i member. Lucy and the boys gratefully agreed. They held a small, intimate service, just for the family.

Stan read aloud a passage from David's journal that described the pain that drove David to death:

> Times are tough, diary. Aren't they always for me. I wish I could give you some good news, diary. It's about time, isn't it? But these kinds of things don't change, booby. I knew that when they first began. I knew it way back then.
>
> Times have changed a bit, though. I'm getting closer to the end. I'm twenty-six and the walls are closing in. Every night when I go to bed, I shudder at the thought of waking up and starting another day. I don't get enough out of it. I dodge and I squirm and I die of anxiety and exhaustion and pain and suffering. It is amazing that one person should have to endure what I do.
>
> God, give me some relief. I've been enduring long enough. Please give me some relief. You know I deserve it. Nobody can take this. I cannot exist in this strange world, anymore.

Then the Baha'i layman who conducted the service spoke briefly. He compared David to a bird in a cage. You open the door, and the bird flies out, and the bird is free. "That's how he felt David was," Lucy says. She liked the idea. "It was really lovely. And it helped. Absolutely."

Both Frank and Stan wanted to know what David and Lucy had talked about that Friday night. Gene didn't ask. Lucy told them a little of it, but she knew what they were wondering because she wondered it herself: What did David want from her in that midnight conversation the night he died?

She worried about this a lot at first. "I really wondered what I could have done for him the last night. I can truthfully say I did as much as I could while he was alive. I don't have any regrets that I didn't do enough. I really felt that I did all that could be done by any human being.

"But that last night. What was he asking me, what did he need from me? Did he need me to say something that would keep him going?"

She went to David's doctor, Jim Massey. He told her that David was one of the 15 percent of manic-depressives who are not helped by any kind of medication. "There is nothing you could have done," he said. "After the shock therapy didn't work, it was only a matter of time."

Lucy allowed herself to let go of guilt and pain, to feel comforted. How could she feel guilty or unhappy that David's long agony was over? She tried to face realistically what had happened to David. In spite of what she had told David about the hope in new drugs, new cures, she had to admit to herself that she really believed "there wasn't going to be anything that would work."

She could not make sense for David of the ordeal his life had become. It had not made any sense to her! David had had to handle it, and he had handled it in the way he thought best. She detached herself from responsibility for what she couldn't help. Lucy gave herself permission to be relieved that David's suffering, and her own, were over.

The example of David's life and the tragedy of his death had positive effects for the mother whom he had loved so much. She became much more appreciative of the normal life, the life without tragedy. Her son had been destroyed senselessly, but for some indecipherable reason she was alive and well. How ungrateful it would be of her not to enjoy what David would have given his life for, what he gave his life for the lack of—the simple, available pleasures of the world.

With her new insight, Lucy suddenly felt smothered under the burden of negativism she'd accepted from her husband for so long. As she detached herself from David's tragedy, she detached herself from Frank's narrow view of the world. And she told Frank so.

"I became very much less tolerant of my husband's chronic complaints, of his finding fault with so many things. He is blessed with a very good life, and health, and other things. As I tried to explain to him one day, it would be sacrilegious to David for him to continue his attitude."

This confrontation with her husband represented a real change in Lucy. "Before, I felt that I needed to keep everybody happy. Mother had to keep everything going. I had to keep everything nice and easy as possible. Now I don't feel that way anymore, really. He has to uphold his end too. . . .

"I had fear before. I didn't want to make waves. I didn't want to cause problems. I don't worry about that now. Whatever I think is the right thing to do, I do it. Let the chips fall where they may!"

Lucy still cries for the waste of David's life, but she cries for David, not for herself. She has detached her own life from that of her child. But she has not, even after his death, detached herself from her child. One of her favorite places for quiet and reflection is David's grave in the cemetery. "I go, I plant flowers in the summertime, and then I go to water the flowers. It's very peaceful there.

"And while I'm there I talk to him. I did as much as I could for David while he was here, and I feel that I'm continuing to do something for him.

"And for me."

9

Detachment as Strategy

As the story of Lucy Carpenter illustrates, sometimes a mother must detach her view of the world from her child's for the sake of her emotional survival. David despaired of life. For him, life was hell, an unremitting cycle of depression and mania. He chose to die.

After his death, Lucy made a decision also: to live. David's suffering had taught her something of the value of normal life, and she determined to seize the days that she had left. She didn't love David less when she recognized that she and her son were separate persons, with separate destinies.

Reasons other than a child's suicide call for a mother's detachment for her own sake. Like Lucy, Marian James eventually had to detach herself emotionally from the fate of her son Lanny. Lanny had become a criminal. Because Marian had no control over his illegal activities, she learned to quit identifying herself with him. Why should she be ashamed of what she could not prevent? At twenty-six, Lanny is not dead like David, but his separation from his family is almost as complete as if he were. "Because of all the damage that he's done to the family over many, many years," his mother says, "it's really more comfortable when he's not around."

On drugs since the seventh grade, Lanny created turmoil for his parents, who talked to him, cried over him, gave him years of counseling, and eventually sent him away to a special school for troubled children. Nothing helped. When Lanny was seventeen, he was expelled from school for dealing drugs. Shortly afterward, he robbed, beat, and nearly killed a service station attendant.

Lanny expected his parents to run interference, as they had in other brushes with authority their son had had. Instead, the Jameses let the law take its course; they neither bailed him out nor hired an attorney for him. "You can't keep bailing kids out of things forever," they told each other.

When the case went to trial, Lanny told his mother he was "embarrassed" to face family friends. He implied that she could have saved them all from "embarrassment" by covering for him.

She wasn't having any. She detached herself emotionally from his "embarrassment." "If you're ashamed to have somebody else know it," she asked her son, "then why in God's name did you do it? You've got to face up to that—don't lay it on me.

"If you can't handle seeing these people later, tough luck, Charlie. That's your problem, not mine."

"Your problem, not mine" sounds like the consummate brush-off. It is also the simple truth. A mother may reach that level of detachment from some instinct for survival even more basic than the maternal instinct.

But her own emotional survival is not the only reason a mother needs detachment from her child's problems. She may at the same time practice the art of detachment in order to help her child. Detachment was the strategy that Kate Barnes used to force her child to take charge of her life.

KATE, WATCHING FROM TWO WINDOWS

Home is not always the best place for a troubled young person to be. Kate and Nicholas Barnes are convinced that if they had not sent their daughter Debby away from home at fifteen, today Debby would be dead. Debby is adopted. Her emotional problems, the Barnes family eventually learned, stemmed from ontological causes: she felt uncertain about her identity; she was deeply confused about her relationship to the natural parents who had "abandoned" her; she desperately feared being "abandoned" again.

Yet, paradoxically, Debby came to trust her parents only when she realized they cared enough about her to send her into an environment that could provide the structure she was not getting at home. Detachment saved Debby's life. "It was absolutely a dead-end road," her mother says, her long fingers nervously twisting the gold chain at the neck of her beige cashmere sweater. "I don't think that you can sit by and watch a child absolutely self-destruct, which is what she was doing. I think anyone would react! She was crying for help, crying for someone to do something with her."

In her thin intense face, Kate's dark eyes appeal for understanding. "She was destroying herself, and probably, in the process, destroying me. Because I was allowing her to do that."

The second of the Barneses' three children, all adopted, Debby had troubles from the time Kate and Nicholas brought her home, at five weeks old. No sooner was the new baby settled than Kate began hemorrhaging. She became very ill, and over the next months suffered a staph infection, hepatitis, a D and C, a complete bowel obstruction, and eventually a hysterectomy. "I almost didn't live for many months. For my daughter's first year of life I was out of the house, in the hospital, much of the time." Nick Barnes and the grandmothers, first one and then the other, had to do the mothering that Kate had done for Tim, Debby's brother, who was two years older, and was to do for the youngest child, a boy they adopted two years later.

In the hospital, Kate worried constantly about her children. Tim was strong and sturdy, a robust, precocious child. But what effect would her absence have on little Debby? First of all, there was the very real fear that the adoption agency would learn the situation and take Debby away. And what about Debby herself? "In any adopted child there is a problem with separation," Kate explains. Debby had already been separated from her natural mother. Now Debby had been forsaken again.

At last Kate, weighing under a hundred pounds and feeling completely exhausted, came home from the hospital for good. By that time, she had also worked herself into a load of "tremendous guilt." She assuaged her guilt by pouring attention on year-old Debby, attention which didn't stop even when she and Nick went on, a year later, to adopt another boy, Brian.

Eventually what Kate calls a symbiotic relationship grew up between her and her only girl. "I really had an unusual attachment to my daughter," she says, "and she to me."

As the Barnes children became old enough to understand, they were told that they were adopted. "Our children have known always," Kate says. "They grew up knowing. We talked about it a lot, always with pride. . . . For us, adopting children was essential because we would not have had children otherwise."

Neither Tim nor baby Brian seemed to be troubled by the idea, but Debby was. She moved closer and closer to her mother. "A very pretty child, pleasing in her way with people, warm and sensitive," Kate remembers. Tim was extremely advanced, and Kate and Nick made "a tremendous effort to make no comparison" between the two oldest. Debby, they decided, was a happy average, an endearing daughter.

Even as a youngster, however, she complained of terrible stomach pains. The pains were real, they and the pediatrician could see, but they had no identifiable cause. Only much later did the family realize that Debby was expressing physically the overwhelming fear of separation which had already become her constant companion.

By the time Debby was in the seventh grade, other troubles presented themselves. Her grades had been high average. Now Kate could see she was slipping. Her grades were falling steadily, but that wasn't all. A gregarious child, she was choosing friends from "lower and lower groups where she could feel better" in comparison. Kate went to Debby's counselor, who laughed at her concern. "Debby is a normal, healthy, delightful child," he told her. "She doesn't have a problem; *you* are the problem."

Kate tried, unsuccessfully, to convince herself that the counselor was right. She knew she tended to hover over her daughter. Perhaps things were okay after all. She arranged tutoring and some informal counseling for Debby and hoped for the best.

The following fall Debby went into the eighth grade. She was prettier than ever and physically mature, and she had no trouble attracting friends. Kate was happy that Debby seemed to be coming into her own. Then, during the first football game, Debby slipped off into the woods behind the school with several of her friends. In a little over an hour, she downed an enormous amount of beer and vodka. "It was a self-destructive sort of thing," Kate says.

When they saw the state Debby was in, her friends got frightened and left her. A police officer who was patrolling the grounds found her, barely able to speak. She was rushed to the hospital and her stomach was pumped. After a long night of terror for Kate and Nick, the doctor came out and told them that Debby would live.

From that episode on, Debby got in worse and worse trouble. Her grades were terrible. At home, she retreated to her room. She had friends, apparently, but they didn't come to the house, so Kate didn't know them. She was still seeing a tutor and a psychologist, but they couldn't seem to help. Nor could her mother. "I was trying to help," Kate says, "but I could see things were just getting out of hand."

When Debby went to high school a year later, things were very much out of hand. Her peers didn't offer much inspiration. From grade school on, Debby's class had been identified by teachers as the worst ever. "There were an awful lot of kids in that class who have been in a lot of trouble of one sort or another," Kate says.

Even in a "bad" class, Debby did badly. Because of her poor record and low test scores, she was put in the slow group, and that bothered her. Before long she began skipping school. Her family knew she was drinking. Several times the school administration called Kate or Nick and asked them to come and pick Debby up, because she was causing trouble. On one occasion the police were called in, and the Barneses learned their daughter had gotten involved in drugs.

That time was a nightmare for Kate and Nicholas. All Kate's guilt came sweeping back. "I take on all the responsibility and all the guilt for everything," she says. "I'm trying to get rid of this [problem], but I do. Guilt is a terrible thing with me. . . . That's part of me."

She responded to this bout of guilt about Debby as she had responded to the guilt she had felt about her long hospital stay during Debby's infancy: she showered Debby with attention. Before long, Debby and Debby's behavior had become the focus of Kate's life. "I know I overreacted," Kate says. "I like control, and I could not control my daughter."

Yet she wouldn't relinquish authority either, even to Nick. Kate approvingly describes Nick as "the strong one" in the family: "I was always very happy to have Nick make the decisions—except where my daughter was concerned. Where Debby was concerned, I somehow thought I was better." Debby was her problem and it was a problem she couldn't handle.

Family life deteriorated badly. Debby might come home from school, go directly to her room, and fall into a heavy sleep. Then Kate would know that she was "on something." "We would try to awaken her for dinner," not always successfully.

On other occasions, Debby wouldn't come home from school. Six o'clock, then seven, came, and no Debby. The family gathered uneasily around the dinner table. After dinner, Kate might ask Tim and some of his friends to drive around the neighborhood and look for his sister—"which I wish I had not done, but I was so desperate to find her some of those nights."

When Debby went out socially, it was even worse. If, as frequently happened, the girl stayed too late at a party, Kate would send Tim and his best friend on a "rescue mission." "They could go to these parties and go in, and of course Nick and I could not."

Sometimes the hour grew very late and Debby hadn't been found. Neither Kate nor Nick could sleep. They would go to bed and lie there listening, waiting. When Nick dozed off, Kate would get up and walk the floor. She tries to describe the horror of those nights of waiting with an image "that haunts me . . . like a bad dream."

> There are two windows in our house [that I think of].
> One is a dining-room window, which is a low window. I used to get up in the night, when she wasn't home, and I would, on my knees with my arms on the windowsill, just watch up the street praying that she would come in sight.
> Then there was another window, which was a tall window, and I would lean with my arms on the sill, looking the other way down the street.
> I would just move between those two windows, waiting for her to come home. Sometimes she would and sometimes she wouldn't.

As she watched from the two windows for Debby, Kate, who had never relied much on the church or the clergy, muttered desperate prayers for her daughter: "God, please make her come home from the party, please make her come home." Her prayers didn't seem to be answered.

Unhappy and disturbed already, Debby felt tremendous pressure from her mother's constant, unproductive concern. In retrospect, Kate realizes that Debby would probably have responded favorably to the stronger hand that Nick would have provided—"a structured situation and rapid feedback, which is easy enough to provide in a family setting. It was just not a part of our family setting." But Kate's reproaches, Kate's dependence on Debby for good behavior, Kate's inability to cope, drove her daughter away. At fifteen, Debby began staying away from home for days at a time.

> She usually would call and say, "Just want you to know I am all right, but I can't come home, I can't deal with it. I don't want to be around home."
> So she would be gone, one time for about five days.
> Her psychologist knew someone, in a crazy "small world" sort of way, who knew the person she was staying with. So we were able to observe that it was just nonstop drinking. . . . She had not been going to school, and she was drunk all the time, she and her friend.

Throughout all this, Kate was not acting assertively. Debby went or didn't go to school, she saw her doctor, she ran wild—she called the shots. Kate waited, watched, and suffered. She remonstrated with Debby, tried to reason with her, but she didn't succeed in bringing order into her daughter's chaotic young life.

As weeks went by and Debby didn't improve, Kate grew more and more frantic. She seriously, and justifiably, believed that Debby might drink herself to death at fifteen. But she had gotten so involved with her daughter's feelings that she had lost herself in Debby's drama. Debby was writing the scenario and playing the lead, and her parents had been assigned bit parts. Or, to put the problem more simply, Kate had lost the adult detachment necessary to help a disturbed child.

DEBBY, "SENT AWAY"

One afternoon something happened. Some power deep within Kate moved her to see the situation at last not as a reproach to her as a mother, but as a problem that could be solved. "A light bulb went on," Kate says, and she knew quite suddenly that Debby *had* to be brought under control. If her mother couldn't do it, someone else could. Kate paid attention, and then she took action.

> I can remember exactly where I was and what I was doing when I decided that we could go no further with Debby [as she was]. It was about two o'clock in the afternoon. I was pacing my kitchen, which is what I did many afternoons. Literally just pacing, waiting for the phone to ring and the school to call and say that she was drunk, or that she was something else.
>
> And I stopped in the middle of my walking and put on my coat and went to the library.

At the library, she spent several hours going through reference material, looking for something that could help Debby. Though she turned up nothing, the effort had broken the syndrome of ineffectuality in which she had been trapped.

Her mind working better than it had in months, Kate raced back home when the library closed and leafed through the phone numbers of her friends and acquaintances. Who could help? Something must be done for Debby! She would see to it that it was.

Taking her courage in her hands, Kate at length decided to call Jennifer Johnson. She didn't know Jennifer that well, and a phone call of this kind was a breach of a certain social distance maintained in their circle. But Kate remembered that Jennifer's daughter Jackie was away at school. Jackie and Debby were exactly the same age, and Kate knew that Jackie had had "problems" for years. Kate had always respected and liked Jennifer too much ever to ask her about Jackie directly, but she must put tact aside now, for her own child's sake.

She dialed the number and Jennifer answered. "Jennifer," Kate said, "this school Jackie is in, would this be a school for children who are just out of control?"

Jennifer began to laugh—"hysterically, if you can imagine," Kate says.

> I mean, I thought she would never stop laughing, and she said, "Yes, just *slightly* out of control."

I said, "Well, I didn't know; I knew that it was a special school." And I said, "Let me tell you a little bit about my daughter this past year."

Then Jennifer said, "She sounds perfect for the school. Just get on the phone."

And Kate did. She called the local representative for the school, then began calling the school's director at intervals throughout the evening. About midnight she reached him. Quickly she explained the situation. He understood at once. He told her, "Come on. Come tomorrow."

During all this frantic phoning, Nick came home from work. He watched Kate in amazement. After months of inactivity, she was finally doing something. "I think he was sitting in wonder. He was very much in agreement, but I think he thought I was moving a little quickly. . . . But I had really reached a decision."

After a sleepless night of planning, the next morning they faced the problem of getting Debby to the school, which was halfway across the country from the Barneses' home in Houston. The boys left for school at the usual time. Kate's telephoning began again. She called her mother and asked her to pick up twelve-year-old Brian after school and explain the situation to him as well as she could. Then she called Tim's private high school and got him out of class; she had just realized that she and Nick would probably need Tim's help with his sister. Last she called the airline and made four reservations on a noon flight to California, where the school was located.

But where to find Debby? She was on one of her extended drunks. They hadn't seen her for four days. Nick thought of the police. Debby had never actually been arrested, but the police had come to the school a number of times because of her and they "were very aware of her," Kate says. Sure enough, "they had an idea where she was."

Nick and the police officer, tailed by Kate and Tim, found Debby parked in a car at the back of the high school. It was ten o'clock in the morning, but already Debby was drunk and "she was wild." Debby is a small girl, slight and short, but "terribly strong." It took all four of them to get her in the car. Then the police officer left and the Barneses raced down the Texas freeway toward the airport.

They created a scene at the airport. Tim was in his school uniform, a coat and tie, looking very proper, like Nick in his business suit. Kate had dressed neatly, but she was "teary and distraught." Debby, in jeans and denim jacket, with long hair falling over her face, looked anything but proper. "We dragged her screaming obscenities through the airport," Kate recalls, "I running ahead and trying to tell people that my husband and son were trying to take care of her and that she was emotionally disturbed.

"I didn't tell people that she was also drunk. She was very, very drunk."

RUNNING

The Rampart School (not its real name) did for Debby what Kate and Nick hadn't been able to do—gave her time to dry out, specific and stated rules, the sense of structure that the desperate girl needed. Debby wanted help, Kate believes; her behavior was a radical way of getting someone to bring her under control. "I absolutely believe that these children 'set up' situations in which to get caught so that they will receive some care or direction or family attention that they need."

But for a long time Kate had been so intent on her suffering, so emotionally identified with Debby's successes and especially Debby's failures, that she couldn't see Debby's need clearly. Now she believes that someone else, some presumably objective expert, should have been able to respond to Debby's plight.

She remembers with particular bane the seventh-grade counselor who sent Kate home with the cheerful message, "Debby's not the problem—you're the problem!" "For a while I could hardly drive by that school. I had to keep saying to myself"—she laughs bitterly— "'It's not the school.'" She knows now that she should have had greater faith in her own feelings of alarm than in someone so obviously insensitive to the children for whom he was responsible.

She also feels critical of the doctors at the time of Debby's nearly fatal overdose of alcohol. Why didn't they suggest that Kate and Nick aggressively seek help for their child? That night, Kate and

Nick had stayed in the hospital with Debby during the hours her stomach was being pumped, when the doctors weren't sure whether she would live or die. Both parents were of course "very upset."

Yet, seeing their concern, the medical staff did not tell them that Debby needed help, but, out of a foolish and misguided compassion, said that she didn't.

> Three doctors and two nurses came to us because we were very obviously upset, and said, "Please just forget that this ever happened. It happens all the time, and just forget it and go on. Just forget it."

"I think that is just mind-boggling!" Kate says.

> They should have advised instant, immediate reacting to something of this sort. . . . I believe the medical profession was remiss. They could have done something with my daughter, right then, and she probably would have been responsive.
>
> She was terrified, and of course terribly ashamed, but at the same time just belligerent and mean as hell. [She was probably wondering], "What do I have to *do* to get someone to listen to my grief?"

By some miracle of insight that afternoon in her kitchen, Kate herself at last was able to move beyond her own stress to pay attention to *Debby*, not to Kate's feelings about her. Putting herself out of the picture, she saw only that her child needed help. Then she acted. Sometimes over the next two years she was to wonder, as most parents do, whether she had done the right thing for Debby. "It was terrible for Debby," she acknowledges, "to be sent away." And Debby, quite naturally, still feels some resentment toward the school, if not toward her parents. Even so, Debby herself believes that being "sent away" saved her life.

For Kate, action was and always is better than passivity: "I think you make the decision that you are going to fight . . . whether it's the right action or not. I feel good that we took some action."

When they had gotten Debby to Rampart, the whole family, except for Brian back in Houston, met with the young, vital director, Jim McClain (not his real name). McClain told them that Debby was "very like a lot of other teenagers; she was truly a teenager in crisis."

After McClain had met Debby, he talked with Kate and Nick. "We spent about three hours with him, which was an incredible experience—talking about our family, talking about our daughter, talking about our expectations."

McClain and Tim talked privately for a while. Then they left Debby. "This was in March of her sophomore year, so she was fifteen. We left her. But we were in constant contact with the school. . . . It was wonderful to be able to communicate our concerns and have them communicate their concerns, keep us in touch with where she was. And we talked to her often."

Kate also talked often with Carolyn Shubert, one of her best friends. Soon after the Barneses got back to Houston, Carolyn called to find out how Debby had made it at the school. Kate found herself pouring out her fears and hopes to the sympathetic ear of a mother who was going through the same things herself.

Like Kate and Nicholas, Carolyn and Monty Shubert had adopted children, Sally and George, whose problems were much worse in every way than Debby's. Sally, with minimal brain dysfunction and learning disabilities, had at least a three-year developmental lag. The brain disorder left her with "a total lack of judgment." From kindergarten on, the other children made fun of her, and Sally had no social life. When she reached adolescence, desperate for attention from people her own age, Sally discovered boys. She began to cause enormous problems for her parents and herself. In the sixth grade the Shuberts sent her to a special school; Carolyn had begun to realize that Sally would always need to live in a supervised environment.

George, Sally's younger brother, was becoming even more difficult to deal with. At thirteen, he was completely antisocial. A quiet, passive child, he was capable of alarmingly hostile and destructive acts at home. He had recently begun the drift of unhappy children toward drugs and alcohol. The Shuberts had not put George in a special school, but already they wished they had.

Carolyn was as glad to find a confidante as Kate. The two women, who were casual social acquaintances, had worked together years earlier as volunteers with emotionally disturbed children. Now, working with their own emotionally disturbed children, they found tremendous support in each other. An intense friendship developed between the two mothers, which Kate describes:

> We talked on the telephone; some days we must have talked hours and hours, maybe a dozen times in some days. Or we would get in the car and go to each other's house if we needed to. I didn't have to get out of the house. Sometimes Carolyn had to leave her house [because of George], and would just suddenly be at the door.

And their friendship has lasted. At the time of the interview, four years later, Kate says, "We absolutely are *there* for each other. I don't think there is anything that we would hesitate asking of each other."

Kate needed all the personal support she could get during the two years Debby spent at Rampart. The school didn't have instant and complete success with Kate's headstrong daughter. Far from it. In fact, when Debby began to feel that the counselors at the school were getting close to the source of her problems, she responded in a maddening fashion: she ran away. And because the counselors were good, because the school was able to bring the light of objective analysis into the dark and hidden corners of Debby's young psyche, she ran away often.

> She has covered the west coast from California, where the school was, to southern Canada, I think, three times. She could run away while they had all sorts of people watching her. She ran away from the school in the middle of the night, with the state police providing her ride. I mean she can talk her way in and out of any situation.
>
> Once or twice she got a truck driver—it's just wild; Carolyn and I just couldn't believe it—to drive her, and then he would give her fifty dollars and take her to a Greyhound bus station. . . .
>
> She ran away so many times I cannot even tell you how many; she has the school record for sure. But she never did anything illegal. She never stole money, for instance, but she would get little old ladies to give her money in restaurants all over the place.

Debby had been sexually active since the age of thirteen or so, and often when she ran away, it was with a boy. Some of those periods of freedom in flight remain pleasant memories for her, though not for her mother.

Every spring she tells us about the lovely ten days she spent on the beach, and how they got money; they collected bottles along the roadside and would turn them in and get enough money for a jar of peanut butter and a loaf of bread. It was *wonderful,* and the weather was beautiful, and they were in his grandfather's cottage—which had been closed, of course.

When Debby ran away and things were not so idyllic, she usually called Kate and Nick and begged to come home. They had to learn to say no. Turning their daughter down when she wanted to come home offended their sensibilities as parents. They could probably not have managed this difficult feat without the group therapy they went into at the request of the school.

The school maintained, correctly as it turned out, that when a troubled child ran out of resources, she would return to the school on her own. At that point, she would in effect be asking for help and thus was more capable of receiving what she needed. It worked this way for Debby.

She ran away often, but eventually she always returned. Each of the many times she returned to the school over the next two years, she learned more about herself and her needs. Gradually Debby got a tremendous amount of therapy—group therapy at the school, weekly private therapy with a doctor trained by the Gestalt Institute —and some understanding of her problems.

But she did not quit running. She and her parents often reached a stalemate.

We would not allow her to come home, and she said she would not go back to the school. We believed her—or we believed that she thought she was not going back, but we were equally determined that she was going to go back. Because the school was determined that she see this thing through and that she stop running, and that made sense to us.

We wanted them to hospitalize her, because we felt that she had just to be locked up, so she could face some of these things that were tormenting her. . . . But the group therapist, the school psychologist, and the Gestalt psychiatrist explained that at no time could my daughter ever be involuntarily hospitalized. She is not psychotic. She is not dangerous to herself or to others. She was just mixed up about some things.

Patience was called for while Debby ran herself out. Still, her parents could not help agonizing over her unscheduled appearances and disappearances. Instead of watching from two windows for Debby to come home, as she had done before, Kate found herself with a new post for her vigil: the airport. Debby would be coming home from school for an official school holiday or an authorized visit. Kate would go to the airport to meet her flight.

[I remember] the despair that I would feel. I stood and watched the plane empty, and no daughter. I just stood feeling very alarmed and teary. I waited at the airport so many times when the plane would empty and there would be no Debby.

THE DYNAMICS OF A FAMILY

Detachment had not completely solved their problems. Debby was still not at peace, nor were they at peace about her. Nevertheless, their immediate responsibility for her was easier than it had been for several years. For weeks at a time she seemed to be happy at school. Detached from the constant trauma of her erratic behavior at home, her parents could turn some attention to themselves and the family environment they had created.

From the time Debby was fifteen until she was seventeen, the Barnes family got a lot of help from professional psychological therapists. Few families would be able to pay the bill for this help: Debby's therapy alone cost more than thirty thousand dollars a year for those two years. But then, not all families need to spend so much; less expensive help can be found. But Nicholas Barnes had the money and he later told his daughter he felt "privileged" to be able to spend it to help her.

The Barnes family stayed close to Debby's school. They spent two separate weeks, one week with one son and one with the other, in residence at the Rampart School attending parent-child seminars. Throughout the year the constant communication between parents and school continued. Because of this ongoing close contact, Kate and Nick began to understand better than they ever had the behavior of their strange, unpredictable daughter.

In addition, Nick and Kate went into group therapy, attending weekly sessions with the parents' support group they had joined, of which Carolyn and Monty Shubert were also members. These sessions helped them to discover the ways in which the dynamics of their family could be improved so that the family could function better for everyone's sake.

Debby's problems were largely caused by fear, fear that came from being an adopted child. For years she had been conscious of, as her mother says, "a terrible pain, a terrible fear, inside her. She could talk about this; it was a fear of what she didn't know—her real mother and her real father. It was trying to understand how anyone could leave a child."

Very slowly, by fits and starts, Debby herself began to comprehend the "terrible fear" that had wracked her small frame ever since she could remember. Not all adopted children suffer what Debby did, as Kate says, though "for many children it is very difficult. I would probably be like Debby; I think I would have some curiosity. But it depends on the child."

Kate and Nick began to watch their two sons for signs that they too were affected by adoption anxiety. Neither of Debby's brothers felt as Debby did. Tim, a high school senior on his way to an Ivy League school and a happy, social boy, didn't seem the least bit concerned. "It is honestly just not important to him, he honestly doesn't have any great curiosity," Kate says.

But Tim takes an intellectual approach to life, so he decided, after Debby's problems surfaced, that he should look into his own feelings with a little more care.

> He came to us very formally and said that he thought he would like to go to a therapist and so we said fine. . . . So he went . . . and Tim came back and said, "Well, I don't know if I need to go again or not."
>
> So my husband said, "If you aren't sure, why don't you give it another hour and see what you think?"

After his next session with the psychotherapist, Tim reported that the doctor had said, "Listen, Tim, if you want to come and talk, it's just fine, but you sure don't need to be here." So Tim decided not to go back, though he was happy that the doctor had also left the door open "if you ever want to call me from school, or if there is anything you want to check out."

"It was a very nice way to have left it," Kate says gratefully.

The youngest child, Brian, was only twelve when Debby was sent to Rampart. That he has never expressed any adoption fears and doesn't want to talk about the adoption at all Kate finds disconcerting: "Someday I suspect it will have to come out in some way or another."

Brian wasn't much aware of the way Debby was behaving before she was taken to Rampart, but he remembers his parents' reaction to her behavior—the confusion in the house when Debby was missing, the unhappy dinners, the tears and recriminations.

And he was tremendously affected by the fact that Debby was summarily, as he saw it, "sent away." "We realized a couple of years ago," Kate says, "that Brian was very good and always very careful. We discussed this and he said, 'I will never do anything wrong where I might be sent away.' So we had a lot of conversation about that."

At the time of the interview Brian was sixteen. "He now seems very relaxed, goes out with friends, but it was frightening for him— just the thought that if you do something wrong in our family you are sent away. That's pretty heavy."

In examining the way the Barnes family operated, Kate and Nick found their therapy group to be an invaluable and positive experience. Kate says, "I believe in group therapy, that you learn from others and their reactions much more quickly than you can in individual therapy." But she also recognizes that, for her, the therapy worked "because I like these people so much. If I didn't like them personally, I probably wouldn't go."

Carolyn Shubert, who with her husband Monty belonged to the same group, confirms Kate's sense of the value of the group. "It was a very, very strong support group. You can call anybody in that group any time of day or night, any place. They will come and help, physically or emotionally. Anything that you ask is not too much."

Kate was surprised at how involved Nick, ordinarily a very private person, became with the problems of the other parents. "His work is

very important to him. . . . Nothing, including taking me to the
hospital, would take Nick out of the office. But he came home three
different times to help other families in our therapy group who were
having trouble with their children. . . . Often it was just plain need
of a muscle. Just like we needed muscle to take my daughter to
school, these people needed muscle to remove a child from a situation or whatever." And Nick was there when he was needed.

From the group, the Barneses and the Shuberts also became
friends as couples, spending, as Carolyn puts it, "Friday night after
Friday night together, just talking about our problems." Much of
what they talked about had to do with the specific problems of
adopted children. Being adopted clearly was a central issue in Debby's difficulties, and the Shuberts thought in Sally's and George's as
well. Carolyn believes that the problems of adopted children have
not received as much attention as they should from child experts.
She also faults some adoption agencies for being less than candid or
knowledgeable about the children they present for adoption.

On the basis of her own experience, she thinks prospective parents ought to be told clearly by the agency, in advance, that adopting a child is a calculated risk. Although recent research indicates
that adopted children have no more problems than other children,
Carolyn's point is well taken:

> I would not say, "Do not adopt children." I would say that
> . . . you are taking a risk, and that . . . it requires special
> parenting in many cases.

But in the larger group, family problems discussed were more
universal and the solutions hammered out applied to families with
adopted children as well as to others. One of the first things Kate
and Nick learned was that they functioned exceptionally well as a
couple—"better than most people," Kate says proudly, "and we
were fortunate and strengthened by that, I would say."

Nevertheless, they quickly recognized that Debby's difficulties
had risen from the family environment they had created. As Kate
acknowledges, "We're part of our daughter's problems, and they
developed in our family. It's not that she went out and did something; it was a developmental thing." So they set out in therapy to
understand what had gone wrong with their family dynamics.

The first problem they realized was the lack of limits set up for their children. Debby needed structure, and she didn't get it. Kate and Nick are strong, independent people who needed very little external structure or overt support from each other. They were, to use David Riesman's self-explanatory term from Chapter 1, "inner-directed" rather than "other-directed." "Nick knew I would be all right because that was our relationship," Kate says, "that I was always all right."

They patterned their family on their own relationship and on the family Kate had come from. "Our family is actually a very structured functioning family, but it was sort of inner structure." Like Kate's parents, Nick and Kate made few demands of their children and set up few rules.

A similar situation existed in the permissive school environment of the seventies. "Since this whole thing," Kate says, "I have come to value the structured education . . . not only for the education, but more importantly for the self-confidence, the image. . . . [In a structured classroom, a child] has to do things, then when he has done them he has a self-confidence, and he has a discipline."

Instead, Kate believes, her two oldest children were left with too many decisions to make on their own. At home and at school, they were told, "We know you will do right; use your own judgment." This permissive system worked well for Tim, who was strong and independent like his parents. "He could handle it just as we in my family could handle it. But it's a tremendous weight to put on a child," Kate says.

The weight was too heavy for Debby, who had crumpled under it. Already uneasy about her origins, her security in the family, and her own identity, she found herself in an uncertain and confusing world. Testing at the Rampart School revealed that Debby, whose behavior appeared to be untraditional and even anarchic, actually holds very traditional values. "She loved that," Kate says. "She just responded to that, she wanted to hear that. . . . She said, 'They say that I have a very clear idea of right and wrong and of honesty.' That just makes her beam. She *needed* to hear it." Debby was a child who longed for limits she didn't have.

Another problem in family dynamics that Kate and Nick addressed in therapy was Debby's swollen importance in the family and particularly to her mother. Like most of the women in this study, Kate was usually the first person to act on family problems, but with the boys Nick eventually played the stronger role. But Kate had been very possessive about Debby. For intriguing but finally inexplicable reasons, Debby's failures had become Kate's failures and Debby her sole, guilty responsibility. She had almost unwittingly edged Nick out. In doing so, she had made Debby the center of the family and had become fanatical in her concern with her daughter.

Kate's mother helped to bring Kate to a saner attitude. One day when Debby's problems were at their worst, she addressed Kate sternly with "Don't you have to make a decision fairly soon as to whether, if your daughter goes down the tube, you are going to go also?"

"And she pointed out Nick, the other children, and *me,*" Kate says, chuckling. "This was something of course that I had been thinking about, but she said it in a shocking way, and then sort of just left me with it. It brought me up short."

Kate realized that in her parents' family, which she thought "perfect in every way," the children were not central in family life.

> We were a very close family. But I don't think that the children were the dominant part of the family. My mother and father's relationship was very important.
>
> I remember my mother saying, "I adore you, I would do anything in the world for you, but I am raising you to go off and live your own life. And, by golly, your father and I will live ours." It was straight and open.
>
> Nick and I had allowed the children to become the focus of our lives. And I don't think my mom and dad did.

Carolyn Shubert also brought Kate up short on the subject. At one point, Carolyn told their group, she had feared that their problems with Sally and George might spell the death of her marriage to Monty. When she realized what was at stake, she did some serious thinking and made a conscious decision. "The decision," she said solemnly, "was that my marriage came first, and that our children came second, and that I was not going to lose my marriage over my children. I had seen it happen in too many cases, where situations in the home destroyed a marriage, and I was not willing to have this happen."

Through therapy, Kate learned how beneficial a united front from her and Nick would be to Debby. She also came to see what an unfair responsibility she had been placing on Debby herself. She made a decision of her own.

I have done a whole lot of soul-searching, and a whole lot of thinking, [and reached] the decision to go on, the decision that my life is important, and my husband's and my other children's. And that whatever Debby does, I am going to go on.

And, for heaven's sake, it's a good thing I have finally lifted this burden from her. It's a terrible burden. I am overwhelmed by that part—that we were actually putting the family on her, on how she behaved. The happiness of the individual members of our family, my happiness, my well-being, were on her. That is really cockeyed. I got a little mixed up.

With these insights and others, over the two years that Debby was at Rampart the situation in the Barnes family changed slowly but radically. Kate and Nick shared the family decisions, but, as Kate puts it, Nick became "the mouthpiece" to the children—all three of the children. Tim was in college, but a more structured home environment was set up for Brian, who thrived in it.

"COME HOME!"

Meanwhile, as Kate says, Debby "ran and ran and ran." Finally one night Nick said, "I'm not going on any further with this. I want her to come home."

Kate was surprised but pleased. "I probably would have held out a little while longer, but I was very relieved when Nick said this."

So Debby called, sure enough, just as she often did. She would just beg to come home, and we would say, "No, we cannot see you until you go back to the school. We will be there immediately, Tim and Brian too, we will all be there, but you must go back."

So this night she called. I am sure she expected the same
litany. And Nick said, "Come home!"

And she said, "You are kidding me."

He said, "No."

And she said, "I can't believe it."

He said, "I won't go on any longer with you sleeping in
gas stations."

"If you come home," Nick told his daughter, "you will live according to my rules. We will work on these together, but it will be in
accordance with my wishes.

"And you will receive therapy, and you will no longer run."

Debby was with a boyfriend at the time, and she knew this meant
leaving him behind. "I'll have to think about that," she told her
father. "It will take me a couple of days to decide."

"Fine," he said. He hung up. He and Kate looked at each other.
Could they do it? They believed they could.

Two days later, Debby called again. "I'm coming home," she said.

Of them all, the most thrilled to have her home again was Brian,
who was fourteen. Glad as they were to have her back, Kate and Nick
were understandably nervous. Brian felt no such reservations. "It
was the happiest day of Brian's life," Kate says. "My mother says
that Brian was a new person when Debby came home."

And home turned out to be the best place for Debby to be. At the
time of Kate's interview, Debby had been living within the family
setting and abiding by the family rules for over a year and a half. Not
once in that time, Kate says happily, has she gotten out of control. "I
think she has started on a track and I just want to keep her going. I
am less worried about Debby now than I have been since she was in
the sixth grade. . . . She will have ups and downs, but I think she
can cope."

Her education essentially stopped when Debby was thirteen or
fourteen, so her first move at home was to go back to her tutor for
help in passing the high school equivalency test. She passed the test,
and "she is very proud of that," her mother says.

Debby was very conscious of the expense she had been to her
family, so she got a job immediately. For a year and a half, she
worked as a waitress and cashier in a coffee shop. She received many

raises and more than once was named Employee of the Month. Her salary enabled her to begin buying a car.

She also took and passed several classes at a local community college. Debby had dropped out of therapy, which worried her parents, but "we knew we could not force her to do it," Kate says. Then she talked to her parents about the prospect of college. Nick said, "Debby, I don't know why you want that. You said you hated school."

"Well, yes, Dad," she said, "but I have to get someplace, and I have to be able to earn money to live." She kicked this idea around for a while.

After several months, she went back to the therapist with a plan. She had gotten very bored with her job at the coffee shop, and she wanted some testing to find out what she is suited for vocationally.

"This is all very exciting to us, and to the therapist also," her mother says.

> We want her to initiate things on her own behalf. . . . The therapist has gotten so carried away, it's a riot. As of last week, Debby has started going to a rehabilitation vocational counselor, trying to figure out what it is she wants to do.
>
> And it might very well be that she would be better off in a six-month training program, where she can see the end and get some feedback, then get a job. They will place her. . . .
>
> It would be something where she would have some dignity, which is very important to my daughter. . . . She needs to be able to tell her friends, "I'm in computer school." She needs to have something that is acceptable to her in the eyes of others, and that [allows her to] live on her own and be independent.

Independence is a goal for Kate too. "I want my independence and Debby wants her independence. It's very important to both of us."

Kate has realized that, if Debby dreams of being independent, her mother can now "allow her to be. That's new in me. I absolutely can now. It's more than insight. It's ability. I can let her go."

In the meantime, the family are enjoying each other's company.

No longer does Debby retreat to her room when she is at home. "She is with the family all the time now," Kate says cheerfully. "She sits around with us."

And Kate is catching up with the nurturing Debby missed out on. "We don't want to hurry this step," she says, "so that Debby knows that she was sent away to deal with a problem, not sent away to make our lives more comfortable."

Kate cooks good meals for her daughter and is ready to do Debby's laundry, but Debby won't let her. Kate was prepared to make concessions of all kinds, having learned in therapy, for example, that if teenagers won't clean up their room, a mother should neither badger them nor do it for them. "And I did get so I could simply close the door, and the dirt would pile up and everything else."

To her pleased surprise, she doesn't have to do this. "For the first time since seventh grade her room is clean, and she is pitching in and helping the family too."

As Kate backed off and let Nick and Debby get closer to each other, Debby's "wild flirtatious streak has just calmed down. She has boyfriends, but her girlfriends are more important at this time." Debby has gone back to her old, good friends. "The therapists have commented on her ability to make and sustain relationships," Kate says. "Unlike lots of children who have gone through what Debby has gone through, that is one of her real strengths."

Debby has also learned to articulate the fears about her status as an adopted child which still plague her from time to time. Not long ago when mother and daughter were driving to the Gulf together for a weekend, the subject of abortion came up. Kate asked Debby what she thought about it.

Debby turned around "with the haughtiest look," and told her mother firmly, "Mother, you shouldn't even have to ask. Of course I don't believe in abortion. I could have been an abortion."

USING WHAT SHE'S LEARNED

Kate frequently tells Debby, "Honey, I know what agony you have gone through, and I'm terribly sorry you had to suffer. But I'm grateful to you for what I have learned from you and your experiences."

"I think that makes her feel better," Kate says. "It probably relieves her mind." But Kate means every word.

The last year that Debby was at Rampart, Kate decided to work. She had discovered that if detachment helped her daughter, it also helped her. At first, to take her mind off Debby and Debby's problems, Kate "scrubbed a lot of floors and cleaned a lot of cupboards." But she needed more: "to think of others" and "to get outside myself a little bit." There ought to be some use beyond her own family circle, she thought, for the insight she had gained into troubled young people.

Before long she landed a position interviewing applicants for a private school for troubled children. Her job at first was modest but vital: to help parents evaluate whether the school could really serve their child's best interests, whether it would only be a stopgap measure, or whether, in some cases, it could actually be damaging. As time passed, however, she demonstrated such tact and sensitivity, such a firm grasp of the issues involved, that she began to be consulted also for students in the school who got in trouble.

> I can often talk to those families and provide some real
> insight, and not only insight but solace. I tell them that they
> *will* get through situations when they don't think they can.
> And that some good can come out of it.

Kate has what every counselor needs: detachment and empathy. Through her initial failures with Debby, she has acquired a certain objectivity which helps in examining a child's behavior. Yet at the same time she knows how these people feel because she's been there herself. With skeptical parents who think of her merely as a professional who doesn't understand the full horror of what they are going through, she is ready to share her own experiences with Debby.

Once "a really rough, tough blue-collar type of man" with a very troubled and, as it happened, adopted daughter turned on her angrily. "What do you know about it, lady?" he challenged her.

"There isn't anything you can tell me that I can't tell you one better," she told him. And she proved it.

"And we sat down and had the most fabulous conversation," Kate says, laughing at what she calls their one-upmanship. "He just poured out his soul. And I knew it was good [for him.] It was good."

Her work has brought her a greater pride and sense of accomplishment, Kate says, than anything else in her life. "I had to get myself going and get out of the mucking around in my own mind and just take some action. It's getting up in the morning and simply going and doing a job. I'm doing something; I am influencing other people in some areas that I know something about."

Kate paid attention to her child. She took action, which demanded giving up the mutual dependency that was crippling her and her daughter. She chose instead the detachment that was necessary for their psychological strength. And in the movement from dependency to detachment, Kate received a wonderful bonus for herself: autonomy.

"I had to make a life of my own, apart from my family, and it was the best thing I ever did," she rejoices. Her dark eyes sparkle, and she smiles. "I want to send everybody to work!"

Now she and Debby are happily establishing a connection that will last because it is based on strength rather than on weakness.

PART II

SECOND SELF

SECOND SELF

Stage Five

AUTONOMY

Shaping the only life for which a mother is completely responsible—her own

10

The Tremendous Mercy of Autonomy

Once, not so long ago, middle-class mothers in America presumably fell prey, as they approached middle age, to something called "the empty nest syndrome." The children, on whom the lives of these women had centered, had grown up and left home. Thus "the empty nest." Mother, abandoned to her own devices, found those devices startlingly, traumatically thin. Thus the "syndrome." The traditional housewife and mother spends her youth on family duties. She might well spend her last thirty years in a state of chronic regret at the loss of those duties, which have given her life its only meaning. Or so the theory goes.

The experiences of the mothers interviewed here give the lie to the theory. Not a single woman in this study suffers from "the empty nest syndrome." "Traditional" these mothers are, certainly. They devoted most of their energies to home and family. None of them held a full-time job when their children were young; none pursued a career or practiced an art in a way that interfered with family life. They have paid attention to their children and taken action for them in trying situations. Much of the drama they have known in life has come through motherhood.

But only briefly here and there do they confuse the lives of their children with their own lives. Overwhelmingly, they don't want to live *through* their children, or, beyond a certain necessary point, even *with* their children. They understand instinctively that, as Simone de Beauvoir says, "living by proxy is always a precarious expedient." To a woman, they would agree with Mary Gordon on "the other part of mother love: it was not all of life." As she puts it in her novel *Men and Angels:*

> And that was wonderful; it was a tremendous mercy. For there was so little you could do for them, even if you spent every moment with them, gave them every waking thought, there wasn't much that you could do. You gave them life, you loved them, then you opened them out to the world. You could never protect them; so you left them to themselves. That was the mercy, that you could turn from them to something else, something they couldn't touch or be a part of.

Everyone, a mother perhaps most of all, needs a "something else," an individual province which has nothing to do with family life. Every mother is first a woman, every woman a person. The "something else" may be the study of art, as it is for Gordon's heroine, or something far more mundane. Anything will do, so long as it satisfies the person in the mother.

Then the empty nest becomes a busy workshop, studio, or office. Rosemary Dixon sells real estate from her empty nest. Sharon Marsh runs a sewing shop in hers. Suzanne White has become a commercial artist, Kate Barnes a counselor, Margot Morrison a cellist. These middle-aged women and countless others like them have discovered the tremendous mercy of autonomy.

WHAT IS AUTONOMY?

Autonomy doesn't automatically come with every job, of course, in spite of Kate's pronouncement that she'd "like to send everybody to work!" Millions of women who can lay no claim to autonomy have full-time jobs outside their homes. Poorly paid, unpleasurable, their jobs help to enslave mothers who feel that by working they are sacrificing themselves for family financial needs. Whether or not a job confers autonomy depends very much on a woman's attitude toward what she does and the reasons for which she does it.

The autonomous woman makes conscious choices which give her control over some area of her life. Autonomy is, more than anything else, a state of mind. No one is completely free, no one has complete control of her life. But control can be sought, can be worked toward, can be achieved.

Dr. Jane Loevinger, the psychologist at Washington University who created the test for ego development which was given to the women in this study, distinguishes six full stages of development, with numerous transitional stages. The first two stages, the Symbiotic and the Impulsive, followed by a transition stage, the Self-Protective, are associated in adults with serious emotional problems. None of these mothers scored at these levels.

Nor did any of the mothers score purely at the level of the third stage, the Conformist. The Conformist level is characterized by conformity to external rules and by an emphasis on "niceness," appearance, and social acceptability. Conformists are unoriginal thinkers. The majority or a large minority in most social groups scores at the Conformist level.

But the women studied here who gave Conformist endings to some of the sentence completions on the test ("What gets me into trouble is . . ." *my big mouth*) showed in other sentences sufficient development to justify a higher rating. All of these women were post-Conformist.

Over half of these mothers scored purely at the fourth level, the Conscientious. The Conformist thinks that rules are necessary and require rigid adherence. The Conscientious sees rules as general guidelines for conduct, and feels free to change rules when the situation warrants. The Conscientious looks to internal standards, internal criticism, as guides for behavior, and is concerned with good mutual communication with others, and highly discriminated feelings and motives.

At the post-Conscientious level exists the transitional stage of the Individualistic, where respect for individuality is added to the Conscientious. The Individualist recognizes that emotional dependence may continue even in the absence of physical and financial dependence. Over a fourth of these mothers were rated at this level by Loevinger's expert scorers.

Practically speaking, the Autonomous stage is the highest level of ego development. The sixth, the Integrated stage, is so seldom achieved as to remain something of a hypothetical construct; if it were achieved, inner conflicts would be reconciled, the unattainable renounced, and individuality and identity cherished. The Integrated can only be attained, if at all, by way of the Autonomous stage, just as the Autonomous is attained only by way of the Conscientious.

The Autonomous adds to the qualities of the Conscientious a respect both for autonomy and for connection (or "interdependence," to use Loevinger's self-explanatory term). At this level, one has a heightened sense of one's own individuality and a respect for that of others.

The Autonomous mother no longer needs the safe world of the Conformist. She has the ability to tolerate paradox and contradiction in life. She is aware that a "good" process may yield a "bad" result, and vice versa, and that the simple rules of the Conformist may be irrelevant or misleading. Furthermore, the Autonomous capably acknowledges and copes with her own inner conflicts.

Autonomy is rare. Though the scores of the women here were regarded by the experts as exceptionally high, only one mother, whose story will be told in the next chapter, had reached the undiluted Autonomous stage.

But, accurate as psychologists claim the Loevinger test to be, what do these test scores signify, anyway? What do such cold test results have to say to us about the experiences of a warm, breathing woman who has been forced to deal with life? And what help, if any, is here for other mothers and fathers?

Simply this: a higher level of autonomy can be achieved. The preceding somewhat technical discussion of the levels of ego development reveals that strength can be *developed* which will enable one better to contend with life, to meet its ordeals realistically, imaginatively, and courageously. One can progress from level to level, as the scores of these women indicate. Younger mothers in the interviews, new to their problems, who described themselves as incapable of coping with their untraditional children, scored lower in ego development than the women who knew themselves to control their own lives although not the lives of their children. These experienced women had not been brutalized by the often brutal experiences they had gone through. On the contrary, dealing with problems, mastering themselves, taking control of their lives, they had gained strength of character. Aeschylus was right over two thousand years ago: Wisdom comes through suffering. The experience of these mothers confirms it.

Often autonomy begins simply, basically. Sometimes the only control a woman can envision in her life is control of her own body. Many mothers in this study found exercise a bastion against the terrible feeling of powerlessness that often accompanies a parent's trauma. If I can't control the external world, they reasoned, at the very least I can control myself. And the reasoning works.

Ruthanne Mowbray's daughter Beth succumbed to crippling mental illness after a series of bad drug experiences. Unstable, unable to care for herself, Beth nevertheless went on to have a child. Ruthanne adored her grandchild and "worried much more than before there was a little one." Yet she could do almost nothing to control Beth's erratic behavior or to help her grandchild. Finally, her own health was at stake also. What could she do to protect herself against futile worry?

"I figured out a way of coping," she says, "which was to have physical exercise. . . . I did aerobics and I swam and I would come home with the tensions relieved. I made a point of doing this twice a week, which seemed to be about all I could fit in, but I really made myself do that, and it was very helpful."

Autonomy breeds autonomy and respect for autonomy. A woman who gains control of one area, however small, of her life will almost miraculously see that control extend itself into other, larger spheres. Mrs. Ramsay, Virginia Woolf's mother of eight in *To the Lighthouse,* wants to shout out, "Life stand still here!" She knows that it is the flux of life, its constant change and movement, that is the enemy of order. Life itself will carry her children away from her and the unity of the family. To fight it, she needs a realm of control.

Mrs. Ramsay copes with change and loss by finding symbols of permanence in parts of her life which she can arrange to some extent as she wants—a story read to a child, a civilized dinner party, a perfect sonnet. "Of such moments," she believes, "the thing is made that endures." The novel validates her faith.

What's more, the mother who realizes her own autonomy, who

clearly comprehends that she alone is responsible for her life, accords that same privilege, that same responsibility, to her child. Like the three women whose stories are told in this chapter, a truly autonomous mother doesn't want a passive, docile son or daughter. As she respects the human person in herself, the "I" in the mother and wife, she respects the human person in her child. She recognizes his right to succeed or to fail because of his own choices. She acknowledges his responsibility to determine his own life.

"THEN GO BACK TO THE MOONIES!"

Marilyn Greene is such a mother. Marilyn almost lost a child to the Moonies. Her daughter Jill, like young Bob Rourke, was indoctrinated by the Unification Church at the age of eighteen. Jill spent three months with the Moonies and was well on her way to becoming a convert.

Marilyn is a tall, sophisticated woman, with straight bronze hair, vivid green eyes, and creamy skin. Her straight bronze hair swings across the shoulders of her tweed jacket as she describes the Greene family ordeal which began during Jill's first semester in college. Jill, the second child, had left her native Indiana to go to school halfway across the country. A shy, religious girl, lonely in unfamiliar surroundings, away from family and friends, she met the Moonies at church. By Thanksgiving, with two weeks left to go in the term, she had decided to pass up her exams and had signed out of school.

Jill called home from the Unification Church. "Mom," she told Marilyn, "my friends are out in the car with the motor running waiting for me, so I can't talk long. We're on our way to a training center. I've decided to give my life to Mr. Moon."

The Greenes reacted very much as the Rourkes had reacted to a similar message from Bob. "We were crazy," Marilyn says. "There's no question about it. This wasn't our child doing this." Convinced that Jill had undergone a rapid and completely inexplicable personality change, the Greenes jumped in the car and drove through the night.

Late the next day, travel-worn and exhausted, they arrived at the

Moonie retreat. They found a former Catholic monastery on the Hudson River "surrounded by acres of rolling grassland with a huge tall fence and iron gates and cobblestone courtyard. And we just walked in there like lambs to the slaughter because they were ready for us."

Jill refused to leave with them, but she did agree to come home at Christmas. That visit was a failure. "She was perfect," Marilyn says, tossing her bronze hair sarcastically, "had her little plastic smile in place and was determined to show us what a wonderful thing being a Moonie was for her. . . . It was horrible, it was just horrible. . . . This was my child and yet it wasn't my child."

When Jill left to return to the Moonies, Marilyn broke down. "I just felt we might never see her again. My husband and I tried to tell each other that we still had two wonderful children, and that if it took six or seven years for our daughter to live through this and become herself again, we were not going to let it ruin our lives or the lives of our other children. Well, I don't know whether he really believed this, but I didn't."

Jill had gone into a forty-day workshop. The Greenes wrote and called, but someone was always listening in on the phone and Jill said they opened her mail. "She would have to stay up until three o'clock in the morning in order to write us and then go in and sit on the bathroom floor where the only light was, because she had no time during the day," her mother says.

In February, as the workshop ended, Marilyn pulled some political strings through a contact in her governor's office. Her contact called Jill's Unification leader and asked, "Is she free to come and go? Her parents are worried about her." The result was a three-day pass for Jill, a very unusual, almost unheard-of move for the Moonies to make so early in an indoctrination.

Jill came home for three days in the middle of February. As her "furlough" came to an end, she began to develop doubts about going back. "She couldn't go and she couldn't stay," Marilyn remembers. "She and I spent a whole day sitting in the family room with her bags packed. I had a terrible muscle spasm in my back, so that I could hardly move. I was in my bathrobe because I couldn't move enough to get dressed. We sat there confronting one another for the whole day."

At one point, Jill put her hand on the phone to call a taxi to take her to the bus station. In spite of her pain, Marilyn moved across to take the phone from her. "I can't let you go back, honey," she told her daughter, "until I can feel good about what you are doing."

"And how are you going to stop me?" Jill asked, looking down at her disabled mother.

"I thought, well, Moonies use this sort of thing so why can't I?" Marilyn says. "So I said, 'Jill, when a mother bear knows that her cub is in danger, she has superhuman strength. I am concerned that my cub is in danger and I don't know how I'll keep you here, but I'll find a way to keep you from going back.' And I didn't have the foggiest notion in the world that I could do it."

Jill didn't leave. "I guess the breakthrough came when she said, 'If you hold me here against my will, then that's kidnapping.' And I just snapped out, 'Right, it is. Call the police if you want to.' And she said, 'MO-OO-THER!' the way kids do. And that was the first kid sound that I'd heard from her since she'd gone off to college." Marilyn laughs. "And I thought, 'Aha! there's something still there.' "

For the next eleven months, Jill deprogrammed herself. Her first step, at Marilyn's suggestion, was to sit down and write out "something like two hundred and seventy questions that she had in her mind about the Unification Church and mail them off to them." Of course she didn't expect—or receive—an answer.

In a few days, she went into what Marilyn calls "a total psychotic break."

> We thought she might commit suicide. She wanted to go off to a cottage at a lake that belonged to some friends of ours, all by herself with the dog. I thought she'd try to dig a hole in the ice and fall in, and yet I could not somehow say no. So we let her go. I felt all along that we could not exert control, that we had to let her find her way back.

Neither Jill nor Marilyn wanted a deprogrammer like Ted Patrick, who since the early seventies has used controversial methods to break down the mental conditioning of cult members. "I felt this might blow Jill's mind," Marilyn says, "and I just decided to rely on my own intuition."

Jill went to the lake but it didn't help her. All she did for three or four days at the lake was to sleep. "She slept and slept. Then she came home and it was as if she didn't know who we were. She ran into things."

The next step was a phase, as Marilyn describes it, "like cold-turkey withdrawal from drugs. For weeks we went through what I would have described as an exorcism."

> It was the darnedest thing I've ever seen. She would stiffen out on the bed and she would shriek at the top of her lungs, shriek obscenities. It was as if she were in absolute mortal pain. And she would do this for an hour at a time.
>
> And I would just sit and hold her hand. She'd shriek these questions and it took me a little while to realize they weren't for me. . . . They were for her.
>
> And I'd hold her hand and just try to rub her back and then all of a sudden it would be just "boom" and she'd sit up and say, "It's over."

At first this behavior horrified Marilyn, but as time went on, she says, "I got so I didn't even dread it because it was fascinating." It was also working. According to her mother, Jill was fighting fire with fire.

> The thing about the Unification Church is that they people their world with spirits and demons. So she'd have these awful nightmares, nightmares that she was clawing my face!
>
> Oh, it makes me *mad*, just literally *mad*, every time I think about what they can do to someone. She would have spirits and demons around her. I didn't really leave her for more than half an hour or an hour for weeks and weeks. I should have kept track, but at the time I wasn't thinking about keeping track. It could have been months before I left her for more than an hour.

The next step, as Marilyn describes it, was for Jill to relive the stages of growth in her past life, "all the stages of becoming a person." Like a young teenager, she decided she couldn't be the least bit tactful because tact was affected. "Then she was so brutally frank she was obnoxious to be around."

Like a baby, the only time Jill felt really alive, she said, was when she was eating. Only a little over five feet tall, she quickly gained a most unattractive twenty pounds.

"It was remarkable to watch the human mind work out something on its own," Marilyn says. But the toll on Marilyn was heavy. Jill "shouted and raged and ranted" at her mother through this whole process. Jill and Marilyn had the benefit of a psychiatrist whenever they needed him. One day, in desperation, Marilyn called him. "You're having a problem," he told her, "because you're trying to be fair. You don't have to be fair. Your daughter hasn't been fair with you and the Moonies haven't been fair with her, so you really don't have to be fair."

After that, Marilyn tried some detachment of her own. She still listened, still consoled, but "my coping mechanism was to look at her not as my beloved child, but look at her very clinically as if this were someone that I was doing this experiment on. I made a real distance—a personal distance—between her and me.

"I was manipulative and I was firm and I was objective and I couldn't have done it without help, couldn't have just stayed with her all that time."

Finally, the showdown came, the time when Marilyn immediately, instinctively, and correctly brought into play all she had learned about detachment and all she believed about autonomy. Late one afternoon, Marilyn was setting the dinner table. Jill came in with her usual litany of complaints and problems. "She started yakking at me about how I had always brainwashed her. How could I find fault with the Moonies when I'd brainwashed her all the time she was growing up?" One can imagine the scene: the serene room, the neatly laid table, the tall, slender woman with the pale skin and the sheaf of dramatic bronze hair, and the pudgy, pasty girl, her own pretty red hair a tangled mop in her eyes, her whining voice going on and on and on.

Marilyn drew herself up to her full height; no muscle spasms would spoil things this time. "Jill," she said, in her deepest, angriest voice, "if you can't tell the difference between your growing up in your family and what Mr. Moon and his group have done to your mind"—she slammed the saltcellar down on the table—"I think perhaps you'd better go back to the Moonies!" And she walked straight-backed out of the room, went upstairs to her bedroom, and slammed the door decisively behind her.

Then she quietly dialed the psychiatrist and told him what she'd done. "Beautiful, wonderful, perfect," he said. "You gave her a free choice and you proved your point by the way you said it."

"Wait a minute," Marilyn told him. "I couldn't have done it if I didn't mean it." She wasn't playing a game. She was just trying, in the most dramatic way she could think of, to get Jill to realize what Marilyn had believed from the beginning: that Jill was responsible for herself.

"That was the turning point," Marilyn says. As she hung up and sat down at her dressing table to cool off, she heard a timid knock at the door. Jill came in, her face abashed and fearful. She stood behind Marilyn, looking at her mother's face in the mirror.

"Mom," she said, "I didn't mean it, I didn't mean it. I'm sorry I haven't confided in you more and trusted you more."

Marilyn saw Jill hadn't quite gotten the point. The last thing she wanted was to take over with Jill where the Moonies had left off. She laid down the hairbrush she'd picked up idly. "Good Lord, Jill," she said emphatically, "you have your life, and I'm certainly ready to start with my own again. We are going to grow in different directions, and you're not accountable to me, *at all.* You're your own person."

"But, Mom," Jill said, "do you realize what you've done to me? You've taken away everything I believed in and that I was giving my life for. And I don't have anything to put in its place. You haven't given me anything to put in its place. Do you realize what you've done?"

"Yes, I do," Marilyn told her, "and it's worried me to death. But you know why I did it? Because I have so much confidence in you that *you* will find something to put in its place.

"Because if I tried to give it to you, it wouldn't be yours."

Jill picked up her mother's hairbrush and slowly brushed her red mop back out of her eyes, studying herself in the mirror as she did so. "Okay," she said. "I guess that makes sense."

Eight years later, at the time of Marilyn's interview, both Jill and her mother have put their dramatic talents to use. Jill finished a degree in broadcasting and works in television on the West Coast. An intelligent, worldly, successful young woman, she has no regrets about the events of that landmark year in her life. "You know," she has told her mother, "I was headed in the direction of a very narrow, fundamentalist, ingrown religion. That's why the Moonies could get to me so easily. I wonder what would have gotten me out of that if this Moonie episode hadn't happened?"

Marilyn too has reevaluated her religious beliefs in these eight years. The experiences she had with Jill have given her a horror of any sort of religious fanaticism or attempts at mind control. She continues to work for her church, but often she finds herself, she says, "sitting in a sermon and saying, 'Says who?' I tend to be something of a maverick in the church circle."

Marilyn, her husband Richard, and Jill have all felt strongly enough about the individual's right to autonomy to warn the public about the methods the Moonies use to win converts. Together and separately, the Greenes have spoken to various groups. Marilyn has found herself to be an effective public speaker. The first time she was nervous, but she followed her instincts. Putting aside her prepared talk, she says, "I just got up in front of the microphone and told my story, and that seemed to be what they wanted to hear."

As Jill took charge of her life, her mother, as she had threatened, got on with her own again. Marilyn first wrote a historical play about the Renaissance for classroom use, and worked it into a four-week program which she conducted herself, for a fee, for interested elementary schools. Inspired by the success of this project, she has since gone on to take classes in theater at a local university.

Recently she had a role in a major university production. At the age of fifty-three, she found herself taking curtain calls. "It was really fun," she gloats. "I just turned on, all my lights blinked, I was on a high. I didn't get very much sleep for a while, but I had more energy than I've had in years. And now I think maybe my field is theater rather than education. I don't know. I've got a choice."

"OUR OWN WOMEN"

Marie Lowry is a tough person, a survivor. She survived a poverty-stricken, violent childhood. She made it through the painful and totally unexpected death of her first baby. She flourished as a business partner of her husband Harry in his clothing firm on New York's Seventh Avenue. She coped with Harry's death and has managed the loneliness that followed. But the marriage of her daughter Betsy nearly threw her. Betsy married a black man.

For some mothers, the biracial marriage of a child might present no problems. But for the purposes of this book, the behavior of a child is defined as untraditional if a mother believes it to be untraditional. And Betsy's marriage blew Marie's mind.

To understand why, one must understand Marie. As she talks about herself and her daughter, Marie is a formidable little figure dressed in an old tweed skirt and sweater, a short wiry woman with a fiery expression and a stubborn chin. Marie grew up in Brooklyn during the Depression. Her father owned a small plumbing business. The parents didn't get along well. Marie's mother was a difficult woman. "She would withhold love when she was angry," Marie recalls. "Sometimes for a week at a time, she wouldn't talk to my father."

But her father was moody and unpredictable also. One night when Marie and her mother came home from a movie, her father jumped out of some bushes by their apartment building and began hitting her mother. "He used to whip my older brother, but he never touched me, because I kept away from him," Marie says proudly.

But she saw violent things. Her father kept a gun on top of the china cabinet in the dining room. Once Marie's mother began screaming at her father because he had bought something she didn't want—"they were always screaming at each other"—and her mother grabbed the gun and said she was going to kill herself. Marie, who was about six at the time, got between her parents as they wrestled for the gun. "I was afraid, because I thought she would really do it, and I loved her. She was my *mother.* That kind of stuff—horrible."

When she was eight, her parents divorced. Her father was so bitter that he refused to pay alimony. Marie's mother would take her out of school to go down to the Friend of the Court with her, and they would appeal for help in getting some money from the father. But Marie's mother refused to press charges. "He's your father," she would tell the children. "I can't put him in jail." So no money was ever forthcoming.

They had a very hard time in the heart of the Depression. Marie's mother did domestic work by the day when she could find it. She made doughnuts and the children peddled them on the street. Somehow they made it through.

When Marie was fourteen, her brother left home. Shortly afterward, her mother married again, and her new husband moved in with them. He was very jealous and became more and more unstable, so Marie's mother decided to divorce him. When the legal papers were served on him to get him out of the house, he turned nasty and stabbed his wife with a kitchen knife. Then he stabbed himself, dragged himself from the kitchen into the bedroom, bleeding profusely, and locked himself in.

Marie's mother lived, but her stepfather didn't. After the two had been taken to the hospital, Marie had to take her little sister home, clean up the mess, and carry on with their lives. "I remember rolling up the rug," she says, "and taking it into the basement and cleaning up the other blood around. . . . And I remember sleeping in that bed and looking at that lock they'd broken to get to him." By the time Marie's mother came back from the hospital, Marie was the mother. She cooked, got herself and her sister off to school, and even talked to the police when they came to investigate.

In a few months, her brother returned. Marie graduated from high school, and with the two of them working, as Marie says, "we had money, and we could take care of ourselves, and so life was better from then on."

Marie determined that life for her was going to stay good. By the age of seventeen, she had experienced all the disorder she ever wanted, and she made up her mind to run her life in her own way. She got a job in the garment district and went to business school at night. "I was a hard worker. I wasn't very smart, but I was ambitious, and I did my very best and learned." Before long, she was promoted. She lived on nothing, put her money into two little pieces of property, sold one at a profit, and began to build a bank account.

She married Harry Lowry, who was just starting out in his own business. "He had been working for a firm, so he didn't have much money. I had more money than he did. But he had great potential, and I loved him." The two built a fine business and a fine life together.

In business, they were partners. "He put a lot of responsibility on me, and I helped him in his work. He had a lot of confidence in me."

But Marie deferred to Harry, because she wanted to, as "head of the house. Women nowadays think that's not the thing to do. I liked a head of the house." Having grown up in a tumultuous family, she wanted her own family to be hierarchical and controlled.

Harry's business grew, and he had a knack for making money. He made investments, most of which paid off handsomely. But he kept Marie informed about what was going on.

> A couple of times he made the wrong decision, and he apologized to me, "I shouldn't have sold that stuff."
>
> I said, "Hey, who's got a pipeline to God? We don't know," and he appreciated that, he said, because so often it's easy to say, "I told you not to do that."
>
> But I figured he and I both were doing the best we could as we went along.

After a couple of years, when Marie became pregnant, she quit going in to work, though she still helped Harry at home. She had a little girl, normal and healthy. "We just adored her," Marie says.

When the baby was about six months old, she developed a cough, nothing much, but Marie didn't like the sound of it. The pediatrician took an X ray of the lungs, and discovered an enlarged heart. He told Marie and Harry to rush her right over to a big hospital on the Upper East Side with a children's cardiac department. "I just want them to look at her," he said.

When they got to the hospital, a doctor was waiting to examine the baby. Marie was not allowed to go into the room with her. After a while, other white-coated figures appeared and converged on the examining room.

Then the doctor came out. "It's very serious," he told Marie. "I'd like you to leave her overnight, and we'll give her a little oxygen to help her out."

> So I said yes, and he took her off, and it was so terrible. In those days you didn't stay with your child. I would never leave a child alone in the hospital now, but, you know, I wasn't willing to believe that it was anything urgent.

So we went home, and we got a call at one o'clock in the
morning. She had expired. It was terrible. It was terrible.
She had little wrinkles in her wrists, you know, a fat baby.
And so anyway, we went through the funeral. She looked
like a little doll. And I couldn't cry. I just had to accept
it. . . .

But what I noticed was, you know, empty arms. For six
months I had carried a baby, then there's nothing. . . . I
used to dream I would be carrying her, and after I woke up
I would feel so good, so comfortable.

Marie wondered what she had done to cause her child's death, but
the doctors assured her that what had happened was a fluke, and
that she should have another child right away if she wanted. She lost
no time in having Betsy.

From the first Betsy was a dynamic, outgoing child. The whole
world loved her. In school, she was only an average student, but she
was a leader among the children.

At home, she could be a handful. Betsy didn't like authority, and,
as Harry left day-to-day discipline up to Marie, "she and I were often
at odds," her mother recalls. They both tried not to spoil her. In
fact, Marie thinks maybe they were too scrupulous in this respect.
"She always wanted a four-poster bed with a canopy, but I was going
to get that for her after she graduated from high school. Which is
foolish, because then they couldn't care less." In spite of minor
disagreements, however, they were good, loving parents, and Betsy
was a more than satisfactory child.

Betsy made friends easily and brought the world into the Lowrys'
life. "She comes into a room and immediately she starts things
going," Marie says. As she grew older, and they could arrange it
around school, her parents took her with them when they traveled.
They went to Mexico, to Italy. They took her camping, spent two
weeks on a dude ranch. "We had good times together."

Marie particularly remembers a trip to Yugoslavia and Greece
when Betsy was sixteen. In Istanbul, the family ran into two young
men Betsy knew who were traveling through Europe together and
they all joined forces for a while. Marie smiles at the recollection of
the adventures they had. "Betsy always opened up so many new
experiences for us."

Harry died the year before Betsy graduated from high school, a loss to Betsy, a body blow to Marie. She had lost a friend, a business partner, a husband, a lover. Once again, however, she couldn't take the easy comfort of tears. Even at the funeral, "I couldn't cry. I was greeting people like it was a social thing and saying to myself, 'What's the matter with you?' But I'm a very private person and I couldn't cry."

Marie began to pick up the pieces. Betsy graduated from high school and decided against college in favor of computer training. She did well, as always. When she finished her course, she went to visit a cousin in Chicago. While she was there, she found a good job and decided to stay.

Marie missed her daughter and she missed Harry. "Betsy has the sense of humor her father had, and this is what I miss. While he was introverted and very serious, he would make me laugh. I miss that. The things he would say were humorous. Most of us, after the party's over, we think of the things we should have said. Well, he could say them in a minute. And Betsy is that way."

Some important element of her life had vanished. Together she and Harry had had goals—what they would do, where they would live. Without Harry, she didn't much care what she did or where she lived. As time passed, she began to develop a social life, but something was missing. She took comfort in the fact that Betsy at least had goals and was doing well.

Like her mother and father, Betsy was a go-getter. She was determined to earn her own living, spend what she made wisely, build some investments. The frequent letters and phone calls from Chicago always held good news. This went on for two years; then the letters began to talk about Peter.

Marie knew who Peter was: a young black lawyer who lived in Betsy's apartment complex. "When she had come home at various times, she had mentioned him, along with other young men she had been dating. I didn't pay much attention. She's always had many boyfriends, like most young girls nowadays. It was just another facet of her life."

But Peter began cropping up more and more frequently. They went out to dinner together. Peter had gotten tickets for the ballet. Peter was buying a Mercedes. Betsy's cousin began to talk about

"Betsy and Peter," but Marie still didn't think much about it. She thought it was like Betsy to have a good black friend.

"I didn't know any blacks socially," Marie says. "I knew about blacks only through the news media—crime and drugs. We did have two black ladies at the firm, seamstresses, and I used to go to their home sometimes years ago to pick up fabric. We all did everything in those days. I'd get off work early and run out to pick something up. Those two ladies were charming; they had comfortable homes way up on the West Side—they were probably scared to death of the situation there, just like I would have been if I lived on that street.

"And I worked in an inner-city hospital in Emergency as a volunteer for two years before my husband died, so I met drug pushers, the poor blacks, that type of people, so that was my experience with them."

But it never occurred to her that Betsy could be romantically serious about a black man. She was totally unprepared when Betsy came home for Thanksgiving during her second year in Chicago, and announced, "Peter and I are getting married at Christmas." The two of them were having dinner at a favorite French restaurant at the time.

Marie choked on her *boeuf en daube*. "You're *what?*" she said.

"All the plans have been made," Betsy said. "I'm going to do it, Mom."

"She picked the worst possible time and place," Marie says. "I started to cry. I don't *ever* cry in front of anyone, even at home. I didn't cry at my little girl's funeral or at Harry's. I just don't do that.

"But here I was, in a public place, and the tears were just streaming. I didn't say anything. I just couldn't believe what I was hearing. I started crying and I couldn't stop."

Through her tears, which had startled Betsy as much as they had Marie, Marie begged Betsy to wait a while, reconsider, spend some time away from Peter.

"No," Betsy said. "We tried that. We were apart. We dated a little bit and then we didn't see each other for a couple of months, and both of us couldn't stand it. So we agreed. When he asked me to marry him, we talked about it, and how to do it, and this is what we want to do."

Marie was shocked to her core. "I guess what I thought about white girls who married blacks was that they met in college, and the girl wasn't so attractive, and, you know, she settled for this. That was my idea.

"But Betsy wasn't like that. She didn't *need* him. He has a nice position, but so do a lot of the men she dated. She just didn't need him."

Sobbing, Marie pulled all the stops.

I said, "You're going to have nigger children." I *never* use that word, I don't even feel about the black people like that, but this is something I said. I said *everything*.

I begged her to wait. I said, "Well, if you will wait till spring, until April, you can come home and be married at home, and I will give you both a wedding, and I will accept it." I did that with some reservations, but I thought if she had a little more time to think—

But she said, "No, all the plans are made."

And then the thing that hurt me the most is, I said, "You haven't said anything about me attending your wedding."

Well, it was going to be at a friend's house, and, uh, "I don't think you would want to be there, Mom." And she made so many excuses, I dropped it right there.

I said, "Okay, you leave and you do this, and I never want to see you again. Never."

And I meant it.

Betsy and Peter were married in Chicago at Christmas. Marie sat in her brownstone in Brooklyn, devastated. "I just felt, 'Well, I've already lost one daughter, and now I've lost two. I've lost both of my children, and I've lost my husband.' I was more feeling sorry for me than worried about what was going to happen to her."

Marie's next thought was that the marriage wouldn't last. After her unhappy childhood, she was no stranger to divorce, and she tried to think that Betsy had simply made the kind of mistake Marie had seen her mother make. "Don't get hung up on this," she told herself, "and don't tell anybody, because she may be divorced before anyone has to know." She knew that basically Betsy was a commonsensical and conservative girl. As hard as Marie and Harry had worked to give her the advantages in life they had not had, surely Betsy wasn't going to blow everything with a marriage to a *black.* Her heart turned over in relief at the prospect of Betsy's imminent divorce.

While she entertained these thoughts, she had no contact with her daughter. When Betsy called, Marie refused to talk with her. Nor had she met Peter. After several months of this stalemate, Peter called Marie at the shop on Seventh Avenue. "I want to talk to you," he said, "and I'll fly to New York if you'll talk to me."

What would Harry do? Marie asked herself. She was trying to be especially tough in her dual role of mother and father to Betsy. Well, Harry would certainly see the man, she thought. So she agreed to meet her son-in-law at a coffee shop on Madison. She didn't want anyone she knew to see them together.

Peter turned out to be a handsome, gentlemanly man, everything a mother could have wanted for her daughter if his skin weren't black. But it was. How could marriage to such a person make Betsy happy, give her the place in life that her parents had planned for her?

Marie let Peter have it. "I was not very complimentary to him or his race. I told him there was no way I wanted to see Betsy while she was married to him, and that I thought that he could have prevented such a mess—that the blacks and whites I knew anything about just didn't get along."

In spite of herself she was impressed with Peter's reaction. "Betsy is very unhappy," he said, "and I'm unhappy because she is."

"I don't care," Marie said hotly.

"Think about it," he told her in parting. "Betsy says you're some lady. She misses you."

Marie thought about it. Suppose Betsy were to get sick, suppose something were to happen? She knew she'd never forgive herself.

Besides she missed Betsy. They had always had an open and volatile relationship. Because of her own mother's coldness, Marie had never before held herself aloof from her daughter as she was doing now. "If I didn't like something she did, we had it out and I told her, and then I would hug her and say, 'Okay, now, you know how I feel, let's leave it at that.' But I balked on this marriage, because I thought that if I didn't approve, she might divorce him sooner."

Maybe that would still work, she thought. At length she called Betsy. "Why don't you come home, and we'll talk about it? Don't bring Peter, but you come and let's talk. And I want you to know, Betsy, that *no one* knows about this."

Betsy came home. But she came home *pregnant*, and "just delighted that she was pregnant, so happy." Marie knew she was beaten. Betsy had laid claim to her own life. Her mother bowed her head to fate and got on the phone to call her friends.

"What I realized about Betsy," her mother says in the interview six years later, "was that she doesn't see Peter's color. She didn't marry him to prove anything or to show anybody that she was open-minded. She did it because she was crazy about him. I asked her not long ago if she were happy and if she loved her husband, and she said, 'I'm the luckiest woman in the world.' She just doesn't see him as black."

Marie herself sometimes forgets the color of Peter's skin. "If I don't see them for a while and I go to visit, I walk in and see him, and it just kicks me—because my eyes register a different thing than my head does.

"Even with my little grandson, I adore him, he's so sweet and so nice, and I look at him, and he's *black*, you know. I keep forgetting, he's black.

"But Betsy doesn't see them as black. She just doesn't see it."

Betsy has proved not only her autonomy but the wisdom of it in her mother's eyes. She and Peter have two children, a nice home, and a useful and happy life. By marrying a black man, Betsy has once again, as she used to as a teenager, "opened up so many new experiences" for her mother.

For one thing, Marie has over the years come to understand more fully the problem of racial prejudice and the scars it leaves. "I'd hate to be a black person in white America, wouldn't you? It would be terrible to be black in America. I'm sure they've all, no matter who they are, felt discrimination, and it's hurt. I hurt for my son-in-law. Many times I just feel for him, but there's nothing I can do. And that's one thing I've learned through this marriage—that I haven't changed things much."

Nor has Marie herself changed in some basic ways. Theoretically, she still doesn't approve of biracial marriages. "I still think it really isn't the best way for a couple to go. The circumstances have to be perfect, almost, for it to survive."

About Betsy, however, Marie isn't worried. "Betsy takes care of herself. She can handle any situation and she comes out on top. She's got a very strong will.

"I tell my friends that if Peter and Betsy get a divorce, it won't be because it's a biracial marriage, but because she's so hard to get along with that he can't stand her. . . .

"If she sets her mind on something, you cannot change it."

Betsy is, in fact, a lot like her mother. Marie likes to visit Betsy's little family, but on her own terms. So she has bought herself a camper complete with all accommodations, and she can come and go as she pleases. She insists on her independence, her autonomy.

She and Betsy have occasional blowups that are very alarming to Peter. The last big one came when their baby daughter Harriet was born and Marie went to Chicago to help Betsy. Mother and daughter had a spat about some housekeeping procedure.

At last Betsy put her hands on her hips. "Well, it's *my* house, Mom!" she said with finality.

> "Fine," I said. "I'm leaving."
>
> I packed up everything. My son-in-law was there; he was flabbergasted. He said, "Do you have to leave, Marie?"
>
> I said, "Yes, Peter, I have to leave. You wanted her; she's yours. You've got her. You stay home and take care of her."

And she left. "I don't want to be hurt by her, and I take nothing from her," she says decisively. "She tells me she admires me. I think we're both our own women."

Strong-minded daughter, strong-minded mother. Marie doubts she will ever marry again. "I could have been married, very definitely, four times, but I always say to my friends, 'I already had Mr. Right, and now I'm looking for Mr. Perfect.'

"I won't have a boring man. So many, as they get older, are so boring. It's not that I'm such an intellectual, or that I'm so much fun, or anything. It's just—I can't get the same things I had with my husband, this communication we had. . . . I just can't seem to find that."

So she tends to her investments, runs her business, and drives her camper across the country to see her daughter. When she wants to.

"IT'S HER CHOICE"

Granting a child autonomy sometimes means, as it did for Marie Lowry, coming to accept a course of behavior for one's child that would be unthinkable for oneself. Some forms of untraditional activity, such as drug addiction or alcoholism, present physical dangers that few mothers can tolerate for their children; others, such as membership in a cult, offer fairly clear-cut psychological hazards.

But biracial marriage is another story. Although it took Marie a while to see such a marriage even as a possibility, like most Americans she believes in marrying for love, in choosing a mate freely. She herself married for love and refuses to marry again without it. She understands what it means to love a man. In spite of her racial prejudice, Marie came to respect Betsy's right to choose as she herself had chosen, and even to feel a grudging admiration for her daughter's incomprehensible color blindness. She would never marry a black, but she accepts Betsy's marriage because it works for Betsy. Betsy has not been damaged because of it.

Homosexuality is another such gray area for traditional middle-class mothers. How do women of the kind represented here respond to the knowledge that their child is homosexual? To answer this complex question as simply as possible, they are more interested in the effect on the child than on anything else. Of course, they would prefer that their children be straight, just as Marie would have preferred that Betsy marry a white. But, convinced that a child has freely chosen his sexual situation and that he is not injured by it, these women acknowledge the necessity of sexual autonomy.

"There is so much confusion about sexuality anyway," Ellen Kincaid says. "I think we're moving away, medically and theologically, from the 'sick' connotation that homosexuality has had. We're learning that it's not the fearsome dread aberration that we thought it was."

When Ellen says "we," she means herself as well as American society. No one could have been more shocked, more distraught, than Ellen was when her daughter Trudy began a lesbian relationship her second year in college. For Ellen, however, that blow was one of many that she received that awful spring and summer of 1975.

For the interview, she has come home early from her present position as manager of a large ski-clothing business in Chicago. She is nattily if casually dressed in her work uniform, designer ski clothes and after-ski boots. A graduate of Vassar College, Ellen worked part-time when her children were growing up, and took a full-time position as soon as possible. A cheerful, competent woman, tanned and vigorous-looking, she flashes a warm, accepting smile as she describes her emotional adventures with her daughter.

Trudy, the oldest of Ellen and Joseph Kincaid's three daughters, was born in 1956. She grew up happy and gregarious, a good student and an "extremely involved, loyal, and non-judgmental friend." Her grades suffered during her last two years in high school when she began making friends among those "on the periphery of school life," as Ellen puts it, and questioning school and parental authority.

The summer Trudy graduated from high school, the Kincaid family took a European vacation with another family. Trudy asked for permission to bring her boyfriend along, and the Kincaids agreed. When the family left, Trudy and her friend wanted to continue traveling for another month or so.

Ellen and Joseph were reluctant. They didn't like the young man much, and thought he and Trudy would have a poor introduction to the relationship between men and women. "We wanted to say, 'Absolutely no, you cannot do this,' " Ellen recalls. "We've asked ourselves since, if we had said that, what would have happened. But, with the oldest child, the thought of saying an absolute no was just too frightening to us. I think we felt that she'd run away."

The permissiveness of the early seventies influenced them also. "As parents we were sort of in limbo. . . . How much control should we exhibit? . . . Because it was all unknown, uncharted ground, as far as we were concerned. I think we were trying to be good parents without being punitive or unjustly harsh."

Perhaps most important of all, the Kincaids are "politically fairly liberal, I more than Joseph." They subscribe to the liberal's "sense of people acting out their own destiny and living their own lives," as opposed to the conservative's concept of "sort of repeating their families' lives." So they agreed, with trepidation, to Trudy's continued European jaunt before she settled down to college. As they had feared, Trudy came home jaundiced with "men" and had to enter college late.

The college she entered in January of 1975 was a small private school in rural Illinois. Completely uninterested in "making it" economically, she decided on a major in philosophy. Before long, she took a stand among campus activists; the issues she was most concerned with were environmental and feminist. "She never broke the ties with her family," Ellen says, "but there were some trying and tortured confrontations that we had with her because she wouldn't do things the way we felt she should."

The first big blowup came early that summer, when Trudy had stayed on in school to make up some of the credits she needed to reach sophomore status. She decided to live off campus, but not until Ellen and Joe drove to see her one weekend did they realize how really off campus she was. Ellen describes her shock:

> She chose to live in something that a migrant worker would live in . . . , just a little shack . . . , completely cut off from the rest of the world. She had no car, so there was no way of transporting herself other than hitchhiking. It had no electricity, no heat, and she said she was going to live there the rest of the time she was in college.
>
> We were so frustrated at that point with her decision, that she was just rejecting everything that we felt she should be doing, that we left with the idea that that was *it*.

"All right," they told Trudy. "Do what you want. We're through worrying about you."

As they drove down the dirt road that led to the county road, they agreed they would just cut themselves off from this difficult child of theirs. But Ellen couldn't stop crying. Finally Joe turned the car around. "I'm going back," he said. "She probably feels as bad as we do."

He drove back the way they had come, got halfway down the dirt road toward Trudy's little shack, and there was Trudy, "jauntily walking along the road." Ellen laughs at the recollection. "I wouldn't say she was unconcerned, exactly, but she was certainly not as shaken as we were." The parents realized two things: that they couldn't just put Trudy out of their minds, and that they probably couldn't do much to change Trudy's mind.

Late in the summer something happened which probably did more to influence Trudy's subsequent life than any other single event of her family history. Her sister Jane, two years younger than Trudy, and Jane's friend Sherry were raped by two young black men after a Grateful Dead concert. The girls called the police and the men were arrested.

Both men had criminal records for similar offenses and had only been out of the state prison for about six months at the time of the rape. It was an ugly rape; the girls were abused and their lives were threatened. Sherry became pregnant because of the rape, and had to have an abortion. Jane and Sherry decided they wanted to prosecute; they were convinced they had a case, and would be doing the right thing by putting the rapists out of circulation.

Trudy came home for the trial, which turned out to be "a complete fiasco," Ellen reports. The public prosecutor who handled the case was "totally inept." To make matters worse, the trial was conducted in front of an all-black jury in an inner-city court.

The defense attorney seized the opportunity to make a case against little rich white girls who venture into foreign territory. In a strategy all too familiar to victims of rape, Jane and Sherry inadvertently found themselves under attack in the trial. "The defense lawyer mistreated the girls by the kind of testimony that he brought out—you know, it was after a concert by the *Grateful Dead*. The whole implication that he made was that the girls didn't belong there anyway, and what were they doing down in that part of town, and what kind of clothes were they wearing, and you know, that kind of thing. It was just bizarre."

The trial went on for five days. "The agony of it for Jane and Sherry was terrible," says Ellen. After five days, the defendants, in a crazy miscarriage of justice, were acquitted.

Except for Rachel, the youngest, who didn't quite grasp what was going on, the Kincaid family was seriously affected. Jane, basically a smart and sturdy girl who'd been caught up in some rebellious teen behavior, came through her ordeal better than the family dared hope. At first she was rocky—went to school, dropped out, couldn't concentrate. But she had taken immediate steps to get psychiatric help. After several months, she left Chicago to study abroad for a year. Then she came home, continued therapy, and finished college with Phi Beta Kappa status. At the time of the interview she is engaged, has a fine job, and is "pretty much going on with her life."

Joe, Ellen says, "found [the experience] devastating—that terrible feeling of not being able to protect your child." He felt his manhood and his paternal power had been compromised by the rape, the trial, and the acquittal.

In Trudy, who valued loyalty and justice, and who had already had one unimpressive relationship with a man, a free-floating contempt for men was engendered. Appalled by the rape, horrified by the way the girls were treated on the stand, dismayed by the prosecutor's ineffectuality, Trudy later suggested to her mother that that's where her lesbianism may have begun.

"It's hard for me to think," Ellen says, "that something that happened to somebody else could trigger that much reaction, could make you take that kind of [radically different] direction with your life as a result of it. But certainly it affected and colored her thinking very strongly." That fall, back in college, Trudy began her first sexual relationship with a woman.

The woman, a visiting professor, was more than twenty years older than Trudy and "a bright light on the campus as an ardent feminist," Ellen says. "She became Trudy's first [female] lover. I was extremely resentful of that, mostly because of the age difference. I thought this was not only an infringement on the relationship between student and professor but also a very unfair advantage of a young girl."

Both Ellen and Joe found it difficult to remonstrate with Trudy about the affair. For one thing, Trudy didn't tell them outright what was going on. Oddly enough, the girl, who hadn't hesitated to confront her parents about her other maverick decisions, let them figure this one out for themselves. "There was never a confrontation," her mother says. "It was more just a process of wearing us down [till we realized] that this is how she was choosing to live."

Surprisingly, shocked as she was, Ellen also found herself ambivalent. By this time, she had been through enough trauma with Trudy to see that Trudy's sexual life "was more or less beyond our realm, so far as being able to change it. And I suppose, when I'm thinking the most rationally about it, I think it really isn't my business. It's her life, her decision.

"But I can go from that point to almost one hundred and eighty degrees the other way and be horrified and upset about it."

Joe took Trudy's lesbian relationship harder. Coming as soon as it did after Jane's rape and the acquittal of the rapist, he felt even less capable of protecting and guiding his daughters. Besides that, he blamed himself. As Trudy's father, he felt responsible for having shaped her attitudes toward men. "I think that was very threatening to my husband," Ellen says, "that somehow he had projected a male image that turned her off."

It didn't help matters that Trudy, laboring under her new feminist ideals, tended to identify her father with the oppressors of women through the ages. "She was very antagonistic to Joe and really gave him a hard time, but"—Ellen laughs at the recollection—"because of her feminism, she could find almost no fault in me. She would extol the fact that I'd gone out and I'd worked and I'd done this and that; it was a very lopsided point of view."

More than anything else that pained her, Ellen was disturbed by the break between her husband and her daughter. Loving them both, she saw how basically much alike they are, "in the way they appeal to people, their openness, their gentleness." She could not bear to see hostility between them. The Kincaids had had family therapy after Jane's rape. She remembered gratefully how beneficial it had been to all of them, even to young Rachel, who had gone in protesting, "I'm not crazy!"

Now Ellen used her influence with Joe and Trudy to arrange counseling for them. As a result of this help, Joe soon became more able to put his feelings of responsibility in perspective. Like Ellen, he chose to detach himself from Trudy's lesbianism sufficiently to see it as her choice for her life, not some sick alternative to which he and the rest of the male sex had driven her.

Trudy too changed over the next several years. Her affair with the older woman ended with Trudy's graduation from college. Gradually she began to drop some of her more militant feminist attitudes, while maintaining an active role in the concerns of women. She became an officer in the National Organization for Women, and volunteered to monitor a rape hot line for the community.

But at the same time, to Ellen's pleasure, Trudy again developed several friendships with men. "She's quit repudiating all men; she's not nearly as judgmental," her mother says. "Matter of fact, she has a friend, a young man from Philadelphia who's a horticulturist, whom she's traveled with to an environmental study group."

But Trudy quickly let Ellen know what *not* to expect of that relationship. "I asked her about this young man who calls her and that she goes out with sometimes, and she whirled on me, 'But, Mother, there's nothing to that.' And we both laughed afterwards, because it was as though she didn't want to hold out any hope."

Once out of the college setting, Trudy also began to collect several older friends, longtime acquaintances of her parents. "Some of the men within that group," Ellen says with obvious relish, "she enjoys and likes to be with. She's perfectly natural with them, and to me it lends a certain amount of normalcy in her life. What she's chosen about her individual sexuality doesn't seem so outrageous.

"I think she's just maturing. She doesn't need to lash out at her father all the time. She doesn't need to fight all those battles that she was constantly fighting. And that lends greater credibility to what she's doing."

Trudy continues to have homosexual relationships, and the whole family has tacitly agreed to include her friends in family activities with Trudy. They were all relieved when she formed her second serious lesbian attachment with Marian Duckett, a young woman her own age. She and Marian lived together for two years. During that time, Marian was always "welcome in our home," Ellen says. "Because Trudy had this previous relationship with a much older woman, I was much happier that this was a contemporary. It just seemed healthier to me." It meant to Ellen that Trudy had made a free choice.

Nor does Ellen permit herself any regrets about Trudy's sexual direction or any longings that she change. If she were to express anything of this kind, Trudy's champion Jane, herself a strong feminist, would straighten her out quickly. She recalls one such recent episode:

> I said, "Well, you know, Jane, sometimes I think that if Trudy had had a better heterosexual relationship with a young man in her early twenties, this would not have happened, that she would not have—"
>
> And Jane really turned on me, as though I was not giving credence to what Trudy had supposedly opted to do on her

own. [She let me know] that this was a freely chosen personal preference on Trudy's part and not due to any disappointment or unhappiness or abuse suffered at the hands
of men.
     Jane said I was way off base, and she chided me for it.

Ellen feels no guilt, she says emphatically, about the direction
Trudy's life has taken. "That's a word I have almost eliminated from
my vocabulary. I believe very strongly that people take responsibility for themselves . . . and I don't assume guilt in much that happened."

She attributes this belief in part to the fact that she always had
some autonomy herself when her children were growing up. When
the children were still young, she took on a part-time job, and "it
was almost a foregone conclusion that I was expecting them to be
independent. I never felt that my working meant there was real
neglect of them.

"You know the old bromide about the time you spend with them is
quality time. I'm not sure it was that so much as the fact that I knew
that I needed to do what I was doing, needed it for myself."

Because she held a well-paid job, she was able to afford a house-
keeper. "That meant that the time I spent with them was time that I
wanted to spend with them."

Today, she describes her own career as "for me, the best of all
possible worlds. It gives me the freedom to do what I enjoy doing
much of the time."

She pauses to reflect. "I'm pleased with my life," she says cheerfully. "I'm proud of my marriage and proud of my career."

The autonomy that she has maintained for herself in marriage
and motherhood over the past thirty years she is eager to see in her
children. She accepts Trudy's autonomy, her right to take charge of
her own life. "She is a grown person now, and this is her free choice.
If I respect her, I have to accept her decision."

Thoughtfully she continues. "You have to look at the person who
makes the decision. Trudy is a sound person, doing many credible
and exciting things with her life, and that's terribly important to
me."

At the time of the interview, Trudy is living at home again, pursu-
ing a graduate degree in horticulture. "We're enjoying having her

home," Ellen says wryly, "as much as one enjoys having a child come home. She's very good company."

But she makes no bones about the fact that she is ready to have all her children become financially and emotionally independent. She believes that parents today continue an emotional responsibility for their children later than her parents' generation did. "It's surprising to me that our lives are so closely tied to each other still."

Jane, engaged and living away from home, Ellen acknowledges, "still very much needs us emotionally. I don't begrudge this. I know that until she marries, until she makes that connection with somebody else, that's going to be the case." She is pleased to contemplate the increased autonomy that Jane's impending marriage will, and should, bring to Jane and to her parents.

Ellen recognizes, however, that the connection between mother and child never dies. "You never ever 'get rid of' your children, you're never through with that concern. My mother was still anguishing over me two days before she died, always wondering, 'How's she doing? Is everything all right?' I think you just have that with you forever probably.

"But nobody can tell you that. You have to live it to know what it means."

And Ellen is pleased that the connection will last. "I'm certainly glad that I married and had children. I wouldn't have missed these associations and relationships."

Just the same, she is also glad that Rachel has almost finished college and will soon be on her own. She wants to see Jane "married off" and emotionally independent. And she'll be happy indeed to have Trudy finish her studies and leave home for any little shack she chooses to live in, with any companion she likes. Ellen is looking forward to an empty nest.

Not long ago, the writer Jane Adams described the sensations she had as a mother when her two children finally left home, to assume responsibility for their lives and to leave her free to take charge of her own. "I am a mother," she writes, "who never feared an empty nest. I have a life, a career, an agenda, and it seems as if I have waited forever to get back to it."

Yet in the midst of her relief, she feels the natural anxiety of the mother that she has left something undone, "some essential parental task I neglected." As she tries to think what it is, she drifts through her children's empty rooms, cleaning, tidying, rescuing favorite sweaters and replacing broken glass.

Then she realizes that she is performing futile tasks.

> It occurs to me that I am repairing a past they have put away, and that though they will return to this house, to these rooms, they will not be living in them again, merely passing through. And that, whatever I forgot to do for them—to teach, show, notice, praise, give or honor—they must do for themselves, or do without.

Jane Adams reveals what most women know: that, after nineteen or twenty years of constant and concerned mothering, a good mother wants her children to fly. The empty nest is her reward for a job well done.

And she wants to use her own wings. Adams's children left home on schedule, in the natural course of events. For the women in this study, the task of mothering was rendered longer and harder than usual. Yet for them too the happy time comes when the children "must do for themselves, or do without." In the twenty or thirty years likely to be remaining to them, these mothers, grateful for the tremendous mercy of autonomy, contemplate the joy of their own lives.

Stage Six

CONNECTION

Forging a new bond with the child and with the
world

11

Family Connections

BOTH THE CHILD AND THE GARDEN

Yet women want connection. For women, loving relationships are the ground of being. Naturally and instinctively, they rely on an ethic of caring, as the psychologist Carol Gilligan puts it. However much a mother desires autonomy for her child and for herself, she counts on its being an autonomy that doesn't rule out their lifelong connection. The female vision conjures up a "both-and" world, in which *both* autonomy *and* connection are possible, a world with the rich multiplicity of life itself.

What keeps connection between mother and child alive, what makes it vital? What is connected matters as much as the mere fact of connection. "Only connect," "all you need is love," "love makes the world go round"—these shibboleths are shortsighted. Instead of *love,* think *strength and love:* a strong self, a loving concern for others. "The woman who must love for a living," Vivian Gornick wrote in "The Next Great Moment in History Is Theirs" in 1969, "the woman who has no self, no objective external reality to take her own measure by, no work to discipline her, no goal to the illusion of progress, no internal resources, no separate mental existence, is constitutionally incapable of the emotional distance that is one of the real requirements of love."

Emotional distance a requirement of love? Yes, it is. Through autonomy is forged a new kind of connection, a mature love, the respectful connection between equals. Neither mother nor child exists solely for the convenience of the other. Their relationship must take its place, make its way, in the hierarchy of values which every autonomous adult establishes.

High on the scale of values is fidelity to oneself, fidelity to one's private image of the thing in life that endures. In one of her poignant little stories about her mother Sido, the French writer Colette recalls an occasion when, homesick and craving her mother's company, she urged Sido to visit her in Paris. Sido put her off. As much as she would like to see her beloved daughter, she wrote, she couldn't leave the provinces just then. One of her plants, a sluggish shoot which rarely flowered, was about to bloom, and Colette would understand that she could hardly miss *that!*

Colette, a wise daughter, did understand. Sido often called Colette her "masterpiece," but it was in her garden that Sido's inviolate, independent soul resided. To Colette's imagination, her mother grew to be herself a kind of garden. In *My Mother's House,* the daughter described Sido as "swept by shadow and sunshine, bowed by bodily torments, resigned, unpredictable and generous, rich in children, flowers and animals like a fruitful domain." Because Sido, alone, stood for something, Colette prized the connection between them. Even after Sido's death and after the daughter herself was an old woman, Colette still felt, humbly, not "at all sure that I have discovered all that she has bequeathed to me."

Perhaps the most important of those bequests was a sense of balance, the ability to moderate between the rival claims of child and garden, of city and country, of solitude and connection. Sido saw that she lived in a "both-and" world. She could go to Colette when she liked, could stay at home, busy with the concerns that enriched her hours there, when she liked. And because she saw that she had the freedom to choose, and to vary her choices if she wished, she could remain faithful to her own image of what her life should be. Thus she could, and did, create for herself a life that included both the child and the garden.

JOY ABOUNDING

"I am responsible for myself walking through this life," Joy Baron says firmly. "I have lots and lots of choices, if I care to take them. With every choice there will be goods and bads. But I am free to choose, within the capabilities of my mental and physical well-being."

Anyone looking at Joy would conclude instantly that her mental and physical capabilities are pretty great. A tall slender woman with reddish-gold hair carelessly piled up on the top of her head, Joy fairly radiates energy and goodwill. Her candid blue eyes shine with intelligence and amusement out of her lightly tanned face with its "good bones" and discreet sprinkling of golden freckles. Casually but smartly dressed in a long plaid flannel dress and worn leather boots, at fifty Joy knows what she thinks and feels. "We all have choices," she says. "I could have chosen not to do this interview, because it would be too painful." But she is ready to talk. She wants to tell her story, because she believes knowing what she experienced, the passage from pain and fragmentation to peace and wholeness, might help other mothers.

Even after eight years, every detail is fresh in her memory during the interview, emblazoned there permanently by the intensity of the pain that she and her family suffered when her unmarried daughter became pregnant. "The pain was like an explosion; it was like I was fragmented, like the part of the rocket that goes to the moon. It was awful, awful, awful.

"Yet I know I put the pieces back together. I may not have put them back in the right way for somebody else, but I put them back in the right way for me. I am whole and my family is whole."

To another mother, the problem in Joy's family might seem minor, a relatively small slip, easily corrected. In comparison with drug abuse, alcoholism, mental illness, crime, and other varieties of aberrant behavior, pregnancy out of marriage might seem tame. Abortions on demand are legal and common. The social stigma against unwed motherhood itself appears, statistically at least, to be disappearing: according to government reports in 1983, one baby in every five in the United States is born out of wedlock. In 1984, more than three-fourths of American women were reported to begin sexual activity before marriage. Both those figures are climbing.

No longer is unwed motherhood, as it was for years, almost exclusively the province of poor black women. Many independent single white women, like Carol Easton's daughter Anne, now choose to have a child out of marriage and to raise it alone. Anne got pregnant at thirty, had no desire to marry, but was eager to have the child. "I'm doing something I really want to do," she told her mother.

"She did it for herself," Carol says, "and she is very happy." The Easton family went along with Anne's decision. Anne's sister told her mother, "Anne is a big girl now and this is her decision. Accept it." And Carol has. "My biggest goal these days," she says, "is to get back out to California to see that little baby as often as I can."

Janet Crocker's daughter Laura also had a child out of wedlock. Like Anne Easton, Laura was thirty and "not interested," her mother says, "in marrying the father." Janet and her husband Marshall urged Laura to have an abortion, but Laura too was adamant in her refusal. When the child, a male, was born with Down's syndrome, Janet was terribly concerned about the difficult course her daughter had set for herself.

To Janet's surprise, however, Laura's devotion to her son has made her a different, better person. "She's never wanted any help from us," Janet says. "She wants to do this on her own." Having to focus her life has strengthened Laura. "In a sense, she has profited by it."

If illegitimacy is a problem, it is a problem that many American families will face, more and more an ordinary problem even for middle-class people. But it wasn't ordinary to Joy, and Joy is our guide. In every story in this book, the paramount element is the perception of the individual mother, the ruling consciousness and conscience hers. When a mother finds her child's behavior painful, what the rest of the world thinks hardly matters, at least for the purposes of this study. To Joy, what happened in her family was "the very worst thing that could happen."

She told her daughters so five or six months before the pregnancy became a fact. Bill Baron, Joy's husband, was recovering from a heart attack followed by open-heart surgery. The whole family—Joy and Bill; Rena, eighteen; Beverly, seventeen; Danny, fifteen; and Toni, fourteen—were visiting a quiet, rustic resort in New Hampshire, not far from their home in Boston. The children had had a scare that was, as Joy says, "the worst thing so far in their lives. They thought their father was going to die." Their retreat into the mountains was recuperative for them all, for "a family who wants to get in touch with itself."

Coming back to their cabin from the communal bathhouse, Joy and the three girls were talking quietly about the terror of Bill's illness. "Mom," Bev asked her mother, "now that Dad is getting better, what would be the worst thing that could happen to you?"

Joy paused for a minute. "Well, Bev," she said, "I guess it would be that one of you girls would get pregnant before you were married." The girls got quiet. Rena, the oldest, blushed and looked away. Toni, the baby, came over to her mother and linked arms, and they walked arm in arm up to the cabin.

"THE WORST THING"

That scene had taken place in July. About ten o'clock on a snowy Friday night early the following January, Bill and Joy were sitting at the kitchen table drinking a cup of cocoa before bedtime. The two oldest children were away at college, their son Danny had gone to a school ball game, and Toni, who had just begun dating, was out with her boyfriend Mike.

Rena's fiancé saw the lights and stopped by for a minute. Then Toni came in, right on schedule at eleven. While Mike waited in the living room, Toni came back to the kitchen. "Her immediate target, as usual," Joy wrote in her January 9 journal entry, "was the refrigerator. She opened the door and stood with her back to us, surveying her choices."

Her mother studied her idly. "Her hips were certainly expanding," Joy wrote. "Her fourteen-year-old body was thickening more than I had realized. The thought flashed out of nowhere: 'My God, she's pregnant.' " Then, looking at Toni's innocent, laughing, freckled face, Joy forced the "hideous presentiment" out of her mind.

The following day, a Saturday, the presentiment became reality.

Joy describes what happened in her journal entry dated January 10, 1975.

> Toni had offered to help me take down the Christmas tree and clean the family room. As we packed away the holidays, carefully wrapping each memory, we talked about the family. How good it had been to have the girls home. What a difference it made in the communication within the family group when they were with us.
>
> I watched her as she teetered on the little ladder, plucking a high ornament. She had always been very graceful; her balance was not so good anymore, as if her center of gravity had shifted. And the previous night's hideous thought came back.
>
> I began questioning her. When was her last period? She wasn't regular yet. Was she gaining weight? Maybe it was a buildup of fluids because of the irregularity. And then the awful question asked out loud: "Toni, could you be pregnant?"
>
> "I don't think so, Mom."
>
> But if she only "thinks" not, then it could be: the act has been performed. My stomach turned and my head buzzed. My voice was toneless. "When, Toni?"
>
> "During the big snowstorm, the first part of December."
>
> Six weeks! Oh, my God!

Quickly Joy called the family doctor and arranged to bring Toni in for a pregnancy test later that afternoon. The results would be ready Monday. Frightened and tearful, Toni called her boyfriend, who rushed over. Joy couldn't stand the sight of his ashen face. She ordered him out of the house and told him never to try to see Toni again. Toni ran upstairs, sobbing hysterically.

Joy was about to follow her when Bill called. The Barons are a country family. Their sprawling white house north of Boston sits on a large, prosperous farm which the family owns and operates as a nursery. Joy, Bill, and the children as they are available divide their time between house and business. This weekend morning Bill and a salesman were in the nursery, and they were out of cigarettes. Would Joy mind bringing a pack across the field? "Cigarettes!" Joy wrote in her journal. "Trivia! My world was crumbling around me, and he wanted cigarettes!"

Slowly she walked on upstairs to check on Toni. Toni was "curled in a fetal position on her bed. Her sobs had subsided, and her breath was coming in hiccups as it does after exhaustion in tears."

Joy came back down, pulled on her heavy coat, and took a pack of cigarettes across to Bill. One look at her face and he pulled her into the privacy of his office. "My God, Joy, what's happened?" he asked.

She told him. He put his arms around her. Joy vowed never to forget his words at that moment: "We've been through a lot together. We'll beat this, too."

"It was to be during this year that, after twenty years," she recorded in her journal, "I learned to lean on and love my husband."

Sunday was a blank day, a day to get through before the test results came back on Monday. The Barons are Catholic, and they went to Mass, at which three members of the family prayed frantically for the same thing—only Danny didn't know what was going on. After lunch, Bill and Danny took their shotguns and went rabbit hunting. Joy and Toni drove into Boston to see a movie, *The Little Prince*. Just right for a fourteen-year-old, Joy thought sadly, and just right for Toni. She recorded the theme in her journal, "The story of taming: love fulfilled and love betrayed."

On Monday, the test results came back. They were positive. "That night," Joy wrote, "when it was time for bed, I tucked Toni in, kissed her, and sat by her bed until I was sure she was asleep." Toni slept but Joy didn't.

The next morning, sleepless and exhausted, she packed the children off to school and sat down at the kitchen table, surrounded by dirty dishes, to confront the full horror of their situation. Before long, she was crying hysterically. Bill came down on his way out to the field where some men were waiting for him. Joy looked up at him through tear-swollen eyes. "I just can't take it," she told him. "I'm just going to ship Toni off to my sister, and let her handle this. I just can't even look at her anymore."

"I have to leave, Joy," Bill said. "They're waiting. I'll call you in a little while, okay?" An hour later he called. Joy was still crying. An hour later, when he called again, she was still crying. Bill put the phone down in his office and tried to think what to do. He had never seen Joy like this before.

DEALING WITH SHOCK

Bill Baron is a solid, analytical, careful man, slow to make a decision, inflexible once he's made it. The clerks in his office find him a hard man to work for, Joy says; he demands perfection and is unwilling to overlook a mistake. He and quicksilver Joy, who have worked together and lived together over thirty years now, are a union of opposites. From Joy's point of view it's not always been too happy a union. "I thought I was so bright and so beautiful and he was so lucky to have me."

She thought he didn't appreciate her, and Joy is not a person to suffer slights cheerfully. "Ten times a year for twenty years," she recalls during the interview, smiling faintly, "I did things like, in my mind, dividing up the furniture. I never divided up the children. I always told myself that I would never leave till Toni, the youngest, was sixteen, because I wouldn't do that to the kids."

But that fatal year of 1975, the year that Toni was fourteen, Joy put leaving Bill out of her mind forever. For the first time in the two decades they had spent together, she realized how lucky she was to have him. "I learned that year," she says, "that he is a marvelous, supportive man, a wonderful husband, a fantastic father—I just can't say enough. I wouldn't trade him for anything.

"I still know that one of my choices is to leave him, but I never will and I know that now, and I didn't know that before."

Bill had thought Joy would come to Toni's aid in the unwanted pregnancy with her usual dispatch and assurance. She had a quick instinct for the right thing with people, seemed to know what to do instantly. Beside her, he felt awkward; he had always been both dazzled and dismayed by her snap decisions.

This time, however, she was completely out of control, of herself, of the situation. He listened to her crying, then put the phone down and stood irresolutely in his little office. Toni was six weeks pregnant. *Somebody* had to do something. Hastily he picked up the phone again and dialed a customer who had become a friend. Phil Connolly (not his real name) was a priest and a family counselor for the Catholic Church; he would know what to do.

"I have to see you immediately, Father Connolly," Bill found

himself insisting, sounding, even to his own ears, completely unlike
his usual reserved self.

"But I'm leaving town tonight," the priest objected.

"That's all right," Bill urged, "see me right now. You have to see
my wife and me."

Father Connolly misunderstood. "For God's sake, Bill," he ex-
postulated, "you've been married for years. I can't do anything
instantly to help a marriage on the rocks."

"It's not my marriage," Bill said. "It's my daughter. She's pregnant."

The priest sighed with relief. "Oh, is that all?" he said. "We can
take care of that today. Come on in." But he reckoned without the
depth of Joy's feelings.

Bill drove back by the house and picked Joy up. She had managed
to get dressed and comb her hair, but her swollen face and dis-
tracted manner alarmed him. He hoped that Father Connolly could
help. If he couldn't, he thought, he didn't have one problem on his
hands; he had two.

Joy recorded the meeting with Father Connolly in her journal
entry for January 13, 1975.

> "My God is a god of love. He wouldn't let a fourteen-year-
> old be pregnant," I screamed at Father Connolly when we
> entered his office. And that was only the beginning. I
> screamed; I cried; I cussed. I damned our Church and my
> God. Bill tried to shush me, but once the dam had broken
> in my control, I was unable to hear or see anyone or any-
> thing except my frustration.
>
> Father Connolly was very gentle. He served me coffee
> and listened to my tirades. He neither lectured nor ser-
> monized. When I finally sat down to sip the cooling coffee,
> he called a friend of his, Rosa Miller (not her real name), a
> counselor and adviser with Catholic Social Services. We
> were to be at her office within the next hour.
>
> This quiet lady spent the afternoon listening to our frus-
> trations. She brought me a box of Kleenex and waited each
> time I broke down until I was able to gain control of myself.
> She presented some alternatives to us, among them abor-
> tion and separate education facilities available for preg-

nant girls. She began our education in the legal ramifica-
tions for Toni, the father, and the child if it were to be
born.

By the time we left her, we had made an appointment for
Toni and Mike to see her in two days, to begin the steps
involved in establishing paternity legally.

For the next week, Joy was a zombie. Miss Miller called her every
morning before ten o'clock, mostly just to listen to Joy, to hear what
was happening in the family. Sensitively, she made few suggestions,
asked few questions, at this point; she just let Joy spill out her
confusion and pain.

Joy's other outlet for her emotions in these first difficult days was
sleep. "Every day," she wrote, "I slept twelve out of the twenty-four
hours. It was a way to escape . . . , a welcome drug for forgetting
the present."

One night, she records, she woke in the dark to the sound of Bill's
muffled sobs. "If I could trade," he told her, shaking in her arms, "I
would have died when I had that heart attack, if I could make this go
away now for you and Toni."

"It was," she goes on, "the worst thing that ever happened to us."

Toni, a child in her parent's care, seemed less distraught than her
mother felt. One day Joy walked into the kitchen to find Toni standing at the counter with a butcher knife in her hand. Joy screamed.
Toni turned around, puzzled, then turned back to slice a piece of
salami. "Gosh, I'm always hungry these days, Mom," she told her
mother cheerfully.

At Joy's suggestion, Toni and Mike filled out papers to establish
legal paternity of the child, even though at that point Toni had not
decided what to do about her pregnancy. Joy had to renege on her
banishment of Mike. She and Bill realized, she writes, that "we
could not give Mike up for Toni. Only she could do this, and maybe
she never would."

With this decision came a full awareness on Joy's part that, in spite
of Toni's tender years, in spite of the fact that she was Joy's baby,
Toni had placed herself in an adult situation, with adult problems
that only she could solve. To help her daughter, Joy had to give up
the luxury of indulging her own feelings and pay attention to Toni.

PAYING ATTENTION TO A "BRAVE CHILD"

"Why?" Joy asked her daughter. "Toni, why did you do it?"

Toni answered "like the brave child she was," her mother says, " 'I wondered what it felt like.' "

Many of the young people in this study were "brave" like Toni. Like her, they were adventurous, eager for experience, more courageous and less conforming than their peers, ready to have a go at life.

Yet if Toni was undeniably brave, she was also, her mother came to realize more and more, a child, less mature in some ways than her sisters and brother had been at her age. Her own nature had led her into trouble, but that nature had been formed in part by her role in the family scenario.

Joy believes that Toni had not at the time she became pregnant really developed a moral consciousness. From her earliest years, the girl was brilliant. She could read at three without having been taught, and intelligence tests when she went to school categorized her as a genius. Because she was the youngest of four children all within five years of each other in age, there wasn't much time to be allotted for her. "But," Joy says, "she was bright enough to figure out how to get time for herself. One method she used was to allow us to make her decisions for her without our even realizing it."

Take, for example, Toni's choice of school clothes every morning. Joy never made these daily choices for her children. Making choices, she realized, was a part of growing up. But as she began to pay attention to the turns in Toni's young life, she realized that in truth Toni had rarely decided even the simplest things for herself, such as what socks matched what dress.

> She would go to Rena and say, "Which dress should I wear?" and she would go to Bev and say, "What socks go with this dress?" Then she would go to Danny and say, "Which shoes do you think I should wear today? It's raining outside."
>
> Then she came out to the kitchen, and she was all dressed, and I didn't realize that she didn't decide what she was wearing.

Toni's special guardian was Danny, who is just a little over a year older. It was Danny who took her to her kindergarten room on her first day of school and every morning after that for the next eight months. Again, Joy didn't realize what was happening until one spring morning when Danny had a fever.

"You'll have to stay home," Joy told Danny. "You're sick."

The little boy, who was not too fond of school, burst into tears at the thought that he couldn't go. "And how will my sister find her room?" he asked his mother through his sobs.

Joy looked at him in amazement. "After eight months, Danny," she said, "I'm sure she'll find her room."

"But he stood at the picture window and he watched his sister go down the street to the bus stop and you could just see what was going on in his mind," Joy remembers.

Totally secure in her family, the totally loved "baby," Toni was the happiest of Joy's four children. Alone and with the others, she was always "joyful," her mother says. "I remember walking into the hall one time when I didn't expect to see her there, and she was all alone, and she was dancing. She'd never had ballet or anything, but she was literally dancing."

When Toni reached early adolescence she still had the amorality of a child, Joy says. "This is not to say she was immoral, because she wasn't. She was like Pan, the Greek nature god who just joyfully bounded through life smelling the flowers. She was amoral."

She was also closer to her father than any of the other children. Joy, worn out with four pregnancies in five years, was ill after Toni's birth. Bill took care of the baby as much as he could, especially at night. As a result, Joy says, "When Toni needed help, she hollered 'Daddy' instead of 'Mommy.' " As Toni grew up, Bill was very important in her life.

Before and after his heart attack, Bill wasn't available to the children, especially to Toni, as he always had been. In pain but having to go on with business duties, at home "he tuned out a lot of things and was just a bastard," Joy says. Toni suffered from his bad temper and childishly found it hard to forgive him when he got back to normal. "I don't like my daddy anymore," she told Joy. Joy believes that the temporary loss of her father's affection had something to do with the sexual relationship that developed so quickly between Toni and Mike.

Thus Toni was at fourteen both a beloved child who had never learned to make responsible decisions for herself and a little girl who might have felt abandoned by her father. Then suddenly she found herself with a woman's problem.

In spite of the fact that the Barons are Catholic, abortion was not ruled out as a possibility, especially in view of Toni's youth and immaturity. Even before Toni's pregnancy Joy strongly favored the right to abortion on demand, "because I felt that unwed mother-hood was really the worst thing that could ever happen to anybody. I wasn't voting as a Catholic, but out of personal feeling."

What Joy did want to ensure was that Toni would decide what to do about her pregnancy herself. She wanted Toni, who had slid through so much of her short life without making decisions, to understand and to experience the concept of personal responsibil-ity. To have an abortion, to have the baby and keep it, to have the baby and give it up for adoption: these were the alternatives that Toni faced. "I think in some instances the girl doesn't make the choice," Joy says. "Her mother or father makes it." In her family, the girl would choose.

"FAMILY FAMILY FAMILY FAMILY"

The first step, Bill, Joy, and Toni agreed, was to tell the other children in the family. Shortly after Toni's pregnancy was con-firmed, Joy and Bill were supposed to go to California for two weeks to visit her parents, an annual trip which the grandparents carefully planned a year in advance. "We can't go, I can't go," Joy, still in the throes of hysteria and shame, told Bill. They dutifully reported this decision to their psychologist, Rosa Miller.

"Go to California," Miss Miller told them. "This is the only time I will ever tell you what to do. But your daughter will not take her own life, and she has agreed to put off her decision on abortion for the two weeks. She needs to be away from her mother and her mother needs to be away from her daughter. It's necessary. Your daughter will be safe, I promise you."

Reluctantly, Joy agreed. But first the other children must know what was going on. They told Danny right away. He was crestfallen; until Mike came along, he had always screened Toni's friends and protected his little sister. He didn't say much, but they could tell he felt responsible and ashamed.

Next Joy called Rena and Bev, both away in college, to come home. On the Friday night before Joy and Bill were to leave on Sunday, the Barons held a family conference, one of the many they had had over the years.

"Ma, you sound like the Mafia," Danny sometimes teases his mother. "You say 'family family family family.' " "It's true," Joy agrees, laughing. "We are a family-oriented family."

As the children were growing up, in some ways the family was both highly structured and very liberal. Because they all worked together in the nursery, they had an additional responsibility to each other that other families usually don't have. For this reason, they worked out some offbeat practices which became second nature to the children. For example, every member of the family who went out wrote his name, destination and phone number, and expected time of return on a sign-out sheet which they kept on the kitchen table. "It wasn't done in other homes, but it was done in our home," Joy says.

They all understood and took part in family finances. In 1975, the same year Toni got pregnant, the family business suffered because of the economic recession, and Bill Baron had to take out a sizable loan. They were all partners in the business, and they all knew what was happening. They also kept a list of what they owed each other financially, and they paid each other for certain jobs: Joy might get a dollar for hemming Rena's skirt or vice versa.

Rules of conduct, hours, and prescribed punishments they made up together in family conferences at the kitchen table and posted on the refrigerator door, though Bill frequently exercised a power of veto. "We had what we referred to as either an autocratic democracy or a democratic autocracy," Joy says. "We all got to vote, but my husband made the decision."

Neither parent legislated matters of conscience for the children, however. Rena risked a jail sentence to participate in ecology marches on a local factory. The two older children were sent to parochial school, but Joy discontinued that practice with Danny and Toni. All the children were free to attend non-Catholic services, and for a long time Toni went every Sunday to Mass with her parents and to the Baptist church with her best friend. "You'll be sorry, Mrs. Baron," Toni's catechism teacher told Joy. But Joy didn't think so.

Now, on this cold, blustery Friday night, as she sat down with her family at the big pine table where they had held so many family discussions and now were to talk about Toni's pregnancy, she wondered if she had been wrong. Had their liberality with their children been damaging? Was it at the root of Toni's situation?

Joy recorded the event in her journal:

> We sat at the dining-room table Friday night, the six of us, the first time together in several months. Rena was in a bad emotional state. She thought that Toni was being punished for her "sins."

"Rena is very religious," Joy explains. Joy and Bill had suspected that Rena was sleeping with her husband-to-be. Now Rena's guilt erupted. What had happened to Toni was punishment for Rena's sins, and Rena was devastated. "It was worse for Toni to have to go through it than it was for her because she was eighteen and her sister only fourteen."

The family conference helped the other children to bring up their secret troubles also. Danny talked about his guilt and shame.

> We interrupted each other, and consoled one another. We listened and learned. We talked on and on. Bev's boyfriend came and was sent away for another hour. Rena's fiancé came, and was also sent away. I looked into the souls of my children that night, and I loved each one more than I ever had before.

Only Bev appeared to be dealing with the situation superficially. "Bev was looking for solutions, preferably easy ones," Joy wrote. But the next day Joy found Bev collapsed in tears on the living-room sofa. Joy records the conversation that ensued:

> "I feel like such a baby, Mom. I'm the only one in our house who is a virgin. I don't even know the score. My roommates do it. Everybody does. I'm just a baby."
>
> I said a prayer, my first in two weeks, and I started to console my middle child. "Intercourse is a union of two, a

'communion,' and, like the Eucharist that we call Communion, cannot be entered into without commitment. . . .
[When] we participate in the Eucharist, we become one
with Jesus Christ. In 'co-itus,' a man and woman become
one by their physical union. Without relationship, sex is
meaningless. Communion, physical or Eucharistic, presup-
poses *love.*"

Bev's brown eyes cleared, and she hugged me. "Thanks,
Mom."

It was the first time in an eternity that I felt like a worthy
mother.

Early the following morning, Joy and Bill left for California. Joy
took with her the shame as a mother which was the worst part of the
entire ordeal for her. The shame was made harder to bear because it
had to be secret. Until Toni decided about an abortion, they agreed
sensibly not to let anyone else know she was pregnant, certainly not
the doting grandparents. The two weeks in California were anything
but a vacation.

However, during the communion reading at the Catholic church
in California to which Joy's parents took them, Bill passed the missal
to Joy with a passage from Isaiah he had marked: "Look up to the
Lord and smile and you will never be ashamed." "That literally
carried me through," Joy remembers.

FACING THE WORLD

Soon after their return from California, Toni told her parents that
she had decided not to have an abortion. She was unsure about
anything else, but she felt confident that having the baby was right.
Over the next six or seven months, until the little boy they called
Sean was born in the late summer, the six Barons held a half dozen
family conferences, with Miss Miller, the family counselor, in attendance. "We found out that in a family situation like this, everybody is
a part of it. You all almost have to face the world with the same face
. . . and always Toni's needs had to come first."

They decided not to send Toni, always so happy and secure in the heart of her family, away from home during her pregnancy. She would go into a home for unwed mothers her last few months, at the start of the summer, so that she could have constant prenatal care and so that adoption facilities would be available if she decided to put the child up for adoption. But that decision was to be left up to Toni to make whenever she felt ready. In the meantime, having Toni at home, visibly pregnant, meant facing the world together.

The authorities at Toni's school had to be told first. "I couldn't do it," Joy said. "My husband did it." Typically, he handled it scrupulously, preparing for his half-hour visit with the principal as if he were giving a speech, complete with note cards. Toni was too bright to lose her class standing, and he meant to do his best to prevent it. He was successful.

Joy spoke to their parish priest. He surprised her by not giving her "that old saw that 'God gives you only what you're able to handle.'" Instead he looked directly into her eyes and told her that the same thing had happened to his sister. "He didn't have to say anything else," Joy said. A month before the baby was due, he handed Joy a personal gift for Toni.

Encounters for the three oldest children didn't go so smoothly. Rena, who had felt that Toni was a scapegoat for her "sins," had such a hard time with the whole situation that the family decided she would be better off out of the picture entirely. As soon as the spring semester was over, they packed her off to summer school in Arkansas, where she would stay with an aunt.

Bev refused to continue dating her boyfriend unless he agreed to help to keep Toni happy by taking her out to eat and to movies with them and later visiting her with Bev in the home for unwed mothers. He agreed, but he was not thrilled.

Fifteen-year-old Danny was probably hit hardest of the children. Not only was he a year older than Toni, which meant that they had friendships in common, but he had also considered her his special responsibility. He was dreadfully ashamed of what had happened. At first, Joy recalls, he tried to deny it.

> One day I was in the kitchen when he came home from school. I had my back to him, and he came in the door saying, "Ma, I was in the bathroom today, and one of the fellows asked me if my sister was pregnant."

I didn't turn around to look at him, which was a mistake. I just said, "Well, she is pregnant, Danny. What did you say?"

And he said, "God damn it, Ma."

And I turned around and the fellow that asked him in the bathroom was with him and Danny was looking for me to validate the fact that his sister wasn't pregnant. Poor Danny.

"It was an awful time for Danny," his mother says.

He began to run around and smoke pot, which caused trouble between him and his father. This additional family trauma came to a climax one evening when Joy was working in the nursery office and the two men were at home alone together. They got into an argument and Bill pushed his son up against the closet door, breaking it, and blacked Danny's eye. "The closet door isn't fixed to this day," Joy says. "I think my husband has deliberately not fixed it so that he remembers."

Danny got in the car and left. When Joy came home a couple of hours later, she found a note on the kitchen table which read, "Dear Ma, Don't worry about me. I am all right. I won't do anything foolish. I'll be okay. I'll call you. Danny." Briefly Bill told her what had happened, and then he went up to the bedroom to wait. Joy sat in the kitchen, smoking and drinking coffee.

The boy called just after midnight. He had gone over to talk to his girlfriend's mother, and "she sent him back to me," Joy says, "telling him how good we were. Whether we were good or not, he believed her." "Hi, Ma," he said on the phone. "I'm exhausted. I can't come home tonight, but I'll be home tomorrow morning about seven for breakfast." And he was.

Joy and Bill obviously had to tell their friends of Toni's condition, first their best friends, Linda and Sam Rawson. Sam's reaction was surprising. "We sat down at the kitchen table, we poured the wine, and we began to tell them," Joy recalls, "and poor Sam had to go to the bathroom and vomit. He's such a softhearted fellow anyway."

Something Bill said that night to the Rawsons impressed his wife deeply. He was talking about who was to blame. He said, "At first you think, 'My God, it's my fault.' And then, because no man can carry this kind of load and keep his sanity, you say, 'No, it isn't; it's the child's fault.' And then you see the child suffering, so it's got to be your wife's fault. Then you can't stand to be without her because then you won't have anybody. So you blame society, the schools, the teen culture, the boy. It takes a long while until you realize that no one's to blame. It doesn't matter whose fault it is. It only has to be taken care of."

Joy most dreaded telling her parents. Bill's parents are dead, but Joy's family and her parents visit once or twice a year. After Bill and Joy made the visit to California in January, however, the Barons thought they might not see the grandparents for another year, and wouldn't have to tell them anything until it was all over. This plan was blown when Grandma and Grandpa called at Easter. Since they had missed the children in January, they thought they'd come to Boston. Toni was six months pregnant, "very big," due to go to the home for unwed mothers any day. "Mother," Joy said, "you can't come."

"Don't be silly, Joy. Why can't we come?"

Joy paused, her mind racing. What to do? She saw no alternative. "Toni's pregnant." Joy heard a clunk at the other end. "Oh, my God, I've killed her," she thought. Then she realized her mother had dropped the phone.

Her mother's voice came on the line, sounding faint and far away. "I'll call you later, honey," it said.

Two days later her mother called back. "I don't think your dad and I can face this," she told Joy. "You're right. We can't come."

"Okay," Joy said, then she began thinking. The next morning she wrote her parents, "not for me but for my daughter."

If you don't come now, after you called, Toni is going to think she committed the unpardonable sin, and I won't allow this. You have to spend Easter with us, and you're going to have to sit with Toni in church, pregnant, and that's the way it is.

I love you both and I know that you will be able to do it for us because I know that you love us.

Her father called. "We'll be there on Friday," he said. They came. Joy's mother brought with her the good pearls that she planned to leave to Toni when she died. "I think I'll give them to her now," she said.

"No, Mother," Joy told her. "You don't get rewards for what we're going through. You don't get punished, but you don't get rewards either. So save them, Mother, and put them in your will."

RICH REWARDS

But there were rewards for the Barons from Toni's pregnancy, in spite of Joy's protestations. Joy came to recognize the rewards herself. A couple of years ago she told Bev, the child whom she describes as "the friend of my soul," "It was the worst thing we've ever gone through. But it may be the most important experience we'll ever have. Perhaps it also was the best thing that ever happened to each of us individually and to all of us as a group."

Joy was talking about growth. She is quick to add that it's not a method of growth she would advise others to take. "Had God come down and told me, 'Your daughter's going to be pregnant and have a baby when she's fourteen, but out of this will come the most marvelous growth,' " she says ironically, "I would have said, 'Forget it, God, I'm not interested.' "

But she can see the changes for the better in each of them for having passed through what she calls their crucible. "The only one who didn't change," she jokes, "was the dog." It strengthened each member of the family personally, and it strengthened and changed the connections between them.

Joy and her father had been at odds for years. When she wanted to marry Bill, he advised her against it. "You'll never be happy married to this farmer," he said. Joy believed that her father cared for people a lot less than he cared for money and things. His behavior during Toni's pregnancy convinced her otherwise. "I'll never call him a bastard again," she told Bill. "You shouldn't have called him that to begin with," Bill chided.

To her mother Joy had always been close, but they became closer over the next months. Her mother seemed to understand immediately what Joy was feeling, perhaps because her youngest child, Joy's little sister, was retarded. Both Joy and her mother are proud, elegant women, and both care about the appearance of things. At fourteen, Toni looked twelve, but she got as big as a barrel in the last three months of her pregnancy. When Joy took her shopping or out to eat, people stared. Joy was embarrassed, then she remembered her mother's aplomb in public with her retarded child.

Her admiration for her mother grew. "My mother is a very independent woman," she says. "She has a very good self-image. She gave this to me by virtue of her having it. I think that I gave it to my daughters because I have it. We give it to our daughters when we recognize our own intrinsic value, separate from our husbands, separate from our children."

Joy and her mother have formed a connection based on strength and love. As much as she loves her mother, Joy also knows her own strength. "I have reached the point where, if my mother died, I know I could go on without her." She wants to have her daughters feel the same way about her. Treating Toni as a responsible adult was a step in that direction.

Toni went into the home for unwed mothers in May. With their usual organization, the Barons made out a schedule for their visits to her. One day a week she was alone. The rest of the time they visited her routinely. Rena was still in summer school in Arkansas, but Danny, Bev, and Joy and Bill took turns. Toni's boyfriend Mike was put on the schedule. "It was his duty to go," Joy says severely. They never missed a day, "so that," Joy says, "never would she feel like we had abandoned her." She might be away from them temporarily, but Toni was still a part of the family.

And they took her friends to see her. For one outing, Joy and Bill picked up two of Toni's girlfriends and took the three on a picnic at the beach. She laughs at the memory of Toni's childish unselfconsciousness. "Here we were, with the fried chicken and the potato salad. The girls were swimming in the lake and bounding out and up to us, these two beautiful fourteen-year-old bodies, and our daughter with her belly bouncing, running up out of the water just like the others. Toni was not aware that she looked any different from the other two girls.

"Bill and I looked at each other and laughed. I mean, how could we have thought six months earlier that we would be here in this situation?"

From that first January day on, the family had counseling. Joy and Bill saw Miss Miller once a week, sometimes with the children. And

the children visited separately also. Joy recalls that "Miss Miller saw
the baby's father and Toni separately, she saw Rena separately, she
saw Danny separately, she saw both our daughters and our son
together." In addition, once Toni went into the home, she had daily
opportunities to talk with the counselors there. Joy and Bill tried to
keep their promise to themselves; they were anxious to know what
Toni planned to do with the baby, but it was her decision. When she
went into labor two weeks early, they had no idea what she had
decided.

Sean was born at the end of July, a robust child with his mother's
round face, reddish-gold hair, and even a little sprinkling of freckles
across his nose like Toni and Joy. Bill and Joy went in to see their
daughter, sitting up in bed, the baby lying in a little crib at her side.

Instinctively Joy reached out to pick the baby up. "He's going up
for adoption, Mother," Toni said. "You are *not* to hold him."

"Oh," Joy said.

"And so I looked at the baby," she says, sighing, big tears spring-
ing in her eyes. "The little cart was wheeled right by me, and I tell
you without prejudice that was the most beautiful child I will ever
see. But I did not hold him, nor did Toni hold him. This was her
decision." But Bill and Joy spent hours in front of the nursery
window, "looking at that child for the few days he had our name."

As sad as she felt for herself and Bill, Joy felt sadder for Toni.
"She's the one that's giving up her child. I didn't give up my child. I
have my children. They love me and I love them and I have all this
beauty that goes with motherhood. My daughter doesn't have that.
She's the one that had to give it up."

The adoption was scheduled to take place several days after Toni
and Sean left the hospital, days which Sean spent in a foster home.
During that time, once again the whole family assembled with Miss
Miller. "She told us everything she could about Sean's adoptive
parents, without telling us who they were," Joy says. They all faced
together "the final closing," the loss of the first grandchild in the
Baron family. Joy and Bill felt they were prepared. Joy, Bill, and
Toni were to pick up Mike on the day of the adoption, and the four
would go to court together.

The night before the adoption was to take place, Bill, the bulwark
of strength for the whole family, broke down completely. "That was
one of the worst nights I ever remember," Joy says, "and the only

time during the whole thing when I was able to give strength to my husband. Ah, poor Bill! He did not want to let go of that child."

Joy had to lay out the grim alternatives for him.

At three o'clock in the morning, I said to him, "Honey, we have three choices: we can bring the baby home [if Toni will consent], we can allow her to give him up, or we can leave him in a foster home. A foster home is limbo: there are some children who stay in foster homes all their lives because the people who supposedly love them will not bring them home and will not sign the adoption papers.

"This is our grandchild. Do we want to bring him home?"

And my husband said, "That's not good for him; we will not be giving him the life he should have. He will be our grandchild. He won't have a father. He's going to have you as a mother image, he's going to have Toni as a mother image. The whole thing is a mess."

I said, "You're right. Do we want to leave him in a foster home?"

"I wouldn't do that to anybody who belonged to *me.*"

I said, "So do we allow our daughter to go through with it?"

And he said, "I guess so."

They went over and over the alternatives for three or four hours. "We didn't have any good choices," Joy says.

Joy was proud of Toni during the adoption. Her "baby" had grown up, perhaps faster than she should have. "We sat in a room, Miss Miller, Toni, the baby's father, my husband, me, and the judge. And the judge told my husband and me that this was not our affair and that we were to keep our mouths shut. He chose to talk with our daughter. He talked with our fourteen-year-old daughter, and we listened to what she said, and she gave beautiful answers."

Joy realized that "Toni had been there." For weeks and months the once amoral child had been going over the same alternatives that Joy and Bill had faced so starkly the night before. Toni had come to the same difficult moral conclusion that they had reached: for his own sake, she had to give Sean up.

FULL CIRCLE

Soon after Toni gave Sean up, she discontinued her relationship
with his father. The girl had changed radically in the year that had
passed since she had her first date with Mike. "Miss Miller took great
pains to teach her cause and effect," a lesson Joy thinks Toni might
have learned almost too well.

For example, Toni believed so strongly that she should assume
responsibility for all her actions, past and present, that she insisted
on telling all her dates the story of Sean. This phase is almost funny
to her mother now, but it was anything but funny at the time:

> It made no difference who our daughter went out with,
> when he would come to the front door to pick her up,
> before he was allowed in the house, she would say, "I want
> you to know I had a baby when I was fourteen and if you
> can't accept this, I can't go out with you." This went on for
> about a year.
>
> It was horrendous. I mean, you can imagine. Some of
> them left. Some of them came in quickly because, as she
> told me later, they thought then they would have privileges
> with her. She finally learned not to say this immediately.

But "telling," feeling free to share the experience they had gone
through with others, was important to Joy as well as to Toni.

> I think it is necessary, in order to come full circle in heal-
> ing, to be able to tell the truth about what happened, if it's
> necessary.
>
> Now I don't believe in carrying a sign that says, "My
> fourteen-year-old daughter had a baby and I have come
> through it and I am whole, hooray for me." I don't mean
> that. But if something comes up.

For example, she describes an occasion when she and Bill had
gone dancing with two other couples. The other four were talking
about friends whose child was pregnant. "They didn't even get to
the point of saying how terrible it was" when Joy spoke up. She
looked them in the eye and said, "Bill and I have a daughter who got

pregnant when she was fourteen. It was an awful experience. Have compassion for those people. They are going through hell."

If Joy sometimes thought Toni talked too much, Bill thinks Joy talks too much. She doesn't agree. "Each time that I am able to stand up with shoulders straight and a smile on my face and my personhood intact and tell [someone who needs to know] what happened, I am stronger and wiser."

And she believes she owes her testimony to the community of souls on earth, she says. "We live in coexistence with all human beings. This was my crucible, and therefore I give it to you, to tell each person that it is possible to walk through the fire."

She tries to think how to put what she feels. "I'm still paying my dues, and I will pay my dues as life goes on."

Joy has carefully watched the pilgrim's progress that her youngest child has undergone. She and Bill did not, however, monitor Toni's social life or her hours after Sean's birth and adoption. "If a woman gives away her child for the child's good," Joy explains, "that woman cannot be required to be home at eleven o'clock at night, even though that woman is only fifteen."

Toni, subdued and fearsomely responsible, gave them little cause for worry until the night of Sean's first birthday. Joy describes that night.

> She was usually home at nine-thirty and in bed, but that night she wasn't. And she wasn't home, and she wasn't home.
>
> So at eleven-thirty, we were in bed, the light was on, we weren't sleeping, we were both pretending we were sleeping, we were lying there, and our daughter came in the back door. She saw our light on, so naturally she came into our room, which was our intent.
>
> She sat on her daddy's side of the bed, closest to the door, and she said, "Oh, Dad," and she started to cry. He tried to hug her but she wouldn't take the hug. She moved away.
>
> And she stood against the door and she started screaming, "Oh, he's going to think I'm a whore, he's going to think I'm a whore."
>
> I said, "Who, the guy you went out with tonight?"

"No, my son, my son. He'll think I'm a whore because they'll tell him I was fourteen and I was pregnant and he'll think I'm a whore."

And she slumped to the floor and sobbed and sobbed. I thought we would be there all night. My husband and I, we didn't know what to say. We looked at each other and we didn't know what to do for her.

I told her afterwards that I knew she was crying for *her* child, but that I looked at *my* child and I thought she would never be whole again.

But Joy realized later that Toni was going through "the final step of the grieving process. Although her child had not died, to her that child had to be dead, and this was the final agony before the resurrection."

Toni's resurrection came in several forms. First, at twenty-one she met and married Paul, a wonderful man who happens to have a physical handicap. "I love him," Joy says. "He has been so good for her, but I don't think she ever would have married him if it hadn't been for her experience."

And Joy's own understanding and compassion have increased also. "Maybe [there was a time when] I wouldn't have wanted a person with a handicap for my daughter. Then I think of the child's story of the Enchanted Cottage and all the strange people who were beautiful to one another. And you know if you're beautiful to another person, maybe that's more important than anything else."

A second form of resurrection for Toni came in her work. She and Paul don't have children yet, but Toni, always brilliant in the sciences, has gone into medicine. At the time of the interview, she was finishing medical school, looking forward to an internship in pediatrics and eventually to a practice in Boston. She likes being close to her parents.

Danny too has stayed close to home. In fact, he and his wife live in a house on the family farm, and he and his father work together. One of these days before long, Joy and Bill plan to turn the nursery over to Danny, "who is," Joy says, "becoming more and more like his dad, very efficient, a wonderful fellow to run a business."

For all her love of her children and her pleasure in their closeness, Joy keeps in mind the necessity for autonomy that both mother and child have. From the crisis that she and Toni and the rest of the family went through, Joy learned one thing very well: "that you and your daughter are two separate people. Each of you will go through a different crisis. Don't try to tell her what to do. Love her; support her."

By the same token, Joy doesn't allow her child to tell her what to do. On Toni's wedding day, sensing her mother's softness, Toni approached Joy privately. "Mom," she said, "I have a favor to ask you."

"Well, naturally," Joy laughs, "the kid's getting married, so I'm all 'Oh, honey, what can I do for you?'"

Toni looked into her mother's eyes. "Don't ever sell this house. Because if Sean ever looks for me, Mom, this is the address he'd come to."

That was a hard one, but Joy refused. "I said that I could not make that promise. That wasn't fair to her daddy and to me. We have our lives, and our relationship, and we have a right to be able to go on from here. We need now to be allowed to be ourselves as she and Paul will be themselves. And it has nothing to do with my love for her."

All three of the Baron girls have gone into service professions. Bev, the middle daughter, is a physical therapist, now married to the boyfriend who was required to take a pregnant Toni with them on dates. It worries Joy that Bev doesn't want children. She's told Bev she thinks she's making a mistake, "but that's her decision and we haven't talked of it since."

Rena, the oldest daughter, is a teacher. At the time of the interview, she and her husband had a little girl and another child on the way. Joy describes some very ungrandmotherly feelings she had during Rena's first pregnancy. "I was so upset, I can't tell you. You know other women, 'Ooh, I'm going to be a grandmother.' I was so resentful. I think part of it was that I had already turned away from a grandmother role once, and wasn't going to take it on again, because it was just too painful." Now, of course, little Marcia, the image of her grandfather, is the delight of her grandmother's life.

This last episode is just one illustration of a phrase that Joy uses frequently in conversation without ever quite defining—"coming full circle." To come full circle seems to mean to her accepting the bitterness and the sweetness that together make up the liquor of life.

It means walking all the way through the dark tunnel to find the light at the end. "It happens in a lot of things," Joy says. "It happens with faith. It happens with an illness. If you don't come full circle, you die."

It happened to the Baron family with "the worst thing that ever happened." They have come full circle. That doesn't mean the pain they felt has entirely disappeared. Occasionally Joy sees a little boy with reddish-gold hair and freckles, and she wonders if he could be Sean. Sometimes she wants to go up to the mother "and say, 'Oh, what a darling little boy,' and wait to see if she says, 'Oh, well, you know he's adopted.' " But she doesn't do it. "Sean doesn't belong to us anymore. He belongs to himself and whoever's loving him."

She does have a lingering daydream: that Sean will find them someday, "show himself to us just so that we can say, 'We gave you up out of love, your mother gave you up out of love, not out of selfishness. Know this, please know this, please know that we love you.' "

For the most part, however, Joy refuses to allow herself to have daydreams for her family. "For me, yes. For them, no." There was a time when she daydreamed about all of them—that Toni, for example, might be another Madame Curie "and win the Nobel Prize and I get to sit there and know that she did it for me." No longer. "I can't daydream for them. They have to make up their own daydreams."

But she does have a mother's hopes. She hopes to live to see Toni regain some of that brightness she had before morality set in, when, like a young Pan, she danced through life smelling the flowers. "She doesn't realize how broad things are, how broad life really is," Joy says. "But she has to figure that one out."

In the meantime, Joy will settle for connection. The night before the interview, Toni and her husband were on their way home from a party when they saw light in the Barons' kitchen and stopped by for a minute. Joy sat at the kitchen table going over some of the questions she would answer on tape the next day.

Toni looked over her mother's shoulder. " 'Do liberal parents make radical children?' " she read. "Gosh, Mom, that's going to be a hard one for you to answer."

"I know," Joy said ruefully. Toni sat down beside her. "We read the questions and talked and laughed, and Paul was drinking his coffee and just grinning and grinning and generally ignoring us, except really absorbing us also."

After about forty-five minutes they got up to go. Joy stood up too. At the door, Toni turned around and walked back over to her mother. "She put her arms around me, and she looked me right in the eye, and she said, 'I love you, Mom.' "

"And I said, 'I love you, Toni.' "

12

Second Birth, Second Self

Giving birth is a central event in the lives of women. For centuries, women have told each other stories of childbirth, of the universal female drama in which agony and joy, death and life, contend. Birth is not easy for mother or child.

Nor is the second birth easy. When a mother lets an adult child go forth to his own character and his own destiny, that act too carries pain and peril. If most people expected to be born twice, E. E. Cummings once commented, the second time they'd demand "a guaranteed birthproof safety suit." And, he added, they'd probably call the second birth "dying."

But the second birth provides no more guarantees than the first, and calling it "dying" isn't always too far off target. Some women whose stories are told here will never see their sons and daughters reach happy, independent, productive adulthood. Instead, their children are dead; they are incarcerated in prison or commune; or they have been ravaged by drugs, alcohol, or illness. Not all of these children made it.

Their mothers did make it. They were selected for this study because the behavior of their children had not finally worn them down. Oh, they worried and grieved and hoped; at times they were saddened, frustrated, fearful, exhausted; at times they despaired.

But in all this emotional turmoil, they continued—jerkily, with numerous stops and starts and pauses and skips—to move through the stages of the process described in this book: shock, attention, action, detachment, autonomy, connection.

In the long run, responding to crisis and its aftermath made them more resourceful. Faced with the trauma introduced by a child, woman after woman emerged triumphant by calling into play three abilities in particular: the ability to cope with change; the ability to understand and communicate with others; and the ability to trust the healing processes of time and nature.

The women came to recognize and take pride in their strength while not always understanding its causes or effects. Rebecca Winslow, a straitlaced, conservative mother whose freewheeling daughter Kris spent years in a commune, credits her ability to cope with such drastic change to an accident of birth. "I'm from Maine, and we always cope in Maine. Bad weather, bad crops, illness, high seas and a lost ship, whatever—you cope." She might have said Michigan or Mississippi or Montana and made her point. Aside from bad weather and high seas, the social climate of America imposes upon its citizens the necessity of coping with change.

This country was founded in revolution, and it continues to redefine itself from decade to decade. Simply to be an American, from 1776 on, has meant learning how to adapt to frequent and radical social changes. The stages in the process of coping that the women in this book discovered for themselves need most to be understood when traditions are most challenged, as they were in the sixties and seventies. But then traditions are constantly being challenged in America.

From the vantage point of the eighties, we look back to the two decades preceding us as an apex of social disruption, and so they were. The women in this book held their turbulent times responsible, as we have pointed out, for many of the problems they had with their children. But think of the disruptions of the Civil War years, which divided country, state, and family. Think of the rampant alcoholism and gangsterism of the Prohibition years, of the economic divisions and the desperate wandering of the Great Depression. Think of the baneful (from a mother's point of view) "foreign" influences on farm boys from Idaho or Kentucky who went abroad during two world wars and the Korean conflict.

The energy of America is change. Even the word "tradition" may
have inherent difficulties in a country as big, as young, and as diverse as the United States. Similar in background, social and economic position, and ideology as these women are, even they disagreed as to what "untraditional" behavior might be. When we look
to the traditions of our revered past, our minds flash images from
Currier and Ives and Norman Rockwell. But that order, that perfection, that *tradition* which figures in our dreams and our desires may
not have existed as we imagine it. "Every Paradise," Proust wrote,
"is a lost Paradise." American mothers have always had to cope with
change, and while America is America, they always will. The women
in this study discovered that they had that innate ability, which could
be further developed through experience and exchange. They
learned to cope with change by doing so.

Experience taught them also not to give up on a child. Some of
them at the time of their ordeal thought of their children as victims,
others as pioneers. They saw the victims as irresponsible, trapped in
the flux of a decadent society. The pioneers they saw as taking
responsible risks to fulfill the promise of a progressive society. They
were not always right. Some of the children earlier perceived by
their mothers as victims today look suspiciously like pioneers. "It's a
funny thing," one mother said. "With all my worries about my
three, they didn't turn out too badly in the end."

The women here also learned through exchange. They taught
each other. The mothers in these nuclear families no longer had the
habit of exchanging child-raising tales, as women had once, in quilt-
ing bees and church circle meetings. Desperate for attention and
advice, finding the experts often inept, these more recent mothers
also learned to cope with the challenges their children presented by
turning to each other. Thus they gained a sense of common maternal experience. By sharing their experiences in this book, they gen-
erously offered to a wider audience the knowledge that they acquired about the patterns of successful parenting.

In addition to the ability to cope with change, these women discovered in themselves the ability to understand and to communicate
human feelings and perplexities. For some, this ability went beyond
the rational. Where their children were concerned, many of them
believed they had experienced "second sight" or prescience. Elizabeth Rowe saw her transsexual son Nate as the fulfillment of a

promise God made her in a dream when she was thirteen that she would have "a special child." Sharon Marsh heard sirens that existed only in her head, then discovered that her son Russ had been injured in a car wreck. One look told Joy Baron fourteen-year-old Toni was pregnant, two months before anyone else could have seen it. Agnes Price not only knew instinctively that her daughter was pregnant, but that Phoebe was on her way to have an abortion. Such women believed that a "female" intuition peculiar to mothers gave them their conclusions. As Agnes put it, "A mother knows."

Sometimes, trusting what "a mother knows," they defied "male" logic and objectivity. Frustrated with the lumbering rationality of doctor and husband in the play *Joe Egg*, the beleaguered mother of a brain-damaged child exclaims, "I don't want an explanation—I want magic!" "Magic," a suspect concept in a scientific age, was validated by experience in the stories of some of the women in this book. They believed they had been given not just the ability to bear children, a kind of magic in itself, but also a unique ability to see threats to a child and to deal with them.

Thus Sharon Marsh claims she brought Russell back to life when he "expired" from the effects of drugs. "I'll be damned if I'll let you die now!" she shouted as she pushed air into his lungs. Marilyn Greene suggested that animal and human mothers share this capability when she told of trying to prevent her daughter Jill from returning to the Moonies. Comparing herself to a mother bear, Marilyn told Jill, "I am concerned that my cub is in danger, and . . . I'll find a way to keep you from going back."

Aside from these instinctive or intuitive abilities, these women also had the ability to understand and to empathize with their children in more rational ways. The attention they paid to a child was not that of the scientist intent on analysis or the politician intent on power. Women have historically been great readers of novels, and it's perhaps not too farfetched to say that the mothers here *read* the lives of their children. They examined motivation, watched for forewarning, and were alert to the nuances of incident and dialogue, metaphor and symbol. Most important, they kept uppermost in their minds the organic possibilities of personality. They expected their children, like the characters in a good novel, to grow and change.

Once the women had reached the stage of healthy detachment,

they refused to accept total responsibility for their children's failures, just as they wouldn't have taken all the credit for their children's successes. Even Lucy Carpenter, the mother of a suicide,
drew the lines of responsibility realistically. After her son David
decided his situation was hopeless and took his own life, Lucy tack-
led and defeated her guilt. She openly acknowledged that David's
death brought a relief from enormous stress. "He gave us ten years
to help him," she said. She had done all she could, and she didn't
indulge in guilt.

Having looked at their children sensitively and imaginatively, as
the women became autonomous they turned the same kind of gaze
on themselves. They discovered through their experiences that the
growth of their children made it important to have work and connections aside from the family. That the children had changed, were
changing, would continue to change, they accepted. But these
women had learned that they needed something personal and permanent to give continuity to their lives. Interests such as Margot
Morrison's music, Kate Barnes's school counseling, or Rosemary
Dixon's real estate sales banished the fears of "the empty nest." A
woman, like a man, needs a private image of herself by which to live.
No one can answer the question "Who am I?" with "David's
mother." Realizing this, the women in this study turned to the wider
human interaction, the multiplicity of experience, in short to the life
beyond motherhood that comes to every woman with time.

Trusting time and the natural processes in its passage was, in fact,
the third ability demonstrated by these women. Time healed what
reason could not. The mothers here had found no universal answers
which would satisfy the "whys" they had asked about the behavior of
their children. They found no universal formula for solving the
problems their children created for them. But all of them found that
the passage of time helped them to become independent from their
children.

Their stories describe a *process* of coping in which one stage suc-
ceeds another in more or less regular order. Discerning such a
process indicates a faith in time. A pregnant woman knows she must
wait for nine months until the birth of her child; she has a certain
faith in the process. Furthermore, women reassure each other about
the fears of childbirth by saying that time erases the memory of
labor pains.

In somewhat the same way, the women here point to the comforts of knowing that there is a predictable process leading to autonomy and renewed connection. Asked what advice they had for other mothers, in one form or another they said, "Just be aware that time will help." They believed that the pain of coping would be more bearable for a mother who expected a gradual process rather than an overnight miracle.

These mothers had another talent: the ability to laugh. Initially, a mother staggering from the shock of her child's errant behavior will probably *feel* intensely all the tragic implications of the situation. She feels a vast disillusion with the way the child and the world have double-crossed her. She tried to sow order and fulfillment, and she seems to be reaping chaos and despair.

But feelings alone aren't enough for the next two stages. Paying attention to the way the child and the world really are instead of the way she'd like them to be, and choosing a course of action to make both better, challenge her greatest intellectual as well as emotional resources. To respond successfully to this challenge, she must *think* as well as feel.

Feeling requires involvement. A mother feels "with" or "for" her child. Thinking requires distance. She thinks "about" his situation. "The world," according to Horace Walpole, "is a tragedy to those who feel, a comedy to those who think." By the time a woman has moved through detachment into autonomy and a renewed connection with her child, she can usually remember the comic moments as vividly as she does the tragic.

In retrospect, these mothers indulge in healing laughter. They laugh at themselves. Marie Lowry remembers crying into her *boeuf en daube* at the prospect of a black grandchild. They laugh at their children. Joy Baron remembers teenaged Toni, soon to have a baby, with her big belly hanging out over her tiny bikini as she played on the beach with her friends. And Rosemary Dixon, whose daughter died, laughs through her tears at the memory of perfect Polly yelling an obscenity as she fell down the stairs in her tall cowboy boots.

The special genius of human beings allows them both to feel and to think, to be aware simultaneously of the tragic and comic dimensions of experience. The tragic view led these women to rail against the cosmic double cross they believed their children had given them and to exert heroic efforts to set things right. The comic view led them to understand eventually that they couldn't possibly resolve all the ambiguities of a disorderly world. What they couldn't change, they learned to live with: the tragedy and comedy of life itself.

REFERENCES

Adams, Jane. "Now That the Children Are Gone." New York *Times*, October 30, 1985.

Appel, Willa. *Cults in America: Programmed for Paradise.* New York: Holt, Rinehart and Winston, 1983.

Barthelme, Donald. *Snow White.* New York: Atheneum, 1967; rep. 1980.

Beauvoir, Simone de. *The Second Sex*, trans. H. M. Parshley. New York: Knopf, 1953; rpt. Bantam Books, 1961.

Colette. *My Mother's House*, trans. U. V. Troubridge and Enid McLeod. New York: Farrar, Straus & Giroux, 1953; rpt. 1983.

Dickstein, Morris. *Gates of Eden: American Culture in the Sixties.* New York: Basic Books, 1977.

Didion, Joan. *Slouching Towards Bethlehem.* New York: Farrar, Straus & Giroux, 1968; rpt. 1981.

Drabble, Margaret. *The Ice Age.* New York: Knopf, 1977; rpt. Popular Library, 1977.

Ephron, Nora. *Crazy Salad: Some Things about Women.* New York: Knopf, 1975; rpt. 1976.

Friedan, Betty. *The Feminine Mystique.* New York: Norton, 1963; rpt. Dell, 1982.

Gilligan, Carol. *In a Different Voice: Psychological Theory and Women's Development.* Cambridge: Harvard University Press, 1982.

Gordon, Mary. *Men and Angels.* New York: Random House, 1985.

Gornick, Vivian. *Essays in Feminism.* New York: Harper & Row, 1978.

Hawthorne, Nathaniel. *The Scarlet Letter*, ed. Sculley Bradley et al. New York: Norton, 1978.

Janeway, Elizabeth. *Cross Sections: From a Decade of Change.* New York: Morrow, 1982.

Kagan, Jerome. *The Nature of the Child.* New York: Basic Books, 1984.

322

REFERENCES

Levenkron, Steven. *Treating and Overcoming Anorexia Nervosa.* New York: Scribner's, 1982.

Loevinger, Jane. *Ego Development: Conceptions and Theories.* San Francisco: Jossey-Bass, 1976.

Lurie, Alison. *The War Between the Tates.* New York: Random House, 1974; rpt. Warner, 1975.

Miller, Alice. *The Drama of the Gifted Child.* Orig. *Prisoners of Childhood,* trans. Ruth Ward. New York: Basic Books, 1981.

Mueller, Helen. Unpublished journal. All journal entries credited within the text to "Joy" are taken from this source.

Paley, Grace. *Later the Same Day.* New York: Farrar, Straus & Giroux, 1985.

Riesman, David, et al. *The Lonely Crowd: A Study of the Changing American Character.* New Haven: Yale University Press, 1950; abridged rpt. New York: Doubleday, 1953.

Slater, Philip. *The Pursuit of Loneliness.* Boston: Beacon, 1970; rev. ed. 1976.

Thomas, D. M. *The White Hotel.* New York: Viking, 1981.

Tipton, Steven M. *Getting Saved from the Sixties.* Berkeley: University of California Press, 1982.

Woolf, Virginia. *To the Lighthouse.* New York: Harcourt, Brace, and World, 1927; rpt. 1955.